Reforming Women's Fashion, 1850–1920

Reforming Women's Fashion, 1850–1920

Politics, Health, and Art

Patricia A. Cunningham

The Kent State University Press

KENT & LONDON

Frontis: *Harper's Weekly* proof etching by Thomas Nast.

© 2003 by The Kent State University Press, Kent, Ohio 44242
Library of Congress Catalog Card Number 2002001852
ISBN 0-87338-742-2 (cloth)
Manufactured in the United States of America

06   05   04   03   02   5   4   3   2   1

Library of Congress Cataloging-in-Publication Data
Cunningham, Patricia A.
Reforming women's fashion, 1850—1920 : politics, health, and art /
Patricia A. Cunningham.
p. cm.
Includes bibliographical references and index.
ISBN 0-87338-742-2 (hardback : alk. paper) ∞
1. Costume—United States—History.
2. Costume—Europe—History.
3. Women's rights—United States.
4. Women's rights—Europe.
5. Fashion—Political aspects—United States.
6. Fashion—Political aspects—Europe.
I. Title.
GT610 .C85 2002
391'.0097—dc21
2002001852

British Library Cataloging-in-Publication data are available.

For reasons that require no explanation, I dedicate my work
to the memory of my parents, brother, and aunt

Clara Talley Cunningham
Guy Clement Cunningham
Richard Alan Cunningham
Patricia Cunningham Flesh

and to honor family members

William Edward Cunningham
Linda Flesh Brown and Bill Brown
Craig R. Hassler

Contents

Preface

This book began as a project on aesthetic dress in America for a National Endowment for the Humanities Summer Seminar at Yale University and metamorphosed into a broader investigation of women's dress reform in Europe and America. It became evident that not only was the dress reform movement diverse geographically but its major proponents had multifaceted interests, backgrounds, and solutions to what they perceived to be problems with women's clothing. In addition, the period that the various movements were active covered a time span of more than fifty years. In some respects, the broader study came about as a response to claims in costume history literature that dress reformers had no effect on fashion. Primary sources read during the initial investigation of aesthetic dress suggested otherwise.

This book offers the views of women and men who believed that fashion was either unhealthy or unaesthetic, or both. They had differing motivations. Some took a political view, believing that fashion had effectively limited women's roles and thus their potential for any real impact on society. Others firmly believed that women's fashionable dress had become a detriment to good health. Not a few thought that fashion went against true ideals of natural beauty. While various and sometimes opposing viewpoints are represented here, the overarching goal of this study is to reveal the many ways in which people sought to improve women's clothing from the mid–nineteenth century to the early twentieth century and to examine the impact they had on fashion at the time and on dress of the future. This book is arranged according to the types of garments that were promoted to correct or replace fashionable dress. Hence, it focuses on women wearing trousers, altering their underwear, and adopting aesthetic or artistic clothing.

As much as possible, I have sought to allow the ideas of the reformers to come through, to keep the text true to their voices. Although I have offered theory regarding the meanings of dress, I have chosen not to interpret the text from a late-twentieth-century feminist or postmodern perspective. While the construction of gender was central to why women dressed the way they did, during the nineteenth century the approaches to gender issues were different from the ways we might pursue them today. My intention is to offer a sympathetic interpretation or view (the reader may view it as bias) without imposing, or layering, too many twentieth-century notions over already complex nineteenth- and early-twentieth-century ideas regarding fashion, gender, and women's rights and roles.

As in all worthwhile endeavors, there are restraints. The major limitation placed on the subject of this study was that of restricting it to an examination of women's reform clothing worn in Europe and America, specifically England, Germany, Austria, the Netherlands, Scandinavia, the United States, and, to a limited extent, France. Only main garments (dresses or gowns, and their replacements) and underwear are examined, although there is a great amount of literature regarding the abuses of other clothing items, particularly footwear and hats. Also, parallel efforts that were made to reform men's dress have not been considered. My focus on types of garments rather than on themes is an appropriate perspective for a costume historian, who is still interested in the reciprocal impact that changes in dress behavior have on society and culture, especially on women's roles and perceptions of themselves.

If clothing reflects the times in which it is worn (how could it be otherwise?), then efforts to change the status quo of fashion in any way, radical or not, also reflect the times. Certainly reform went against the normal ways of the world. For women to wear unfashionable clothing put them on the defensive; they had to explain why they were transgressing. The explanations that appeared to be the most logical—for improved health, for ease and comfort, for the beauty linked to good health—no doubt gave reform garments some credibility. An understanding of the motivations, rationale, and arguments given by these reformers for altering their clothing certainly lends insight into late-twentieth-century assumptions about dress in general notwithstanding the residual carry-over (greatly transformed by the turn of the twenty-first century) of conservative ideas regarding appropriate dress for occasion, place, activity, and time of day.

The claims of dress reformers that fashionable dress was unhealthy, especially the tight corset, is an issue that scholars have sought to test. Yet, the truth is that if women like Mary Tillotson believed that their garments were causing them ill health, then that was their reality. It is something we cannot test today. Unless they inform us, we cannot know for sure. However, through an examination of the literature of reform, through the reformers' own words, we can discover their attitudes and beliefs and examine their arguments and visual proof of their efforts in drawings, illustrations, and photographs as well as in the actual reform garments that remain.

My goal in writing this book was to determine the extent of dress-reform efforts in America and Europe from the context of the time period in which they took place. One major objective was to reveal the breadth of the reform efforts and thus broaden our understanding of why the reformers felt a need to improve women's dress. Another desire was to reveal the legacy of the reformers—

that is, to show their influence on fashion by uncovering the ways in which reform styles became fixed elements in the repertory of clothing styles worn for different activities.

The reformers' suggestions for new styles of garments were not advanced simply to acquire something new to be "in fashion," or today we might say to be "hip"; their ideas for improved clothing were based on a higher level of motivation and were infused with moral aesthetic notions and health-related arguments. As such, the dress reformers' concerns were very much connected to all efforts toward improvements in social conditions that took place during the nineteenth and early twentieth centuries. These efforts were seen in many aspects of culture and included individuals in many fields such as education, women's rights, temperance, health, as well as the arts: dance, theater, music, fine and decorative arts, and architecture. In many respects these reformers were "fashion futurists." I hope that the reader will want to learn more about these reformers and their ideas and in turn undertake further investigation of their works, lives, and the times in which they lived.

Acknowledgments

There are many individuals and institutions to recognize and thank for their efforts in helping make this book possible. Although I cannot possibly list them all, there are some that deserve special mention. Expenses for travel and release time for research were made possible through a number of grants. I was the recipient of a Summer Seminar Grant and a Travel to Collections Grant from the National Endowment for the Humanities. A sabbatical from Bowling Green State University allowed me to travel in Europe to gather information on the dress reform movements in Britain, Germany, and Austria. The Ohio State University provided me with a leave for one quarter to complete the book.

The staffs of many libraries have been generous with their time. I would like to acknowledge especially the Westminster City Library, London; the National Art Library of the Victoria and Albert Museum; the library of the Austrian Museum of Art and Industry, Vienna; the library of the *Mode Sammlung* (Costume Collection), Vienna City Museum; the Austrian National Library; the Berlin Fine Arts Library; the New York Public Library; Harvard University Libraries; Yale University Library; Smith College Library and Archives; Newberry Library; the Ohio State University Libraries, especially the Fine Arts Library; and Jerome Library, Bowling Green State University.

Museums have also contributed to this effort, particularly the Victoria and Albert Museum; Cincinnati Art Museum; Austrian Museum of Art and Industry, Vienna; Vienna City Museum; Kent State University Museum; Western Reserve Historical Society; National Museum of American History, Smithsonian Institution; Geauga County Historical Society; the Ohio Historical Society; and the Historic Costume and Textiles Collection at Ohio State University.

Many individuals have likewise contributed to my efforts. First, I would like to thank former director John T. Hubbell and assistant director and acquisitions editor Joanna Hildebrand Craig of The Kent State University Press, as well as reviewers Shelly Foote and Sally Helvenston. My major translators were Ulli Aitenbichler Schneider, Brigitte Vadillo, and Thomas Riedl. Individuals who deserve recognition for various acts of kindness and support in their professional or private lives include Ruth Hoffman, Brigitte Stamm, Andreas Ley, Helga Aurisch, Mary Blanchard, Annie Carlano, Nancy Rexford, Ricky Clark, Marian Davis, Lisa Crause, Cathryn Buckel, Joe Hancock, Lynne Kotlarczyk, Beth Dunlap, Linda Welters, Patricia Warner, John M. Pryba, Susan Lab, and Gayle Strege. Those who were always supportive but who are no longer here to thank in person are Otto Charles Thieme, Richard Martin, Edward Praxmere, Donald Stowell, and Elsa McMullen. For his loving encouragement and patience as I put the final touches on the manuscript, I thank Craig R. Hassler.

CHAPTER ONE

Introduction

Fashion, Health, and Beauty

Strive as you will to elevate woman, nevertheless the disabilities and degradation of her dress, together with that large group of false views of the uses of her being and of her relations to man, symbolized and perpetuated by her dress, will make your striving vain.

—Gerrit Smith

Throughout the nineteenth century and in the early decades of the twentieth century in Europe and America the basic silhouette of women's dress went through many permutations, from tubular to full-skirted and back to tubular. Emphasis could shift from the breast, shoulders, waist, and derrière and then back again. The intended shape or style of dress and accompanying silhouette were dependent not on the natural shape of each individual but rather on various undergarments—corsets, petticoats, crinolines, bustles, and other supporting devices that helped to create the fashionable look. Many people viewed changes in clothing styles a natural phenomenon of an advanced society and thus believed that new fashions were an inevitable outward expression of progressive social values, control, and hierarchy; fashion was a sign of modernity. Growing numbers of individuals, however, began to believe that women's clothing, particularly fashionable dress, was harmful to their health. For these people fashion signified and was a major cause of women's political and economic oppression. Because clothing often encompassed artificial forms, some reformers also argued that fashionable dress was aesthetically unpleasing as well.

In the second half of the nineteenth century and early twentieth century it was no longer enough to *look* modern by adopting the latest fashion; many women

now wanted to *be* modern. These women desired simple, healthful, practical clothing that would allow them to be active participants in the public, professional, and economic arenas of society, but fashion and its accompanying rules for behavior were tenacious. Women's minds continued to be forcefully affected by fashion. Changing the course of fashion and the prescribed behavior that seemed so closely linked to it would prove no simple task. Fashion was so pervasive in women's lives that cartoonists frequently depicted women as "slaves to fashion" (Fig. 1).

Since the time of Louis XIV, what was in fashion and what was to become the fashion, whether in dress, architecture, furniture, and indeed in all of the decorative arts, usually emanated from Paris. It is, therefore, not surprising that the art of high fashion, *haute couture*, had its beginnings in Paris. In the mid-nineteenth century fashion decisions became largely the province of English-born Parisian couturier Charles Frederick Worth and a coterie of like-minded producers of fine, hand-made gowns and accessories in Paris. By the turn of the twentieth century, the House of Worth and other purveyors of French *haute couture* were well established as the arbiters of taste in dress. While there were, of course, high-fashion designers of women's clothing throughout Europe and America, these specialists often adapted the new Paris styles. This pattern of copying the dictates of Paris continues to this day, although to a lesser degree. Dissemination of French fashion occurred through the channels of fashion periodicals and general women's magazines, which offered illustrations and, in some cases, patterns of the latest styles. Newspapers also kept the public abreast of the latest fashions worn by Parisian *demimondaines*, actresses, and fashion-conscious wealthy Europeans and Americans.[1]

Women from all levels of society followed the latest fashion, especially for clothing worn in the public sphere. Concern for the latest styles of dress was not an idle pastime, for it was socially important to be considered fashionable and beautiful; clothes could earn one merit in society. Indeed, as interpreted by Thorstein Veblen in 1899, the fashionably dressed woman was a major communicator of family status and wealth. Etiquette books and advice manuals of the time make it clear that being in fashion also meant wearing the correct clothing designated for specific occasions and time of day. It was important to adhere to these rules, for they were necessary to achieve a place in society.[2]

Studies in the social psychology of clothing reveal that following the latest fashion and keeping in touch with social rules are essential to feelings of belonging and fitting into society. Even today people believe that clothes signify the moral and spiritual nature of women. Clothing, therefore, remains an important aspect of an individual's persona as well as a mediator of social relationships. Thus, while clothing has changed since the nineteenth century, some of its basic functions have not. Our understanding of current motivations regarding clothing can lend some insight into nineteenth-century patterns of behavior.[3]

While individuals would not necessarily wish to go against the norms of society or, worse yet, suggest that they might have questionable morals, in the nineteenth century many women did shun fashionable clothing because they believed that it harmed their health. They argued that the amount of under-clothing, the sheer weight of the clothes, and the constriction of the corset were not only harmful to women's health but detracted from women's beauty; in fact, many believed that the clothing was ugly because it did not follow the

Fig. 2 "The First Appearance," from a print issued by Kellogg in 1851 features trousers. Courtesy Peters Collection, National Museum of History and Technology.

THE DAPHNE.

Fig. 3 Umbrella Drawers, one of several reform undergarments offered by the Battle Creek Sanitarium. *Battle Creek Sanitarium Dress System* (Battle Creek, Mich.: Sanitary and Electrical Supply Co., ca. 1890), 52.

Fig. 4 The Daphne Gown, one of many artistic dresses suggested by Annie Jenness-Miller. *Jenness Miller Magazine* 5 (January 1891): 348.

natural form of the human body. For them, the body itself was ugly because fashion had destroyed its natural beauty.

Health and beauty were not the only issues regarding women's dress. For no small number of people linked restrictive clothing to women's limited roles and to what they perceived as women's inferior political position in society. Clearly, many women in the nineteenth century could not, or chose not to, focus their lives on being fashionable. As middle-class women became more involved in the public sphere and attended college, they desired to be more active participants in roles outside of the domestic sphere. For these women being modern meant more than wearing the latest styles in dress. Indeed, in the second half of the nineteenth century increasing numbers of women were attending college and entering professions and businesses. Thus, women sought economic and political power on many fronts.[4]

Reform obviously was not the concern of a single group. Clothing reform was of interest to many organizations and was an international phenomenon, especially from the second half of the nineteenth century through the first decade of the twentieth century. There were many people involved in dress reform, and their persistence over a period of time attests to the continuing interest in creating alternatives to fashionable women's dress. Promoters of women's-clothing reform in America, Britain, and the European continent included men and women who were health or hygienic reformers, educators, feminists, physicians, artists, architects, club women, dancers, actresses, opera singers, members of communal and religious groups, and many other educated people. They all sought in some way to alter and improve contemporary styles of women's dress.[5]

In order to make fashion rational, some advocates of reform suggested altering the underpinnings of women's dress—corset, corset cover, petticoats, bustles, pads, etcetera. They wanted to keep the outer dress in compliance with the styles then in fashion so they devised ways to construct fashionable garments to be less restrictive and cumbersome. Other reformers began to advocate completely new clothing styles that would not suggest an inferior role and that would allow enough ease in movement for work and active sports. These new styles of clothing went against the norm, hence today the term "anti-fashion" often is used to describe them. As such, they were viewed as less than attractive alternatives to fashionable styles of women's dress. Such reform garments took several forms and appeared in the streets and salons of America, in Britain, and on the Continent. They included trousers (Fig. 2), reform underwear (Fig. 3), and artistic "aesthetic" gowns. (Though its significance was not readily apparent, the new underwear was an important aspect of reform, because it allowed women to alter their dresses unobtrusively in order to "make fashion rational.") Subsequent chapters will focus on these three types of reform garments and their arrangement. However, before engaging in a discussion of garment styles and their acceptance, I will offer insight into the nature and function of nineteenth- and early-twentieth-century women's clothing, the inherent problems with it, and the issues of health and beauty that ultimately were responsible for attempts to alter it.[6]

That so many diverse groups and individuals in so many parts of the world have apparently been interested in reforming women's dress also raises a number of questions. While this chapter describes the perceived problems with women's dress, in later chapters dealing with each of the three major types of reform garments, I address further questions: What were the motives and characteristics of the people who advocated the different reform styles? What arguments did they use? How were their efforts received by the public at large? How did their concerns relate to other progressive movements of the nineteenth century? In what way did their persistence impact the ultimate freedom of dress enjoyed by women in the twentieth century?[7]

THE HISTORICAL PRECEDENCE FOR REFORMING WOMEN'S CLOTHING

Reform ideas concerning dress were not unique to the nineteenth and twentieth centuries. There were sumptuary laws in the ancient world, which were rather ineffectual efforts to control extravagant dress. Strictures on clothing behavior also existed in Europe from the Middle Ages through the eighteenth century. These, too, were meant to restrict the extravagant display of clothing by those considered unworthy of the status their clothing might denote. In eighteenth-century England the prominent artists Sir Joshua Reynolds and William Hogarth commented that there were problems presented by fashionable dress.

And indeed in that century, largely owing to the influence of the writings of Jean-Jacques Rousseau (in *Émile*), some effort was made to improve the clothing of children, who at the time were usually dressed as adults. Rousseau and his followers believed that children needed to be comfortable and have more freedom of movement. Children began to be dressed in simple clothing more appropriate to their specific needs.[8]

Likewise, it must be understood that "fashionable" women's dress usually referred to the latest, most current styles acceptable for the public sphere or for social events or formal occasions in the privacy of the family and home. Nineteenth-century etiquette determined what was appropriate. Fashion, tempered by rules of etiquette, called for almost complete covering of the upper body during the day, but allowed women to wear decolletage for the evening. The degree of uncovering, or display, would be determined by the event, place, or time of day. Rules of etiquette also denoted appropriate dress for the home, where women could wear comfortable, loose-fitting clothing called house gowns, wrappers, morning gowns, and tea gowns designed specifically for this use. Etiquette also determined proper clothing for sports and physical activities, for which some women wore bifurcated garments—usually loose, full trousers gathered in to fall somewhere between the knee and ankle. These loose trousers worn for gymnastics, as well as the house gowns worn for comfort in the home, were not designed for public scrutiny and were therefore considered unfit to wear in public.[9]

Clothing for Comfort, Work, and Play

When middle- and upper-class women rose in the morning, they usually put on a loose-fitting morning gown or wrapper, what might be best defined as a house gown. If they then chose to work, they might wear the very loose type, such as the Mother Hubbard style, which became popular in the 1880s. The cut of all these garments, especially the Mother Hubbard, was very simple compared to clothing worn in public; and women might wear fewer, or perhaps looser, undergarments with them. Women could loosen the corset, or wear a soft corset. Some house gowns were made with linings that fit close to the body. The style of these house gowns, the intricacy of construction details, and the type of fabric used to make them defined their use as appropriate for private settings. Since ideally these garments did not constrict the body, they allowed women to move more freely and to feel relaxed and comfortable (Fig. 5).

Tea gowns are the upper end of this class of comfortable "at home" clothing. Tea gowns usually incorporated very fine fabrics and could be quite showy. They became very popular and fashionable in the late 1870s, 1880s, and 1890s in Europe, Britain, and America. In 1893 *The Delineator* observed that "artistic house-gowns are now considered necessary items of a complete wardrobe, and the dressy woman to obtain that individuality which is so desirable, selects her styles from those of past generations and develops them in the most *fin de siècle*

6972   6875

6972   6875

Ladies' Tea-Gown or Wrapper, with a Fitted Lining, and a Slight Train (Perforated for Round Length) (Copyr't): 13 sizes. Bust measures, 28 to 46 inches. Any size, 1s. 6d. or 35 cents.

Ladies' Wrapper, with Fitted Lining (Which may be Omitted) (Copyright): 13 sizes. Bust measures, 28 to 46 inches. Any size, 1s. 6d. or 35 cents.

7180   7180

Ladies' Wrapper or Tea-Gown, with Fitted Lining (Which may be Omitted) (Copyright): 13 sizes. Bust measures, 28 to 46 inches. Any size, 1s. 6d. or 35 cents.

6761   6812

Ladies' Shirred Wrapper (With Fitted Lining) (To be Shirred or Left Loose at the Waist in Front) (Copyright): 13 sizes. Bust measures, 28 to 46 inches. Any size, 1s. 3d. or 30 cents.

Ladies' Princess House-Dress or Wrapper, with Slight Train (Perforated for Round Length) (Copyright): 14 sizes. Bust measures, 28 to 48 inches. Any size, 1s. 3d. or 30 cents.

7290   7290

Ladies' Vassar Gown (To be used as a Wrapper, Lounging-Robe or Night-Gown) (Copyright): 10 sizes. Bust measures, 28 to 46 inches. Any size, 1s. 6d. or 35 cents.

7234   7234

Ladies' New Mother-Hubbard Wrapper, with Under-Arm Gore (To be Made with a Standing or a Rolling Collar) (Copyright): 13 sizes. Bust measures, 28 to 46 inches. Any size, 1s. 6d. or 35 cents.

7147   6699

Ladies' House-Dress or Wrapper (To be Made with Standing or Rolling Collar) (Copyright): 13 sizes. Bust measures, 28 to 46 inches. Any size, 1s. 6d. or 35 cents.

Ladies' Princess Dress or Wrapper, with Slight Train (Perforated for Round Length) (Copyright): 14 sizes. Bust measures, 28 to 48 inches. Any size, 1s. 3d. or 30 cents.

6270   6353

Ladies' Princess Wrapper, with Loose Front and Short Fitted Lining-Front (Copyright): 13 sizes. Bust measures, 28 to 46 inches. Any size, 1s. 6d. or 35 cents.

Ladies' Wrapper or House-Dress (With Fitted Lining) (Copyright): 13 sizes. Bust measures, 28 to 46 inches. Any size, 1s. 6d. or 35 cents.

6272   6478   4342   4116   6725

Girls' Mother-Hubbard Wrapper (Copyright): 11 sizes. Ages, 2 to 12 years. Any size, 10d. or 20 cents.

Child's Sack Wrapper (Extending to the Instep) (Copyright): 10 sizes. Ages, 1 to 10 years. Any size, 10d. or 20 cents.

Little Girls' Wrapper (Copyright): 9 sizes. Ages, ½ to 8 years. Any size, 10d. or 20 cents.

Little Girls' Wrapper (Copyright): 8 sizes. Ages, ½ to 7 years. Any size, 10d. or 20 cents.

Child's Wrapper, with Circular Yoke (Copyr't): 8 sizes. Ages, ½ to 7 years. Any size, 7d. or 15 cents.

Fig. 5 (opposite) An assortment of available Butterick patterns for "Ladies Tea-gowns and Wrappers," from *The Delineator*, mid-1890s.

Fig. 6 House Dress. *The Delineator*, August 1893, pattern no. 6317. The magazine described the dress as an artistic house gown with an Empire waist made of figured challis. "The gown has a short-waisted body [lining] with fitted darts in front upon which are arranged full vest portions of challis" (123).

materials." Although named tea gowns, these artistic gowns were not restricted to teatime entertaining; they were appropriate for informal dining and other entertainments at home. Eventually, more daring women wore them in public. *The Delineator* referred to the gown in figure 6 as an Empire house gown.[10]

The necessities of farm life meant that most rural farm women had to carry out physical labor. To facilitate their work, these women often made adjustments to their clothing according to the requirements of the chores they were performing. While rural farm women often had knowledge of the latest styles in fashion, for work they usually chose to wear more simple versions of what was an acceptable silhouette or a variation of the house gown. The loose-fitting Mother Hubbard, in particular, was not an uncommon sight on the farm; some women even belted it in to pass for "street" use. Farm women might pull their outer skirt to the back to keep it clean and out of the way. They also shortened their skirts. The practicality of loose, full trousers also enticed some to adopt that costume. No doubt, being seen wearing these necessary but quite unfashionable adjustments, as sometimes happened, caused some farm women embarrassment.[11]

Yet not all women feared the ridicule that inevitably accompanied the display of house gowns or work clothes in public. In a report from America that appeared in the English magazine *Knowledge,* the author commented on an instance of intolerance and tyranny that took place in Montana when some women "adopted for outdoor wear a long, loose gown ungirt around the waist, somewhat resembling the Mother Hubbard Mantle." She observed that not only were the wearers "hooted in the streets, . . . the objectionable innovation was suppressed by municipal decree." She continued her account, saying that in another instance, the attention of the mayor of Philadelphia was drawn to women in his city who were wearing the Mother Hubbard costume out of doors. The mayor, however, did not feel compelled to initiate a decree banning the dress from public view.[12]

Gerilyn G. Tandberg has offered still further evidence of the appropriation of the Mother Hubbard by women for street wear. She refers to an article that appeared in the *Monroe Bulletin* in Louisiana (taken from the *Louisville Commercial*) in which the reporter observed that the police were ordered to suppress "Mother Hubbard costumes on the street." Although the *Monroe Bulletin* apparently argued against the Mother Hubbard, Tandberg observed that Louisiana's women "boldly wore these gowns in many variations. They wore them when being photographed but also continued to wear them for chores."[13]

Occasions that mark efforts toward freedom in dress such as these were not uncommon. It is clear, however, that in their determination to make a change in their clothing, advocates of reform drew on existing styles of garments—loose trousers, unstructured underwear, and house gowns, clothing associated with intimate and specific functions or occasions. The house gowns, especially tea gowns, in many respects served as "models" for "artistic" reform gowns, which will be discussed in chapters 4, 5, and 6. In the case of underwear, by adopting garments used for sports, such as equestrian tights, and altering existing garments, even reducing the stiffening in corsets, women were able to make substantial progress toward comfort. The development of the cage crinoline in 1856 was viewed as another improvement because it reduced the number of petticoats and therefore the bulk and weight of garments that hung from the waist.

Reformers' complaints, then, were not about clothing worn in the privacy of the home; rather, the concern was for the physical and mental problems caused by fashionable dress worn in the public sphere, especially the ill effects of the corsets and undergarments that sustained them. Yet the power of fashion was a strong force and no doubt kept many women from airing in public their belief in the need to prevent clothing from harming their health.

Fashionable Dress—1850–1914

Fashion competition in the second half of the nineteenth century in Europe and America appears to have consumed the lives of many middle- and upper-class women, especially those living in urban areas. In "The Economic Theory of Women's Dress," Thorstein Veblen offered his view of American life, arguing that women's fashionable clothing was an indicator not only of their own wealth and position in society but that of their husband and family as well. Women's extremely cumbrous skirts, he believed, indicated their affordable idleness.[14]

In the mid-nineteenth century there is no doubt that Paris was the center of fashion and that English-born Charles Frederick Worth was its leading designer. During the second half of the nineteenth century, when all the Western world looked to Paris for the latest styles, women who could afford to do so purchased their gowns and accessories from the House of Worth, Merlot-Larcheveque, Mme. A. Laferrier, L. Savarre, Mme. Levillion, or Ernest Rauditz. They could go to Paris, or send a representative to the couture house, or purchase from a department store that handled Parisian couture. Of course, only very wealthy women could actually afford a Worth gown, but that did not mean women could not be dressed in the latest style. A contemporary 1880s opinion on the way fashion functioned appeared in *Littell's Living Age* under the title "Modern Dress." After observing that men had finally been able to emancipate themselves from the "tyrannical despotism of fashion," G. Armytage noted that "the weaker sex" were completely under the dominion of dress and had been from antiquity when Hebrew wives "laced tightly" and added colorful fringes to their robes and Greek women "wore body bands and belts to improve their figures." Armytage upheld the belief that the tradition of being a slave to fashion had been maintained and handed down from generation to generation from classical times.[15]

Armytage went on to discuss what George Simmel later termed the "trickle-down theory" of fashion, noting that sovereigns set fashion to the ladies of the court, and the crowd, meaning everyone else, followed suit. Armytage gave credit to Empress Eugénie of France for reintroducing the fashion for hoops and bringing on the reign of the cage crinoline. Indeed, Eugénie popularized the rage for "smart clothes." She dressed magnificently and lavishly, to such an extent that her first clothing designer retired to a comfortable life. It is not surprising that her favorite was Charles Frederick Worth, who, of course, became the most important Parisian couturier of his time and world renowned.[16]

Commenting on the international transmission of fashion, Armytage noted that what he termed an excessive fondness for display on the part of the Parisians spread to the United States because Americans always maintained close ties with Paris. The wave of luxury reached Britain later and made slower progress there. Armytage expressed the belief that a love of fashion is greatest among the opulent middle class and that great ladies of position and name often have no interest in fashion and certainly are not leaders. In *Fashioning the Bourgeoisie*, Philippe Perrot has argued that the *demimondaines* were the first to try out a new Paris style.[17]

There were several ways in which the latest designs from Paris were disseminated around the world so that the women of whom Armytage spoke—in London, New York, Vienna, Berlin, and even the American Midwest—could dress "in fashion." First, there were numerous magazines offering illustrations of the latest styles and in some cases diagram patterns as well, which through measurements could be scaled up to a usable size. Popular magazines in America that offered fashion information, and sometimes patterns, were *Godey's Lady's Book* (1830–98), *Peterson's Magazine* (1849–92), *Harper's Bazar [Bazaar]* (1867–present); *Vogue* (1892–present), and *The Delineator* (1873–1937). Of course, there were many other magazines offering fashion information. In London readers had the *Queen* and in Paris there was *Le Mode, La Vogue,* and *Journal des Dames et des Modes*. Women in Berlin had *Der Bazar* and *Die Modenwelt*. In Vienna women could look to *Wiener Mode*.

Other sources of new fashion ideas were dressmakers who offered patterns of their latest fashions on a limited basis. The dominant American leaders in the development of paper patterns, sized, cut, and ready to use, were Ellen and William Demorest and Ebenezer Butterick, both of whom had thriving businesses in the 1860s. While the Demorests geared their offerings to the trade and a stylish middle-class audience, Butterick appealed to the general public. Both had successful "emporiums" of fashion and publications (*Demorest's Monthly Magazine, The Delineator*) through which they promoted their patterns. The trade in paper patterns was in its infancy during the Civil War, but through aggressive and skillful promotion, the trade grew into a thriving industry by the 1870s, providing patterns to Americans. Newcomers to the industry, like James McCall, the Demorests, and Butterick, improved their methods of production and distribution systems to expand their market. By 1874 Butterick had a shop in London; the Demorests opened a Paris emporium in 1876. Both were successful and grew rapidly.[18]

Every city, large or small, had professional dressmakers who kept up with the latest fashions. And, of course, there were prominent designers in major cities such as Paris, London, Berlin, Vienna, and New York who created exquisite high-fashion gowns with all the expertise and stylishness of a Worth creation. Out of necessity many middle- and working-class women made their own versions of the latest fashion, or had local dressmakers create them. Fabrics and, as the trade advanced, patterns were available in general stores and specialty shops, through mail order, and eventually in department stores located in larger cities in Europe and America.[19]

Indeed, the second half of the nineteenth century saw the development of department stores in all the major cities in America and England and on the continent of Europe. By the 1890s department stores—such as Harrods and Sel-

Fig. 7 Lula Cunningham, Carthage, Mo., c. 1896. Through a study of photographic archives, Joan Severa compellingly argues that all American women were sensitive to the dictates of fashion. See *Dressed for the Photographer* (Kent, Ohio: The Kent State University Press, 1995).

friges in London, Wertheim's in Berlin, Bon Marché and Printemps in Paris, and Wanamaker's, Macy's, and Marshall Field's in America—had become empires of their own, catering especially to the needs of women, who had by this date become the major consumer for their families as well as employees of these great emporiums.[20]

The manner in which Paris influenced the wardrobes of Europeans and Americans did not differ greatly from place to place. In her study of fashion and reform dress in Germany, Brigitte Stamm drew on the observations of Werner

Sombart to explain the means by which Paris dictated fashion to German women in the 1890s. Berlin was the model for the rest of Germany. Sombart explained the process, using the town of Breslau as an example. He noted that while the pattern drawers used existing summer clothes to make up designs for winter clothes, most of what was available in Breslau had been purchased from a leading designer in Berlin like Mannheimer. The Berlin designers made changes in the summer styles. These designs, however, were only partly their own creation. They purchased Paris winter models from the shops that specialized in the distribution of new Paris styles. They called these shops *maisons d'échantillonneurs,* or,

Fig. 8 Classically inspired gowns, 1810–1820: *left,* off-white woven stripe silk, ca. 1820; *right,* white cotton with tassels on sleeves, 1800–1810. Courtesy, Historic Costume and Textiles Collection, Ohio State University.

literally, "sample houses." The shops took their ideas from the masters of pattern design, the *haute couturiers*—Rouff, Laferrier, Piagat, Worth, Doecullit, and Doucet. Sombart observed that it took about one and one-half to two years for a design to reach the little towns on the Russian border.[21]

As urban development continued in Europe and America, and more women, especially in America, had income-producing jobs, they could afford to dress in modern fashionable styles. Even when circumstances placed women in small towns and villages, they managed to be "in fashion" (Fig. 7). And perhaps more important, women could learn appropriate behavior, especially how to dress, from the numerous etiquette books that were available.[22]

Changing Fashions of Dress

For the period of this study, which encompasses the Victorian Age, women's fashionable dress underwent numerous changes in style. The differences in silhouette were not subtle and required specifically designed underclothing to create the desired effect. Indeed, it was the amount of underclothing and its shape and tightness that created the desired look, and that was held in highest contempt by the reformers.

In the early 1800s women continued to wear a variation of the Empire style (Fig. 8). But by mid-century reverence for the simplicity of the Greek-inspired silhouette had been replaced by a style characterized by full skirt, small waist, and tightly fitted bodice (Fig. 9a). Until the invention of the cage crinoline in the late 1850s, the shape of the skirt was created by many petticoats, either

Fig. 9a&b The new "cage crinoline" was cause for much humor in the press, but it actually lightened the load of too many petticoats. *Left:* Fashion plate, *Godey's Lady's Book* (December 1854). *Right:* Cartoon that appeared in *Punch* (August 1856).

Fig. 10 Aqua satin gown, ca. 1863. The skirt would require a hoop or cage crinoline for the proper silhouette. Gift of Ethel Traphagen Estate. Historic Costume and Textiles Collection, Ohio State University.

made of stiff material such as crinoline and horsehair or heavily starched.[23] The cage crinoline, which was a dome-shaped structure of graduated hoops, kept increasing in size until the mid-1860s, creating much cause for caricature in the press (Fig. 9b). In the late sixties the skirt shape began to be flattened in front and the fullness was pulled to the back of the dress (Fig. 10). Eventually, this evolved into a bustle style, which prevailed until approximately 1875 (Fig. 11). This silhouette was soon deposed, and a newer look prevailed, one that was

Fig. 11 "Godey's Fashions for 1873," *Godey's Lady's Book* (1873).

Fig, 12 Fashion plate, *Peterson's Magazine* (1884).

Fig. 13 Fashion plate, *Young Ladies Journal* (July 1896).

Fig. 14 Styles in 1909 were simple with a silhouette that had a subtle S-curve and a mono-bosom. *The Delineator*, January, 1909, 14.

characterized by an elongated sheath-like cuirass bodice. The skirt was narrow and tied back, the back fullness that created the bustle was lowered to form drapery just above the ever-present train.[24]

The 1880s saw a progression in silhouette to one characterized by emphasis on the skirt and a bustle that appears to be higher and larger than bustles of the early seventies (Fig. 12). The skirt hung straight with some drapery, and the bodice was tight fitting with narrow sleeves. By 1896 (Fig. 13) emphasis was again on the bodice, which is best characterized by its enormous sleeves and, hence, substantial shoulder width. Skirts still had a slight back fullness, sometimes worn with a small pad underneath, but toward the end of the decade skirts were made so that they fit smoothly over the hips and curved out just below the knee. The bustle and drapery were gone. A skirt and blouse became essential garments. The look of the Gibson Girl best characterizes the style and the ideal look of the time.[25]

Around the turn of the century the silhouette of the mode again changed, this time to an S-shape, with the bosom protruding in a rather singular expanse that is termed a "mono-bosom." By 1909 the mono-bosom and S-shape were more subtle; the waistline was either at its natural position or slightly higher (Fig. 14).

THE Delineator
*Styles are
reproduced by*
Butterick
Patterns

Fig. 15 Styles for 1916 show
pleated full skirts almost
at mid-calf. *The Delineator,*
November, 1916, 61.

In a few years the mono-bosom disappeared all together and was replaced by an elongated silhouette, which included a long straight skirt. However by 1916 skirts had become shorter and fuller (Fig. 15). Although fashion still prescribed elaborate sets of underwear including corsets, clothing in general had become simpler and echoed aesthetic reform styles.[26]

The Underpinnings of Fashion

As the styles progressed over the years, so, too, did the undergarments that sustained the silhouette. The outward appearance of women was quite dependent on what was worn underneath the fashionable garment (Fig. 16). And what was worn bears little resemblance to what women have worn for much of the twentieth century, especially during the last quarter century. Unlike today, for example, the process of getting dressed in the 1880s was a time-consuming ritual that resulted in a great deal of weight, constriction, and bulkiness being added to the figure.[27]

While women no doubt differed in their approach to getting dressed, our imaginary woman might first put on knit stockings, which, depending on the season, could be silk, wool, or cotton. These she gartered above the knee with elastic bands, which could reduce circulation in the legs. The next two pieces were drawers and chemise. Drawers were knee-length white cotton trousers buttoned at the waist. For hygienic reasons the crotch was left entirely open. Over the drawers she put on either a knitted undershirt called a vest or a loose knee-length cotton chemise. If a hip-length knit vest was worn, a knee-length petticoat would be worn to accompany it. This short petticoat served to replace the bottom half of a chemise and was typically made from cotton, or for added warmth, cotton flannel or wool. Another petticoat was worn over this. It could be white cotton or a more practical dark color that would not readily show stains from mud and other filth from the street. These longer petticoats were washed or brushed out regularly.

The next essential undergarment was a cotton or silk corset stiffened with thin flexible strips of whalebone (or other stiff material) set at very close intervals. This garment encased the wearer from armpits to hips and, even without being tightly laced, provided a firm, predictable shape over which the outer gown could fit with no wrinkles. Corsets hooked up the front for easy entry and were laced up the back to adjust the fit. If a woman had someone pull the laces in very tight to create a fashionable small waist, she risked squeezing her intestines and internal organs backward and downward, creating a bulge below the waist. Her breathing would be restricted when the corset pressed against her ribs. This questionable practice was called "tight lacing."

Our woman would next put on a corset cover to prevent the corset from showing through a sheer bodice or to mask its hard edges beneath opaque gowns. To complete the 1880s look, women needed a bustle to support the outer dress. Bustle manufacturers offered a variety of bustle styles; one was a contraption made of wire coils encased in cotton that tied around the waist and hung at the back at waist level under the gown.

Finally the fashionable woman could put on her gown, which often was made in two parts: a skirt and a bodice. The skirt had extra stiffening added around

Fig. 16 In an effort to make a statement about the artificiality of fashion, dress reformers often compared a fashionably dressed woman, whose dress was supported by many layers of undergarments, with the figure of Venus. This image appears as the frontispiece to Abba Goold Woolson, *Dress-Reform: A Series of Lectures Delivered in Boston, on Dress as It Affects the Health of Women* (Boston: Roberts Brothers, 1874).

the hem and, depending on the fabric, also might be lined. Strings or elastic bands attached inside at the side seams were tied behind the legs to ensure that the back fullness stayed in back. These "tied-back" dresses tended to hobble the wearer and keep her from taking a natural stride.

At this point our woman was ready for her dress bodice. The bodice, which also might have stiffening added to the seams, was fully lined to ensure a wrinkle-free appearance. If it was cold, the fashionable woman might wear a mantle over her shoulders. However, before she donned the bodice it might have been necessary for her to adjust her hair and put on a hat, for once she put on the bodice with its very tight sleeves, she could possibly have difficulty raising her arms. If her mantle was trimmed with jet beading, it could add an additional ten pounds to her clothing. An ensemble could easily weigh as much as twenty-five pounds. The details of this process were slightly different when hoops were worn instead of bustles, but the pain and folly of fashionable dressing had not really changed for centuries. Of course, for many women the effect of the process outweighed the discomfort.[28]

Functions of Fashion

Yet, for all the apparent problems caused by heavy fashionable dresses and restrictive corsets, the perceived need women had for corsets cannot be discounted. Although women's dresses usually had cotton linings and sometimes added stiffening placed along the inside seams, it was the undergarments—cage crinoline, bustles, corsets, pads—that gave a garment its distinctive silhouette. When gowns were made of flimsy materials these garments did add warmth to the body. In cold weather women added extra undergarments made of cotton flannel and wool.

Also, it must be noted, one of the essential qualities and functions of underwear, particularly the chemise, was to protect the outer garment from body oil and perspiration. For it was not until the eighteenth century that physical cleanliness became a part of daily regimen, and then only the educated and wealthy embraced the concept. As noted by C. Willet and Phillis Cunnington, cleanliness in the Victorian and Edwardian eras was a sign of class distinction, and frequent changes of underwear were not uncommon in the leisure class.[29]

It is worth noting, too, that in their research on stays P. and R. A. Mactaggart reveal that corsets, or stays, usually thought of as undergarments, were part of the normal outer dress of English peasants, and worn by the poorest of classes—"those on Parish relief." The stays were not covered by another layer of outer garment. At this time people wore stays because they believed that they could prevent body deformities, a theory that continued to operate, still unproven, well into the twentieth century.[30]

Underclothing also served an erotic function, for many considered slight glimpses of the top of the chemise or the hem of a petticoat erotic gestures and symbols of the act of undressing. Undergarments also accentuated women's physical attributes. For while the corset served to reduce the size of the waist, it also emphasized the breasts and hips. Bustles also focused on the derrière, and, of course, the bust supporter, although it offered relief from the weight of the breasts, also emphasized their size and thus offered more erotic appeal.[31]

If a woman were to reveal a small amount of underwear, the result might be an erotic charge, or at least it would draw attention to the wearer. Going without underwear in public, especially without a corset, even for health reform, would suggest wantonness or, worse yet, that the woman was a prostitute. Prostitutes apparently went outdoors in clothing meant only for use in the home—morning gowns—and without a corset. As noted by the Mactaggarts, there was a historical precedence for these associations: "looseness in dress" was, in the eighteenth century, "associated with looseness of morals."[32]

Studies in the psychology of clothing suggest that the charge of eroticism created by underclothes also is transmitted by the outer fashionable garment. We are aware that women's dress functions to serve obvious needs: identity, modesty, and beauty. More important, scholars argue that sensuality and eroticism also are recognized qualities of women's outer dress. In *Fashion and Eroticism,* Valerie Steele noted Freud's suggestion "that 'the progressive concealment of the body . . . keeps sexual curiosity awake.'" Clothing is erotic because it arouses curiosity about the "hidden parts," and through sublimation, curiosity about the body as a whole.[33]

Clothing theorists J. C. Flügel, James Laver, and Rene Koenig adopted this Freudian belief. Laver offered a theory of "shifting erogenous zones" which maintained that whenever the female body is "habitually covered up, the exposure of any part focuses attention there." The variations created by fashion thus repeatedly allow the viewer to see the body with renewed interest. However, as Steele stresses, the erotic appeal is often more general than Flügel's and Laver's theories suggest. The erotic element may remain inconspicuous; in fact, changes in women's fashions often do not focus directly on sexual attributes, yet may still arouse feelings of fascination and curiosity for the male viewer. Moreover, as Steele observed, changes in fashion do not occur because men become bored with one part of the anatomy, thus causing fashion to alter its course, as suggested by the theory of shifting erogenous zones.[34]

The American experience is most revealing, for as Lois Banner observed, the growth of fashion consciousness in America and the culture of fashion were in keeping with "rampant individualism, materialism, and search for status and success." The quest for beauty through fashion went beyond the search for a husband and a successful marriage, though these were "as much a part of basic American values as the egalitarianism traditionally associated with the rise of nineteenth-century democracy." As women were denied access to power in the developing nation, they retreated into domesticity. Yet, to fulfill their own desires and destinies, they expanded their traditional roles to include volunteer work associated with women's organizations and churches and also to create a "culture of fashion" as a career substitute. For elite women especially, the challenge was to reach an impeccable social position and reputation for elegance of appearance and to know when they had attained it.[35]

The achievement of status was not solely the province of the elite. For women working in shops and factories, and indeed for all women, dress, along with demeanor, etiquette, and hygiene, was a primary means of status distinction. The idea of status appears to be important to individuals in advanced societies. Not only is clothing important to denote group membership, but in many ways it expresses women's sense of self-worth, and clearly it fulfills a fantasy of achieving the American dream of wealth and prosperity. Following fashion was the occupation of the "modern woman," who often rejected old values and roles associated with the home. Fashion reflects the obsession with consumption and display in the public sphere rather than production in the private sphere of the home. A concern for fashion was an escape from a stifling role; a fashionable woman might indeed be perceived as having too much power for she projected an image of being in control of her environment, rather than a slave to the demands of domesticity.

While women of fashion sought to be modern by adopting the newest styles created by the clothing industry and couturiers, they had a counterpart in the women who adhered to more traditional conservative values. If the "ideal fashion beauty" was a contrived and unnatural phenomenon, the antithetical appearance of simplicity was considered "natural." The women who subscribed to simplicity in dress, in keeping perhaps with a Protestant ethic, did not subscribe to what they perceived as the idle worship of fashion; nonetheless, they did not choose to wear radical reform clothing. They wanted to maintain a quiet and proper appearance that rendered them inconspicuous and could be read as moral purity, a religious, particularly Protestant concept. They looked for a middle ground between caring too much about their appearance and showing too little interest and appearing sloppy, which would in their minds also give an impression of being unworthy.[36]

FASHION'S DETRACTORS: THE HEALTH REFORMERS

As noted earlier, there were many individuals and groups who believed not only that women's fashionable dress was immoral but that it was destroying women's health and should be changed for that reason. Their arguments against fashion were strongest against the corset, particularly the practice of tight lacing. In all, women's clothing was perceived to deplete their physical energies and deprive them of good health. The appeals against fashion were clear: advocates of reform believed that corsets adversely affected internal organs, that long skirts swept up filthy debris from the streets, that the weight of the skirts and petticoats impaired movement, that uneven temperatures caused by clothing brought on sickness, and, finally, that faulty suspension of garments put undue stress on the anatomy. Women's health was a critical issue and, indeed, it was the early-nineteenth-century health reformers who set the stage for other groups. Furthermore, promoters of artistic reform dress in the late nineteenth century believed that it was only through good health and a return to a natural, healthy, and fit body that women could ever achieve true beauty.[37]

Although it is clear that many traditionally trained physicians blamed women's clothing for their health problems, most of the articles published by them appeared only in professional medical journals where they did not reach the general public. There were exceptions, of course, like the writings of Dr. Andrew Combe, who first brought notice to the problem of tight lacing in 1832. His works were widely read and accessible. But substantial effort to reform women's clothing grew out of health-and hygiene-reform sects that emerged in response to critical health problems experienced by middle-class society in the nineteenth century. At the time many Americans had lost faith in orthodox, allopathic medicine, which continued to rely on blood letting, calomel, and other harsh remedies to overcome the effects of disease. Instead, they sought treatment through alternative medical practices and home-based cures. The health-reform movement can be viewed as a network that encompassed not only the various medical sects of homeopathy, hydropathy, hypnotism, and phrenology but also vegetarianism, temperance, physiological and hygienic instruction, physical education, and, of course, dress reform. The health-reform movement, and many of its component sects, flourished first in Europe, then was transmitted to the eastern part of the United States.[38]

In America health-reform groups offered a different therapeutic approach to managing disease and often stressed the ability of nature to heal, especially after patients changed to more healthful and hygienic personal habits. For the most part they believed that prevention was better than cure. Unlike allopathic physicians, the promoters of healthful living did not view women as subordinate humans prone by their very physiology to chronic illness. The leaders of these sects believed that women needed to be healthy and sought to improve the conditions of their lives, including the stresses placed on women's bodies by their clothing. Most important, however, these alternative sects welcomed women into their ranks as physicians and healers. While many of them sought good health for women to improve their existence in the domestic sphere, others sought good health for women so they could take their places in society—that is, in the public sphere.

The Rise of Medical Sects

One of the earliest therapeutic physicians was botanist Samuel Thomson, who used native herbs in his patented medicines. His book, which sold 100,000 copies, reached roughly three million followers. Although his medicines included harsh purgatives, the appeal was in the possibilities for home doctoring. Thomson derided apothecaries and pharmacists as purveyors of poisons. The popularity of Thomsonianism, as the sect's therapy was referred to, is seen in the nearly 100 medical colleges that arose to teach the ideology and in the establishment of numerous infirmaries. An offshoot of Thomsonian ideology was an eclecticism that welcomed women to the profession on an equal status with men.[39]

Following the popularity of Thomsonianism, Samuel Hahnemann's homeo-pathic philosophy gained ground as an alternative method of healing. Homeo-pathic medicine likewise minimized the use of drugs and emphasized self-cure and rational living, including fresh air, pure foods, and water. Homeopathy welcomed women in its practice and significantly did not define all women's illnesses as womb-related. This sect also believed in the healing power of na-ture and lent strength to the view that abiding by nature's laws was the best way to remain healthy. Both Thomsonianism and homeopathy increased doubt in people's minds about regular allopathic medical procedures and cures.[40]

Perhaps the most recognized name in hygienic health reform is that of Syl-vester Graham. Graham opposed drugs and allopathic doctors and viewed right living as the way to good health. Graham's two-volume classic, *Lectures on the Science of Human Life* (1839), emphasized frequent bathing, fresh air, regular ex-ercise, vegetarianism, sunlight, personal hygiene, and dress reform. Graham's disciples in hygienic education included two women who lectured to female audiences on hygiene and dress reform, Mary Jane Gove Nichols and Paulina Wright Davis. Both women advocated birth control as a means to maintain women's health and strength, which they believed was so often drained through excessive childbearing.[41]

As a hygienic reformer, William Andros Alcott's contributions were many but he is especially well known as an author and editor. In his journal, *Modern Reformer and Teachings in the Human Constitution*, which began in 1835, and in *The Young Woman's Book of Health* (1855), he argued for woman's education as well as for the need to reform their health, a reform that encompassed improve-ment in their clothing. Alcott altered Graham's health principles and made them more acceptable to a wider audience.[42] The proliferation of Graham's lectures and Alcott's urgings on the subject of health created a suitable climate for the organization of the American Physiological Society in 1837. This group sought to educate people to care for their physical selves. Through this organization, Alcott went so far as to urge women to form anti-corset societies, whose mem-bers "'signed the pledge' not to wear them."[43]

Alcott's and Graham's early efforts soon led Horace Mann, the prominent Massachusetts education reformer, to realize the importance of hygiene educa-tion in the public schools. After circulating several surveys and reports on the state of sanitary conditions and personal hygiene in the state, the legislature was persuaded to pass a bill in 1850 "requiring the teaching of 'physiology and hygiene' in the public schools and the examination of all teachers on their abil-ity to give instruction in these subjects." The passing of this legislation encour-aged other states to follow in their lead and paved the way for all Americans, not just the elite, to reap the benefits of good hygiene and physical education. Instruction included, of course, warnings for girls and young women regarding the ill effects of wearing restrictive clothing.[44]

Phrenologists, as noted by Susan A. Cayleff, also took a stance on health issues: temperance, exercise, fresh air, and reform dress. The sect originated with the writings of Franz Joseph Gall and Johan Casper Spurzheim and spread to America through Spurzheim's lectures and the efforts of George Combe of Scotland, who advocated physical exercise and physiology education. Lorenzo and Orson Fowler also melded phrenology with "Grahamite" dietary and sex principles and became successful publishers of books and journals. Phrenologists shared the health position of many reform groups and, like many of them, denied women's inferiority. Sarah J. Hale, editor of Boston's *Ladies' Magazine*, observed "'Phrenology will do more to elevate women than any other system has ever done.'"[45]

As Cayleff pointed out, many male health reformers delineated the evils of the corset, yet as lecturers to women their way was blocked by moral prejudice against men's discussing female anatomy in a public lecture in front of women. This attitude, in turn, led to more women entering the medical field. The various nontraditional medical sects and the health reformers also welcomed women into their world as equal participants in bringing about health reform through prevention strategies. Women were especially welcome in the area of gynecology and obstetrics. The first woman physician trained in traditional medical practices was Elizabeth Blackwell, who received a medical degree in 1849. Her first book, *The Laws of Life* (1852), emphasized good hygiene and physical exercise for women.[46]

Hydropathic Medicine

It was the medical sect named hydropathy, however, which most heartily welcomed women into its ranks. With a reliance on both hot and cold water as a cure, this approach was similar to therapies practiced since the eighteenth century in Britain and on the continent of Europe. Vincent Priessnitz in Silesia experimented with the curative powers of cold water and after curing a sprained wrist and broken ribs with cold wet bandages, he opened a sanitarium on his property, which eventually became world renowned for its success. Between 1831 and 1841 Priessnitz treated seven thousand patients. The Priessnitz method found its way to America in the 1840s. Again, like other sects, the hydropaths emphasized self-doctoring and healing techniques. Ultimately, many women received medical degrees through training in the water-cure methods.[47]

Since it was clear that "dress reform . . . is synonymous with health reform," hydropathic physicians supported efforts toward reform dress, and many of them adopted some form of rational clothing. These physicians included Mary Walker, Ellen Beard Harman, Harriet N. Austin, Mary Gove Nichols, Rachel Brooks Gleason, Lucretia Jackson, and Ellen G. White. Many of them were active in the National Dress Reform Association, established in 1856, and published articles in water-cure journals and related health literature. A detailed account of these women's efforts appears in chapter 2, on trousers.

The health issue was further promoted by advocates who believed that good health could be achieved only through proper exercise. Furthermore, they argued that only through exercise such as calisthenics and gymnastics could women attain true natural beauty. Calisthenics and gymnastics have their origins in Europe. They became especially popular in Germany and France in the 1820s and 1830s and soon spread to England and America. The beginnings, however, were sporadic. The German nationalistic gymnastic movement initiated by Friedrich Ludwig Jahn spread to America when Jahn's disciple Charles Follen sought political refuge. In 1826 Follen established a gymnasium at Harvard, where he also taught the German language, and, in the same year, took over a public gymnasium in Boston; the latter, however, lasted only through the early 1830s. Another exercise system "transplanted to America" was the "movement cure," the application of rhythmical movements to the human body, which originated in Sweden and quickly found adherents among health-care promoters in America. In 1830, in the *Journal of Health,* Edward Hitchcock, a professor at Amherst College and an early promoter of physical exercise, advocated regular exercise—sports, games, and especially gymnastics. While many of these experiments lasted only a few years, longer-lasting programs for physical exercise in America often were instituted in colleges and academies, especially those that admitted young women. These included "Emma Willard's school in Troy, New York, since 1821; . . . Catharine Beecher's school in Hartford, Connecticut, since 1828; and . . . Mt. Holyoke College . . . since 1837."[48]

The most outspoken advocate of exercise for women in America was Catharine Beecher, a vociferous critic of tight lacing and, between 1837 and the Civil War, author of many volumes of self-help advice literature for women. She disliked corsets, tight shoes, and other "unnatural" forms of dress, and believed that this restrictive clothing was a danger to future generations. In her *Physiology and Calisthenics for Schools and Families* (1856), she included an illustration that showed the natural skeleton of a woman compared to one deformed by "Art": that is, by the fashionable corset.[49]

Calisthenics was the name given to female gymnastics. Men's gymnastics differed from women's calisthenics in that they were more strenuous and used parallel bars, climbing ropes, and other equipment. Calisthenics included stretching exercises, extensions of arms and legs, bending from the waist, deep knee bends, leg raises, high stepping, and the use of some small three- to five-pound weights. Beecher and others warned against overexertion, which characterized participants in men's gymnastics practiced at the popular German Turnverein Clubs in America in the 1830s.[50]

Gymnastics and calisthenics were a positive approach to achieving good health because they suggested that people could and should condition their bodies in an active way. Such action would, many thought, improve the race. This moralistic perspective paved the way for further development after the

War Between the States. Indeed, by the mid-nineteenth century gymnasiums became popular again, especially in urban areas. After the Civil War, with expansion of industry in cities, the gyms served as an escape from mental fatigue and relief from the largely sedentary lifestyles that typified life in urban areas. With so many new arrivals into the city, the gymnasium also served as a community center for those who felt displaced from their families.[51]

Perfection of the body through exercise—calisthenics, gymnastics, physical education, and sports—became an essential ingredient of the system of Christian morality. The "Muscular Christianity" movement, which originated in England, also linked morals and physical culture. The most popular way to become a Muscular Christian was through gymnastics. Exercise, therefore, became more than a prevention for disease: believers had loftier aims—"to raise man to the summit of his nature."[52] It was apparent, no doubt, that calisthenics would do the same for women.

One of the best-known promoters of health through exercise was Dio Lewis, who advocated temperance, health reform, dress reform, homeopathy, and women's rights. Dio Lewis trained with German and Swedish physical educators in Europe in the 1850s. After this preparation he opened a gymnastics school in Boston and published several books on his rhythmic-exercise system, receiving great success with *New Gymnastics for Men, Women, and Children* (1862). Lewis especially encouraged women to participate. He believed that his system was an improvement over Beecher's less strenuous program. Lewis, in fact, trained many women to teach gymnastics-calisthenics in Boston. Caroline Severance, one of the founders of the New England Women's Club, at one time lectured at Dio Lewis's school in Boston.[53]

Lewis promoted dress reform and required women to wear loose clothing for his classes, clothing that did not restrict the waist or shoulders. His program included simple apparatus and exercises that emphasized eye-hand coordination and the element of play. These included throwing and catching bean-bags, exercise rings for isometrics, running, arm pulls, and the use of apparatus such as dumbbells, wands, and Indian Clubs. Music accompanied all of Lewis's exercises, hence the term "Rhythmics" is used to describe them.[54]

The question of what constituted beauty became an issue with the health reformers. They believed that physical exercise was the only way a woman could achieve a true, naturally beautiful body and form. This notion was in opposition to the idea that true beauty depended on the artifice of fashionable clothing and cosmetics. Many reformers believed that any garment that caused a distortion of the body was unhealthy. In *Fit for America* Harvey Green observed that Beecher's goals were to promote health and thus secure beauty and strength. Beecher was one of the first American educational reformers to assert the notion that beauty was a function of health. The ideal was that what is found in nature should take preference over art.[55]

Beecher believed that the ancient Greeks exemplified health and beauty, that they had the most perfect form of human beauty. Advocates of exercise asserted that the body shape of Greek and Roman statuary was the ideal. Beecher certainly was against portliness as a standard for men and recommended gymnastics for them. But calisthenics, she observed, offered many advantages for both men and women. Furthermore, they could carry out these exercises in mixed company. Most physical educators believed that exercise diminished a taste for sensual pleasure, which nineteenth-century reformers viewed as debilitating to both body and mind if carried to excess.[56]

Regarding beauty, Dio Lewis concurred with Beecher, observing that "beauty in women is, in considerable part, a matter of health." Women, from his point of view, need not sacrifice their desire for health in order to be attractive; they would look good, indeed, be beautiful, simply by living the healthy life. The argument that health promoted beauty appears in most dress-reform literature, the most important idea being that the natural body is more beautiful than one altered by the vagaries of fashion. Reformers in America, particularly Annie Jenness-Miller and Frances Mary Steele and Elizabeth Livingston Steele Adams, believed that reform of the body must occur first. This they believed could be achieved by exercise and through the adoption of their reform systems of underwear. The most outspoken promoters of the idea of "Beauty in Nature" were British advocates for reforming the arts, first the English Pre-Raphaelites and aesthetes and later the advocates for reform in the arts and crafts. Taken together, these British promoters of natural beauty were only part of the larger modern design movement that was occurring all over Europe and in America between 1850 and 1914.[57]

The ideas introduced in this chapter will be discussed further in subsequent chapters. Chapter 2 examines the efforts of reformers to promote health, hygiene, and physical and political freedom for women through the adoption of trousers. Chapter 3 details efforts toward maintaining good health through the improvement of undergarments. Chapters 4, 5, and 6 examine efforts of individuals and groups who promoted dress reform through their interest in "modern design" and the application of art principles to the creation of "artistic" dress. Chapter 7 deals with the relationship between reform styles of dress and high fashion, as well as the progress made toward freedom in dress for women during the first two decades of the twentieth century.

CHAPTER TWO

Trousers

The Rational Alternative to Skirts

The enormities of woman's dress, having done their best to deform her
body, will very naturally do their bravest to destroy it.
—Elizabeth Stuart Phelps, *What to Wear.*

One of the first elements of mid-nineteenth-century fashionable dress to
come under the reformers' fire was the long, full skirt. Long skirts dragged
on the ground, sweeping up vermin and debris from the street with every step
and redepositing it in the house. Petticoats hung heavy on the waist; even the
lighter cage crinoline could swing out and flip up in the wind. Trains and bustles
were heavy and awkwardly balanced. Women's skirts made walking up and down
stairs treacherous and running nearly impossible. At worst, they threatened the
wearer's life because they could easily catch on fire in an era when women were
exposed to open wood or coal fires. For reform-minded women, one reasonable
alternative to skirts was the adoption of some sort of trousered garment.[1]

In choosing trousers the reformers sought a solution that they believed was
both practical and modest. Most women did not choose to wear men's clothing
and they did not elect to reveal their legs, for both would have been improper,
indeed, unthinkable. Rather, they chose to wear a dress with a cut similar to
other fashionable women's dresses except for its shortened skirt and its matching trousers, which were either cut straight or gathered in at the ankle. Loose
trousers worn under a skirt seemed like a logical choice (Fig. 17). Trousers were
practical and there was historical precedent for women's adoption of them.
Trousers of some kind had been the acceptable garment for women to wear in

Fig. 17 One of many Bloomer costumes featured in fashion periodicals, book covers, newspapers, sheet-music covers, and fashion plates in the 1850s. *Peterson's Monthly Magazine* (January 1851).

sanitariums, as well as for calisthenics classes and outdoor activities such as mountaineering, but these trousers generally were not worn in public.

In mid-century, the controversy regarding trousers was that some women wanted the freedom to wear a trousered garment in public as an alternative to fashionable dress. The adoption of trousers by women as rational and healthy reform clothing to be worn for all occasions attracted much attention in newspapers, for in the mid-nineteenth century women did not ordinarily wear trousers in public. Women who wore any form of trousers in public chanced being ridiculed or taken for an actress or prostitute. Trousers were associated with men's clothing, not women's. Indeed, in Western cultures trousers had become fixed as a gender-specific garment for men. When some women, such as the American physician Mary Walker, blatantly wore masculine clothing in public, they risked being arrested. Even when women wore loose, feminized baggy trousers under a skirt in public they rarely failed to draw attention and frequently endured harassment. It was hardly a risk for women to adopt trousers for use away from public scrutiny—for reasons of health, comfort, convenience, and especially while engaged in calisthenics and sports—but women who wore trousers in public were making a political statement and accepted the risk of possible ridicule.[2]

In the early 1850s, the American women's-rights advocates Amelia Bloomer, Elizabeth Cady Stanton, the Grimké sisters, and Lucy Stone were among the first women to wear trousers in public. They shortened their dresses and wore loose, full trousers underneath them. However, many women's rights advocates were quick to discard this style of dressing when it became clear that the negative effect of wearing trousers in public impeded their progress toward improving women's rights. Nonetheless, throughout the second half of the nineteenth century in both America and Europe health reformers devoted to rational dress, proper diet, and exercise continued to wear trousers in public. Indeed, their rationality brought them jeers, comments, and looks of distaste. This negative reaction to women wearing pants in public occurred even after trousers became more socially acceptable for exercise, sports, and outdoor activities such as bicycling at the turn of the century.[3]

In this chapter, I consider the reasons that women wore trousers in the nineteenth century. I examine their possible origins in women's apparel in the Middle East and in children's clothing and also their adoption by communal groups and their acceptance as suitable dress for calisthenics in the early nineteenth century. But most important, I discuss the adoption of trousers by feminists, water-cure physicians, and sports enthusiasts who promoted and popularized their adoption, not only in the mid-1800s but throughout the nineteenth century.

A PRECEDENCE FOR TROUSERS BOTH PRACTICAL AND EXOTIC

In "The Gym Suit: Freedom at Last," Patricia C. Warner discusses the precedence for the adoption of trousers by women. She observes that their practical aspects were apparent in the early 1800s when French women wore trousers called pantalets or pantaloons under the simple chemise style of dress then in fashion (figure 18). While this mode was short-lived for adults, pantalets continued to accompany the shorter skirts worn by young girls throughout the nineteenth century. These children's pantaloons were meant to be shown. Later in the century, women devised a similar garment for underclothing.[4]

The practicality of trouserlike pantalets apparently appealed to women in some American communal societies. Several nineteenth-century communal

Fig. 18 "Les Graces en Pantalon," *Le Bon Genre* 42 (1810). Courtesy Patricia C. Warner.

groups devised a uniform style of dress that gave members a familial likeness and distinction. In public their dress marked them as outsiders and thus became a powerful indicator of their community boundaries and shared values.[5] The New Harmony Community, a utopian socialist communal group in Indiana, adopted a shortened dress with full trousers as early as 1824 (Fig. 19). However, not all members admired the trousered dress, for many women thought it improper to indicate the shape of the leg with trousers. In 1848, women in the Oneida Community in New York adopted the short dress and trousers and continued to wear the combination until the 1870s. Women in communal societies

Fig. 19 Frances Wright at age thirty-two in the costume adopted by the New Harmony Community in Indiana.

Fig. 20 French actor
Rachel as Roxane in
Racine's *Bajazet*. Illustration from the lithograph
by Achille Devéria.

adopted the style because it was comfortable for work and because it symbolized the social freedom of the wearer. Yet they felt social pressure, which often kept them from wearing their trouser-style dress in public.[6]

Full, loose pants had long been worn by women in the Middle East, and when actresses depicted Muslim women on the stage they wore the appropriate costume—trousers. In 1838, the French actress Rachel brought attention to the authentic trousers worn by Muslim women when she wore them as Roxane in the play *Bajazet* (figure 20). In 1843, the actress Fanny Kemble was seen wearing pantaloons not on stage but rather while fishing at the resort at Yellow Springs near Philadelphia. On December 1, 1851, comments about Kemble's "male attire" appeared in the feminist journal the *Lily*. Kemble also wore a similar costume in Lenox, Massachusetts, in 1849 and, according to the *Lily*, Kemble received derisive sneers from the local press. By wearing loose, "exotic" trousers in public view, whether on stage or at a resort, these actresses were helping to set a precedent for all women to wear trousers in public.[7] Knowledge of clothing worn in the Middle East was readily available. Turkish trousers had intrigued traders and travelers to the area since the rise of British and French trade with India, Persia, and Turkey in the mid-eighteenth century. Because Turkish trousers were exotic, fashionable young men and women in Europe wore them for leisure wear, masquerade balls, and as the "drapery" (clothing) for informal portraits. Even Mme. de Pompadour was portrayed by Carle Van Loo wearing Turkish trousers. The artist Delacroix returned from travels in Spain, Turkey, and Morocco with works of romantic scenes that detailed the costume typically worn by women in harems—long, baggy pants tied at the ankle.[8]

While the full, baggy Turkish trousers seemed to attract a great amount of attention in western Europe and America, it must be noted that during the nineteenth century women in the provinces of eastern and central Europe also wore a shortened skirt with boots or trousers. A glance through travel accounts and works depicting the "dress of other nations" makes this quite apparent. Indeed, in all of the Ottoman Empire and even in Turkey itself, there were several different styles of trousers worn by women, and these changed over time. The term for Turkish trousers is *salvar*. In eighteenth-century Istanbul women wore *salvar*s with a matching jacket (*anteri*) over undergarments. Although Turkish women wore full, baggy trousers, not all Muslims wore the full style; Persian women preferred a straight-legged trouser.[9]

In the West trousers were, as I have mentioned, worn by young women for exercising. Early in the nineteenth century, as a way to improve the health of young girls and women, educators like Catharine Beecher and Dio Lewis developed calisthenics programs for female students. For this new activity they chose practical pantalets for the students to wear under a shortened skirt. Wearing trousers for such physical activity did not cause a stir because most of these classes were held away from public scrutiny. Also, young girls already had been wearing pantaloons under their short dresses for modesty, comfort, and convenience.[10]

Fig. 21 The typical clothing worn for female calisthenics included some type of trousers. "Illustrations for Calisthenic Exercises," *Atkinson's Casket* 104 (April 1832): 186–87.

The adoption of pantalets was not a new idea even in the 1830s. Indeed, schools in Germany, Sweden, and England adopted the practical pantalets as part of a gymnasium suit worn by young women perhaps as early as 1807. The earliest-known representation of a *trousered* gymnasium or calisthenics dress for women appeared in 1832, when *Atkinson's Casket* recommended the outfit for exercise for urban women, who, they believed, needed to strengthen their arms, shoulders, and backs (Fig. 21). In 1841, the editor of *Godey's Lady's Book*, Sarah J. Hale, quoted a physician from Glasgow, Scotland, on the subject of the appropriateness of young girls being allowed to wear Turkish pantalets or trousers and a short frock while exercising.[11]

It is not surprising that women adopted full trousers and a shortened skirt to achieve comfort, for they were adopting a garment with which they were already familiar, one they might even have worn for exercising as young girls. As many social arbiters saw it, the problem was that in the mid-nineteenth century women desired to wear trousers in public rather than reserving them for the seclusion of a gymnasium, their homes, or sanitariums.

WOMEN ADOPT TROUSERS IN AMERICA

Early Adopters: Nineteenth-Century Feminists and the Bloomer

While it is clear that under certain circumstances women wore trousers early in the nineteenth century, scholars usually credit the feminist Elizabeth Smith Miller as the first American woman to wear the trousers and short skirt in public

(Fig. 22). That is, she wore trousers on the street, not when confined to a health institution or for a theatrical production or masquerade ball. Scholars do not agree on whether Miller first saw the trousers at a sanitarium in Europe, whether she took the idea from the clothing worn at the Oneida Community that was close to her home, or whether she copied the design of a gymnasium costume. What she herself stated was that after spending hours at work in her garden and becoming thoroughly disgusted with the long skirt, she adopted a short dress that was four inches below the knee and full Turkish trousers gathered in at the ankle.[12]

After making the change, Miller visited Seneca Falls, New York, where she introduced the reform garment to her father's cousin Elizabeth Cady Stanton and to Stanton's friend Amelia Bloomer. Stanton adopted the style at once (Fig. 23), and Mrs. Bloomer not long after. Amelia Bloomer, feminist and editor of the *Lily*, a journal devoted to temperance and women's rights, described the advantages of the shortened skirt and trousers in an article in the *Lily* in 1851 (Fig. 24).

Fig. 22 Elizabeth Smith Miller, *From Hoop-skirts to Nudity* (Caldwell, Idaho: Caxton Printers, 1938).

Fig. 23 Elizabeth Cady Stanton photographed wearing a short dress with trousers. "The First of the Flappers," *Literary Digest* (May 13, 1922): 44.

Fig. 24 Amelia Bloomer in 1851 wearing the short dress and full trousers gathered at the ankle, the style that the press soon named the Bloomer.

The local newspaper, the *Courier,* also commented favorably on the style worn by Bloomer. According to Bloomer, the *New York Tribune* noticed that article and "made it known to thousands of readers that [she] had donned the short skirt and trousers"; and from this the news went from paper to paper throughout this country and countries abroad. Bloomer said, "I was praised and censured, glorified and ridiculed, until I stood in amazement at the furor I had wrought by my pen while sitting quietly in my little office at home attending to my duties." It took little time for newspapers across the country to affix the term "Bloomer" to the style. Although the coverage was widespread, Amelia Bloomer later observed that some of her editorial brethren commended the "Bloomers" highly, while others cried out against this "usurpation of the rights of man."[13]

Immediately following its introduction in 1851, commendations of the Bloomer costume were indeed widespread. Supporters in America noted the practicality and convenience of the new costume as well as its healthful benefits. They saw moral and patriotic qualities in its simplicity and modesty. Favorable commentary on the bloomer appeared in many newspapers. The reaction in Ohio, for example, was positive. The *Hancock Journal* in Findlay, Ohio, like other small papers, often reprinted news articles from larger newspapers. On April 25, 1851, the *Journal* quoted Amelia Bloomer on the reasons that she wore a short dress and full trousers. Later that summer, on July 17, they reported their pleasure "that the press generally notices the new dress favorably" and observed that Bloomers were being worn in various cities: New York City; New Haven, Connecticut; Lycoming, Pennsylvania; Manchester, New Hampshire; Newark, New Jersey; Milwaukee, Wisconsin; and Cincinnati, Ohio. An account of Bloomer wearers in Adrian, Michigan, appeared on June 26; then on July 25 the *Hancock Journal* printed two more accounts: the first was a brief statement about 500 girls in Lowell, Massachusetts, wearing the garment for a Fourth of July parade; the second was to report that a young woman in Findlay was seen wearing the Bloomer dress. Feminist and dress-reform publications offered more Ohio opinions, some suggesting the opposition that followed the initial supportive response. In a letter dated February 28, 1853, in the *Lily*, a Bloomer wearer from Mt. Gilead, Ohio, observed that she had worn it for nearly a year and a half and had never been troubled with ridicule. She gave her opinion that other women had not adopted it out of fear of opposition and lack of resolution and energy.

Several Ohio notices appeared in the new magazine devoted to dress reform, the *Sibyl, a Review of the Follies, Errors, and Fashions of Society*, published under the auspices of the National Dress Reform Association, whose supporters were largely associated with the water-cure movement. A woman from Worthington desperately wrote: "Please send something on the Dress Reform to one who can hardly keep her head above the mountain waves of opposition." A writer from Ashtabula noted, "I am wearing the reform Dress. Some laugh, but I still keep wearing it, without strong opposition."[14]

In October 1852, the *Lily* reprinted a letter that had been sent to the *Water Cure Journal* from a "Bloomerite" in Brownheim, Ohio. The correspondent noted that after witnessing a great falling off the previous summer on the part of newspaper editors, and the public generally, "one would naturally have supposed that long before this there would not be one solitary Bloomer to tell the sad tale of their defeat." Yet, here and there, she observed, "We find a Bloomerite, indeed, in whom there is no guile and so far from their becoming extinct, they are steadfastly increasing. In this town, there is quite a number who esteem health, comfort, and convenience, far above fashion or popularity. By wearing the Bloomer they are aware that they subject themselves to ridicule, but they would rather be a Bloomerite, and thank those who invented it."[15]

Books on the subject of women's-clothing reform soon became available. In *Dress Reform, Practically and Physiologically Considered* (1852), Angeline Merritt revealed the "abuses" produced by fashion's corsets and heavy skirts and provided

Fig. 25 Role reversal was a favored device for showing the folly of Bloomers. *Punch* 2 (1851): 3.

Fig. 26 (opposite) "Bloomerism, an American Custom." In this drawing the cartoonist managed to incorporate men's worst fears regarding the effect of the Bloomer.

remedial dress: a body-skimming gown ("sacque") worn over trousers ("petti-loons"). Merritt allowed that there were objections to reform dress and offered reasons for its limited adoption.[16]

Opponents of the Bloomer costume had strong arguments for rejecting it. Some simply believed it was bad fashion. Others saw it as immoral, since they believed that it was worn by some unsavory individuals. For some it was unpatri-otic, because of its foreign (Turkish) origins. Perhaps the strongest argument, the one that did most to bring about its demise as a viable alternative to fashionable dress, was the belief that the Bloomer costume was incongruous with the prevail-ing ideology regarding the role of women. There was a strong gender bias against women wearing trousers, which led to harassment when women wore Bloomers in public. It was not unusual for the Bloomer costume to cause a stir. Indeed, numerous cartoons employed the Bloomer to focus on, and play up to, deep-seated fears of people regarding gender ideologies (Figs. 25 and 26).[17]

In the nineteenth century, when all women wore skirts and all men wore trousers, clothing inevitably came to symbolize the mutually exclusive functions men and women were expected to perform. The ideology of the century was that women belonged in the home, running the household and caring for the chil-dren, while men belonged in the public sphere, running the worlds of business, politics, and commerce. Fashionable women's clothing, especially full skirts worn with many stiffened petticoats or a cage crinoline, could be heavy, awkward, or both and thus restrict movement. This clothing would have been inconvenient for many physical activities, indoors or out. To be active, women needed to make adjustments to their clothing, such as shortening skirts and loosening waists, something they often did for working at home or for farm chores. As such, fashionable garments worn in the public sphere appropriately symbolized women's restricted roles. Cartoons of the period suggest that if women decided to wear pants, it had to be because they wanted to be able to move freely on streets in the public world, and such behavior was often viewed as women's desiring to compete with men for places of public power. The cartoons might even suggest that if women did work in the public sphere there would be no one left to manage the home and men would be forced to stay home with the children.

When women wore trousers or Bloomers in sanitariums and water-cure establishments, the pants were no threat because they were associated with illness and dependence. Wearing Bloomers for exercise also suggested healthful

BLOOMERISM—AN AMERICAN CUSTOM.

benefits. But when Bloomers were coupled with feminist claims and rhetoric, they were a powerful threat to the cultural status quo. The Bloomer gained negative associations when it became connected to the women's rights movement, which at the time was considered a radical cause.[18]

Indeed, many women's-rights activists believed that fashionable dress was a symbol of their oppression. They shared Elizabeth Cady Stanton's opinion that woman's dress perfectly described her condition. "Her tight waist and long trailing skirts deprive her of all freedom. . . . No wonder man prescribes her sphere." Yet, notwithstanding the recommendations given in the *Lily* for wearing the Bloomer style, many feminists ceased to wear it because they wished to focus on other issues related to gaining rights for women. The feminists were not cheered on by other dress reformers for taking this stand. Gerrit Smith, for one, criticized Stanton and other women's-rights advocates for abandoning the reform dress and returning to clothing that "both marks and makes their impotence." Smith believed that dress was "an outgrowth and a symbol of women's oppression rather than a cause. . . . Whatever the moral war, those who wage it must first conquer themselves."[19]

Amelia Bloomer had a response for Smith and others who questioned her motives for abandoning trousers around 1859. In writing to a friend in 1865, Bloomer offered several reasons. First, she had moved to a new community and felt like donning long skirts when she went into society. Second, she found that the high winds easily blew her short skirt over her head and shoulders. Third, she kept the short skirt until the introduction of hoops, finding them light and pleasant to wear because they did away with heavy underskirts (her greatest objection to long dresses). Fourth, it was inconvenient and expensive to keep up two wardrobes—a long and short. Fifth, she felt that there were questions of greater importance than the length of a skirt under discussion at the time—and "I felt my influence would be greater in the dress ordinarily worn by women than in the one I was wearing."[20]

Not all activists ceased wearing trousers in order to promote women's rights. Indeed, many participants in movements for women's rights, temperance, and other causes continued the effort to reform women's dress throughout the late nineteenth century. Certainly, activities continued in upstate New York and in Ohio. Indeed, there were two grassroots efforts toward dress reform that occurred in Ohio during the 1870s. One took place in South Newbury, Ohio, which had been a busy and progressive little hamlet at the close of the eighteenth century and during the first twenty years of the nineteenth century. It began to decline with the advent of the electric railway and later automobiles and paved roads. However, in September 1870, in that progressive town situated in Geauga County a group of men and women organized what may have been the first society for dress reform in Ohio, the Northern Ohio Health and Dress Reform Association. Ellen Munn, an ardent dress reformer, noted that its object was to get rid of "unhealthful, unnatural and inconvenient forms of dress" and to feed and clothe the human body with a view to its anatomical structure. The organizers announced the association's "Dress Reform Picnic" for "all women having courage to lay aside symbols of their servility and don the American Costume of "trowsers and frock" (Fig. 27). All tolerant men, and only such, also were invited. According to the magazine, Ellen Munn wore plaid baggy trousers, secured at the ankle with ruffles embellished with lace or rickrack braid. A full jacket hung over this, knee-length.[21]

The club met regularly at the Union Chapel, a meeting house dedicated to Free Speech and built by residents after the Congregational "Brick" church refused to allow James A. Garfield to speak. The Northern Ohio Health and Dress Reform Association had a membership of seventy, which included: "Elizabeth Fisher, first suffragist; Anna Green, author of a suffrage poem; D. M. Allen, vice president; Ruth Munn, president; Sophia L. O. Allen, leader in every good and progressive cause; Mary Hodges, treasurer; Ellen Munn, recording secretary; and Julia Green, M.D., corresponding secretary." They celebrated the organization of the National Dress Reform Association and women's suffrage every year by having a Fourth of July picnic where women were expected to wear Bloomers.[22]

The dress-reform organization led to the formation of the South Newbury Woman's Suffrage and Political Club, the second oldest suffrage organization in Ohio and one of the oldest in the United States. D. M. Allen (Darius Allen) drafted the constitution, which was signed by twenty-two South Newbury men and women. Ruth Munn was the first president. Many of the early members of the Suffrage and Political Club had also belonged to the National Dress Reform Association. The constitution of the Suffrage and Political Club aimed to place "women on a pecuniary, social and political equality with men." At its inaugural meeting Susan B. Anthony spoke for two hours on impartial suffrage and temperance, and even rebuked tobacco.[23]

The first meeting of the American Free Dress League held in 1874 marked the second dress-reform effort in Ohio. (In Tillotson's words, "fre" for them meant "freedom ov the individual to decide on needs and stiles ov dres, and fisical freedom from waing pressure, restraint and impediment of stiles.") The idea for this organization occurred on the last day of an anti-fashion convention held in January of that same year in Vineland, New Jersey. Faithful friends of Mary E. Tillotson, who had organized the anti-fashion meeting, gathered at her home to discuss the possibility of forming a new organization devoted to dress reform. A number of participants came from outside the New York and Vineland area, including Darius and Sophia Allen of South Newbury, Ohio, active participants in the earlier 1870 meeting in South Newbury. To manifest their regard for equality, the organizers elected a man and a woman to share the various offices. The Allens shared the presidency. The participants planned to have their first meeting in September of that year (1874) in Painesville, Ohio, a village not far from the Allens' home in South Newbury.[24]

The first meeting of the American Free Dress League took place with members of the Ohio press in attendance. In addition to the local paper, the *Northern Ohio Journal*, newspaper reporters covering the meeting were Miss Emma Janes

Fig. 27 The scene may have been much like the painting *Anti-slavery Picnic at Weymouth Landing, Massachusetts,* ca. 1845. By artist Susan Torrey Merritt. Watercolor, gouache, and collage on paper, 74.9 x 100 cm. Gift of Elizabeth R. Vaughn, 195.1846.

of the Cleveland *Leader* and "Editress" of the *Earnest Worker;* Mathews of the Cleveland *Leader;* Gould of the Cleveland *Herald;* and McCormack of the Madison *Gazette.* The *Northern Ohio Journal* carried announcements of the meeting and later reported on its activities, including the resolutions offered by Mary Tillotson, the constitution of the organization, and, later, the text of the speech given by Darius Allen. Although on the morning of the first day the number in attendance was quite small, the paper noted, by the afternoon and evening the number of attendees had increased substantially, to more than fifty.[25]

The local press was not favorably inclined toward the conveners. They admired the conservative wing made up of women such as Stanton, Julia Ward Howe, and Mrs. Livermore but had little regard for the more radical group, officered by females whose zeal they thought was only equaled by their lack of personal charms. It was this radical wing of the reformers that met in Painesville.[26]

Tillotson offered resolutions stating that women should have the same freedom of action with their dress as that enjoyed by men. At the meeting Tillotson's clothing, a short dress worn with loose trousers, was described by one unsympathetic journalist as "aggressively ugly." The newspaper noted that she was the leader of the radical group of reformers. Other speakers included Darius Allen and two female physicians: Sarah Chase, from Cleveland, who professed that, although she did not wear the reform style, she never wore corsets; and Dr. S. A. Vibbert, of Somerville, Massachusetts, who also appeared without Bloomers, although she believed in dress reform in theory. She explained that her husband prevented her from wearing them. Vibbert reportedly observed that there were two thousand women throughout the United States wearing the Bloomer. Clearly, the reporter was biased against the reformers, frequently commenting on the appearance and weight of the speakers.[27]

It is evident that the progressive element in Ohio—those working toward temperance, suffrage, and abolition—also saw the need to improve women's health through dress reform and exercise. The Allen family of South Newbury, like many others in northeast Ohio, had come from progressive regions of New England and New York state. Caroline Severance, one of the founders of the New England Women's Club in 1868, had been active in the women's-rights movement in Ohio before she moved to Boston with her banker husband.

Hydropathic Medicine and Trousers

While both feminists and water-cure advocates experienced insults while wearing Bloomers, the promoters of dress reform in the water-cure movement outlasted the feminists in their persistence. Although some reformers actively involved in promoting feminist issues thought that Bloomers had become counterproductive to their efforts, for health reformers this was less the case. It appears that health reformers could advocate the Bloomer costume with much less public harassment because adopting Bloomers for health reasons admitted to weakness and, thus, was less threatening to the status quo.

Fig. 28 Harriet N. Austin, M.D., in the American Costume of her own design with straight trouser legs. Courtesy Dansville Area Historical Society.

Health journals, such as the *Water Cure Journal* (first published in 1845 and later called the *Herald of Health*), likewise promoted sensible dress for women. Mary Gove Nichols, editor of the *Water Cure Journal*, adopted the Bloomer style herself, testifying that it brought her new health and courage. As editor of *Laws of Life and Women's Health Journal*, (Fig. 28), Harriet Austin likewise spread the gospel of hygienic dressing from 1857 until the 1870s.[28] The *Sibyl*, published between

1856 and 1864, became the voice of women who promoted health reform in the water-cure movement. As such, it was the counterpart to Amelia Bloomer's magazine, the *Lily*, which was the voice of the feminists who promoted reform in the 1850s. However, the *Sibyl*, edited by Lydia Sayer Hasbrouck, an energetic Bloomer wearer and water-cure physician, took the cause of improving women's clothing to greater heights. Indeed, Hasbrouck's journal was devoted almost singly to dress reform.

In an effort to reach a greater audience for dress reform, strengthen the movement, and inform the public, James Caleb Jackson took the lead in sponsoring a dress reform convention at the Glen Haven Water Cure in 1856. The participants all joined the National Dress Reform Association and met the following June with fifty attendees. The association met regularly in central New York, in places such as Canastota, Syracuse, Cortlandville, Skaneateles, Auburn, Waterloo, and Middleton. Officers included well-known reformers Harriet Austin, Lydia Sayer Hasbrouck, Mary Walker, and Ellen Beard Harman, all with medical degrees from Russell Trall's and the Nichols' colleges. The National Dress Reform Association meetings included speeches by widely recognized health and dress reformers and exhibits of model reform gowns. At the Canastota meeting in 1857, Jackson made the claim that more than 6,000 women in America had adopted a reform costume. Despite the hostilities during the Civil War, the 1860 meeting in Rochester attracted six hundred to eight hundred men and women during a two-day session. Twenty-five women from Dansville attended wearing the "American Costume" (with straight-cut trousers), and all participants were dressed in some style of reform dress. Both the *Sibyl* and the *Water Cure Journal* promoted the meetings of the association.[29]

Articles in the *Sibyl* indicate the number of women who adopted Bloomers to better their health. Women from almost every state belonged to the National Dress Reform Association, and many of them reported their experiences in letters published in the *Sibyl*. Wisconsin women contributed reports on difficulties with their husbands accepting the Bloomer and wearing the Bloomer for farmwork. A physician wore hers on her rounds to visit patients, and one woman was married in a Bloomer costume. It was not unusual for lists of the names of regional members to appear in the journal. For instance the names of ninety-five dress reformers from Wisconsin appeared in the *Sibyl* on September 1, 1858, and on July 15, 1859.[30]

The water-cure physicians were some of the strongest supporters of dress reform. Jane B. Donegan, in *Hydropathic Highway to Health*, speculated that hydropathic interests in revising women's clothing might have predated efforts made by women's-rights advocates. Women and men who practiced medicine at the various water-cure establishments, for the most part, believed that dress reform was a necessity. In the early years, for practical purposes during treatment, physicians advised women to wear comfortable clothing during their stay at a water-cure establishment. As discussed in chapter 1, hydropathy was one of several medical sects that promoted reform in women's dress. The *Water*

Cure Journal became very popular and was one of the most widely read health periodicals of its day. Water-cure establishments, which numbered as many as 213 in existence between 1843 and 1900, offered a respite from daily life but also provided a rigorous program that included exercise, a healthy diet (often vegetarian), and water-cure treatments. It was necessary for female patients to be loosely clad in order to benefit from "free and full expansion of the lungs," clearly a function that would not be possible while wearing a corset.[31]

Donegan observed that from the very beginning hydropaths argued against tight lacing and restrictive clothing for their women clients. In 1847, James Caleb Jackson noted that females at his new Glen Haven Water Cure would not be asked to sacrifice health to fashion. And Henry M. Foster, a physician at the Graetenberg Water Cure, declared that "'fashion was a tyrant and women should adapt their clothing to achieve good health.'" The hydropaths ascribed many problems to women's fashionable clothing of the 1850s. Jackson observed that clothing made locomotion difficult, forcing women to avoid climbing stairs and carrying heavy objects, which thus deprived them of exercise necessary to develop a sound circulatory system, which, in turn, was necessary to prevent a wide variety of disorders, including consumption and dyspepsia. Jackson went on to say that women's clothing displaced and crowded their internal organs, causing difficulty in urination and defecation as well as disorders of the organs themselves.

As noted by Jane Donegan, Rachel Brooks Gleason wrote a series of articles on reforming fashion for the *Water Cure Journal* in the 1850s deploring the "'semi-suicidal voluminous heavy skirts, bustles, long waists and longer points that replaced the once onerous practice of tight lacing.'" She described other horrors of dress: "'The whalebone and steels used in corsets were more appropriate for treating broken bones. Layers of petticoats produced excessive heat, and the garments in general were too confining and the skirts hung improperly from the waist causing a dragging down sensation.'" Furthermore, Gleason argued, "'Indigestion, constipation, circulatory problems and a host of other maladies resulted from wearing the corset.'"

Gleason's and Jackson's recognition of the problems associated with fashionable dress was not, of course, original to them. Most water-cure physicians and health reformers shared their views. Mary Jane Gove Nichols, who lauded women for ceasing to tight-lace, warned of the excessive weight of skirts, which, she advised, should be suspended from the shoulders. She also lamented the long skirt that "sweeps the path." Her husband and she cautioned women regarding the consequences of wearing damaging clothing over a long time because of the resulting severe problems that attended childbirth and the "puny and miserable offspring" that was the ultimate outcome. Donegan further observed that Ellen Beard Harman, a physician at Glen Haven, also believed that one could not ignore the relationship between dress and health. Harman noted that flimsy bodices and heavy skirts caused unequal distribution of body heat, heavy clothing weakened the muscles, and exposure of the extremities drove the blood to the internal organs, inflaming and diseasing them.[32]

Between 1850 and 1853, the *Water Cure Journal* proposed a variety of costumes to replace the restrictive contemporary fashions, lauding at various times the "short dress," the "shorts," "Turkish dress," the "Camilla costume," the "American costume," or simply "reform dress." The extent of public use of trousers had begun to include women wearing the costume to temperance, health-reform, and women's-rights meetings, and occasionally for social gatherings.[33]

Regardless of the names they received, the types of trousered garments devised by the water-cure practitioners varied considerably as their wearers experimented with different styles of garments. In a letter submitted to the *Water Cure Journal* in 1850, a "country girl" offered her solution: "stout calf-skin gaiters; white trouser . . . loose, and confined at the ankle with a cord; green kilt, reaching nearly to the knees . . . [and] confined at the waist with a scarlet sash." Her bodice had either long or short sleeves. She noted that this outfit allowed her to ride horseback, row a boat, spring a five-rail fence, or climb a tree, and it gave her the "extra feeling of wild, daring freedom."[34]

Donegan tells us that water-cure physicians tried to come up with a garment that was feminine, beautiful, and, more important, unlike dress worn by men. It needed to be simple, comfortable, appropriate for the season, and attractive. Rachel Gleason suggested a simple walking dress loose enough to permit freedom to breathe and move, and with but one single short skirt, which permitted the "limbs . . . [to] move freely." Gleason advised wearing "pants" to protect the legs and good boots. It was essential to discard the corset and its bones and splints. Like other reformers, Gleason believed that it was important for shoulders to bear the weight of garments; thus she recommended wearing shoulder straps or suspenders. The skirt, she noted, could also be supported by button fasteners on a simple, unboned waist. One should, she further declared, make the dress fit one's form, rather than make one's form fit the dress. She noted that women at the Forest City Water Cure were greatly surprised at the positive effects of wearing loose garments for several weeks.[35]

Jane Donegan discusses the efforts of Harriet N. Austin, another prominent water-cure physician, who adopted reform dress soon after moving to James Caleb Jackson's Glen Haven, New York, Water Cure in 1852. Her efforts to devise a reform dress were not always satisfactory for as Jackson observed, they took the "best parts of men's dress" and united this with the "worst parts" of women's dress. The result was a garment that allowed freedom for the legs but left the upper portion similar to that of the long dress. The sleeves were sewn in so that there was no freedom of motion. Dr. Austin's later experiments were more successful. Her garment had straight-cut trousers wide enough at the knee to be entirely easy yet tapered in at the ankle. "'Never make Turkish trousers,' she advised, 'but . . . cut them straight.'" Austin described the dress as: "'Waist plain, with seams taken up in front, so as to fit not tight, sloping a little lower in front than behind, buttoned up in front. Sleeves . . . loose to give entire freedom. . . . Skirt, for a woman of ordinary height, twenty-two to twenty-six inches in length, about as wide as five breadths of calico, lined, and over this a skirt half, or more than half, as long as the first, and not quite so full.'"[36] An undergarment worn with the costume had long sleeves and a waist, similar to the lining of a dress, to which the pants and skirts could be attached. There were no rigid whalebones used in the dress.

Harriet Austin called her reform garment the "American Costume," and, in her view, it differed from the Bloomer costume in that the latter had a slovenly appearance because of the full-cut trousers. Yet for all of Austin's protests, the feminists' Bloomer costume was not very unlike the other garments described in the *Water Cure Journal* or even Austin's own first efforts. In fact, in the early 1850s, the term "Bloomer" appeared in the *Water Cure Journal* as a synonym for both dress reform and the dress reformers themselves. According to Donegan, the term "American Costume" for reform dress countered the term "French Costume," meaning the debilitating fashionable mode worn by Americans that was derived from Paris styles.[37]

Women who attended one of the many water cures and who wore the American Costume while in attendance often continued to wear it after they returned home. Authors of letters that appeared in dress-reform journals testified to how this new dress improved women's health. In some instances they stated that the American Costume had saved lives.[38]

According to Ellen G. White, founder of the Seventh Day Adventist Water Cure located in Battle Creek, Michigan, modesty in appearance and dress had always been a matter of religion, not health. While she denounced the evil effect of fashion on health in her lectures, she did not embrace the American Costume. Indeed, after she had a vision in 1863 of God showing her that Adventist women should not wear reform dress, White published the story of the vision in one of her many pamphlets, Testimony #10. However, after attending James Caleb Jackson's water-cure establishment at Dansville, New York, she began to have second thoughts about reform dress. Up to this time she recommended that Adventist sisters simply wear their skirts shorter so that their gowns would clear the filth in the streets. She finally altered the American Costume so the skirt would be longer, reaching just below the top of the boot and short enough to clear the ground. She even recommended the garment in her publication *How to Live*. The first time she wore the gown was in 1865 on a visit to the water-cure establishment Our Home. White felt very self-conscious in the "American Costume" and, indeed, never wore it in public (Fig. 29).[39]

White's adoption of the reform dress caused alarm within the Adventist community for they did not know which suggestion to follow, the ones in Testimony #10 or those in *Health, or How to Live*, another series of pamphlets published bound together in 1865. At the Western Health Reform Institute, physicians rejected Testimony #10 and urged incoming patients to wear a reform dress. White finally wrote out Testimony #11, which set the record straight. Apparently, a controversy arose regarding the reference point for skirt length, which was the top of the boot. White referred to women's boots, which were not high, but some readers thought she meant men's boots, which were generally high on the leg. Following the publication of Testimony #11, Ellen White spent considerable energy

Fig. 29 Ellen White in her model reform dress. Taken from Ellen G. White, *The Dress Reform* (Battle Creek, Mich.: SDA Pub. Assn., 1868).

convincing Adventist women to wear reform dress—her reform dress, not the American Costume or other so-called "deformed" reform dresses. In still another revision, Testimony #12, White gave up the boot reference and settled on nine inches from the floor as the proper length of the Adventist reform dress.[40]

Ellen White peddled patterns for her reform dresses as she traveled from church to church. The Adventist health journal, the *Reformer*, advertised designs for sets of reform clothing. Finally, White published a small tract titled *The Dress Reform*, in which she spelled out the do's and don'ts for rational clothing. Despite her efforts, reform dress never won the affection of the Adventist sisters. Eventually, on January 3, 1875, Ellen White had another vision, one that marked the end of her struggle. In this vision she saw that dress reform had become an "injury to the cause of truth . . . even a disgrace . . . to God's cause." When Adventist sisters again returned to more ostentatious dress, however, White recommended simple, loose-fitting dresses that cleared the street.[41]

Although women could wear the short-skirted dress over trousers with impunity when confined to a water-cure establishment, wearing the garment in public could cause alarm, even if the motive for wearing trousers was for improving health. In many cases, it is very likely that those who saw them would be unaware of the reasons that women wore trousers and thus would consider them a threat. The reaction at the time was probably that these women were feminists, people to be feared, or jeered at. Indeed, women's and health journals were full of descriptions of the insults women experienced while wearing dress-reform outfits. When reform dress met with hostility from the public and press, these journals countered by chiding women who renounced trousers. In 1856 Harriet Austin, in a moment of optimism, observed that the opposition was abating. Others did not agree. Despite the opposition, however, many health reformers continued to support the idea of dress reform until the late 1860s, when there was a decline in interest, though even then not a complete suspension of efforts. The harassment women experienced was not the sole reason for declining interest. Russell Trall declared that other aspects of hydropathy and hygienic reform had been overshadowed by the dress question. A single part of the complex issues of health reform, must not, he felt, be allowed to sabotage or sacrifice the whole movement. Yet it was clear that no small number of women reformers would never give up on improving their dress, including wearing trousers.[42]

Indeed, some female physicians such as Dr. Mary Walker lived a reform lifestyle their whole lives. Although she is best known for having worn men's clothing, Walker, a graduate of Russell Trall's Hygieo-Therapeutic College, embraced and designed all sorts of reform dress and continued to wear it for seventy years. Dr. Walker devoted her energy to freeing women "from the bondage of all that is oppressive," but she infuriated her colleagues in the women's movement by adopting tailored, masculine-style trousers in the 1870s. On several occasions she was arrested for appearing in public wearing "unproper apparel." It did not matter that she won the Medal of Honor for her service in Civil War hospitals. In her writings, Walker suggested that women wear pants like a man's, buttoned at the waist or held up with suspenders, and a one-piece knee-length dress made to hang free of the body like a sack coat. She wore these two items over her own emancipation underwear.[43] A physician and classmate of Walker's, Ellen Beard Harman, also wore her version of a health-reform dress into the 1870s, and Harriet Austin, the originator of the American Costume, became one of America's leading dress reformers and wore the costume until her death in 1891.[44]

Mary Tillotson was another dress reformer who never gave up on the cause. As early as 1842 Tillotson adopted a loose-fitting short dress worn with good drawers made like trousers, an outfit, with her health declining from dispepsia, that her sisters called the "grandmother dress." Tillotson's health improved enough so she could continue her teaching and studies with Dr. Trall. In May 1851, after hearing about the short dress and trousers worn by Elizabeth Smith Miller, Amelia Bloomer, and others, Tillotson shortened her own dress twelve more inches. Finding the additional relief surprising, Tillotson remained a dress

reformer throughout her life, and in 1885 she published *History ov* [*sic*] *the First Thirty-five Years ov* [*sic*] *the Science Costume Movement in the United States.* Mary Tillotson charged forth in 1874 to spearhead the establishment of the American Free Dress League, which remained in existence for three years.[45]

Interest in reform dress at the Battle Creek Sanitarium (formerly the Western Health Reform Institute) apparently was revived in the 1890s with several publications and a center where people could obtain reform patterns or have clothing made. One style of garment the center offered was a practical business costume, which consisted of a gored, divided skirt, a dress, leggings, and cap (Fig. 30). It was considered suitable for walking, cycling, rainy days, exercise, office, shop, dairy kitchen, or garden; in short, it was the dress for busy women of any occupation. It was to be worn five inches above the floor.[46]

Scholars tend to separate the dress reformers from the women's-rights leadership on the issue of women's rights; yet most dress reformers, especially the female hydropathic physicians, believed in women's rights and gender equality. They promoted good health in the belief that women needed strength, not just for reproduction but to carry out active roles in the public sphere of commerce, economics, politics, and the professions. Separation of the two groups also slides over the feminists' interest in health. The two groups carried out a debate over what would bring about a change in dress. The dress reformers believed they had a moral obligation to reform women's dress, while the women's-rights groups championed the notion that political, economic, and social institutions would have to change before women could freely choose their own style of dress.[47]

"Reform" for some dress reformers was a style of life. They adopted it as a moral principle and thus eventually isolated themselves. Many dress reformers who wore the short dress and trousers sought to dissociate the name Bloomer from their efforts because it had bad press from being associated with women's rights. People who persisted, like Mary Tillotson, gave the dress a new name— the science costume. Many water-cure leaders ceased promoting dress reform in the 1860s and, indeed, after 1854 less and less information appeared on dress reform in such publications as the *Water Cure Journal*. The *Sibyl* ceased publication in 1864. Tillotson's *History of the First Thirty-five Years ov* [*sic*] *the Science Costume Movement* ends in 1885. Even before that date, reformers began putting their efforts into more subtle means of improving women's dress—through reform underwear and making "fashion" rational. Chapter 3 considers these efforts.[48]

Trousers a Practical Garment for a Sporting Lifestyle and Travel

As part of the overall interest in health issues in the nineteenth century, educators and advocates of physical training continued to promote the philosophy that an indoor life was physically debilitating. They were persistent in promoting women's involvement in a variety of sports activities, for which they needed specialized, comfortable clothing. The trousered garment worn in the early period of the development of gymnastics and calisthenics programs for women and girls continued to be worn, with accommodation made for the different requirements of indoor and outdoor activities. When women's colleges developed physical education programs, the garment worn, called a gym suit, was styled after the earlier models. Magazines began advertising and illustrating trousered garments for hiking, mountaineering, boating, tennis, swimming, biking, and similar sporting activities. Trousers were deemed the perfect garment for travel as well.

Physical Education and Sports. Thomas Wentworth Higginson, a spokesperson for the cause of "manly exercise," was an early enthusiast of gymnastic exercises for girls, whom he felt were in relatively poor health. Others agreed. In

Fig. 31 "The Metropolitan
Gymnastic Costume,"
from *Godey's Lady's Book,*
January 1858.

comparing English women to American women, Catharine Beecher observed
that English women were healthier because they had opportunities for physical
exercise, especially out of doors, which had been denied to American girls and
women. Eventually many colleges shared the philosophy of the health reformers and included hygiene, calisthenics, and sports activities in their curricula.
Health issues were a premier concern of Oberlin College, which called for reform in food, drink, and dress and embraced the crusade for health preached
by Drs. Sylvester Graham and William A. Alcott. The *Oberlin Covenant* (1833),
states that "we will denounce all the world's expensive and unwholesome fashions of dress, particularly tight dressing and ornamental attire." Elizabeth Cady
Stanton was outspoken regarding the need for young girls to have improved
physical education. And by 1865, Vassar College also required physical education and hygiene instruction for women. With the linkage of good health to
exercise and fitness, other women's colleges likewise offered physical education instruction and required the accompanying gymnasium suits.[49]

Whether at Vassar or Mt. Holyoke College, or in Dr. Dio Lewis's Academy of Physical Culture in Boston, for calisthenics classes women wore shortened gowns and loose trousers much like the previously mentioned 1832 design. In 1858, noting that "gymnastic exercises among the ladies have . . . become popular," *Godey's* magazine introduced the Metropolitan Gymnastic Costume (Fig. 31). The similarity of this costume to the Bloomer dress is quite apparent. Indeed, it is more likely that the feminist "Bloomer" derived from the gymnasium dress rather than from the trousered gowns worn in sanitariums. The comfort of the trousered-style gymnasium suit was indisputable; it also became the acceptable style for bathing at American beaches in the nineteenth and early twentieth centuries.[50]

The similarity between the gymnasium suit and the bathing dress in mid-century also served to link the Bloomer-style garment with the idea of physical activity for women and thus gave it cachet, or a semblance of appropriateness, for sporting situations. Certainly, when gymnastics and other physical activities became increasingly popular in schools and colleges, the gymnasium suit became a recognizable and standard uniform. Styles derived from it continued to be worn by women in physical-education classes well into the twentieth century. Indeed, Bloomers and even shortened skirts gained acceptance as appropriate attire for many sports and outdoor activities, even for the public sphere.[51] Wearing trousers for these physical activities no doubt accustomed many women to wearing them and still others to seeing women wearing trousers in public.

Fig. 32 The Sweet sisters in their mountaineering outfits, 1896. Photo by Theodore S. Solomans. In Shirley Sargent, *Pioneers in Petticoats: Yosemite's Early Women, 1856–1900* (Los Angeles: Trans-Anglo Books, 1966).

Although trousers had been worn by individual women as a practical garment, more women began to wear them for pleasurable outdoor activities such as mountaineering, riding, and biking. As early as 1840, Elizabeth Cady Stanton wore a short dress with tall boots while hiking in Scotland with her husband. Trousers worn for mountaineering in 1896 were not an unusual sight. In the mountaineering clubs of the Pacific Northwest, one-third of the members were women, many of whom wore trousers while climbing.[52] (See Fig. 32.)

Bicycling became a popular pastime in the 1890s. The invention of a safety bicycle with drop frame for women made the bicycle available to everyone. Every large community had a bicycle club associated with the League of American Wheelmen. By 1893, there were one million bicycles in America alone. While

Fig. 33 "The Jenness-Miller Bicycle Suit," *Jenness Miller Monthly* (November 1894).

opponents of the bicycle feared female cyclists "would be invalids within ten years," the numbers of women cyclists increased. The problem for women was what to wear in place of the long skirt. Choices included a skirt with leggings, a divided skirt with high-top boots, or Bloomers to the knee (figure 33). Magazines offered a variety of examples, with the more liberal dress-reform advocates promoting Bloomers, especially for women who intended to ride fast. However, many women continued to camouflage their trousers with the ever-present and always acceptable skirt.[53]

By the 1890s, the spirited and independent new woman emerged who enjoyed calisthenics classes as well as participation in outdoor sports. This new woman, as noted in the press, not only rode a bicycle but played tennis, field hockey, basketball, and golf—for which she loosened her corsets and shortened her skirts and sometimes wore trousers. However, when women wore trousers for their athletic activities it was customary for them to wear an overskirt if they were playing in public.

Bloomers for Travel: A Practical Garment. The many articles and notices about the adoption of the Bloomer by feminists gave recognition to the garment and made it a household word. Feminist rhetoric included a great deal of argument regarding the practicality, convenience, and comfort afforded by Bloomers, thus encouraging its adoption as a practical garment. Indeed, during the 1850s some women took the risk of adopting Bloomers to wear for travel; others wore them as a practical garment for physical labor, especially in muddy fields. Women wore Bloomers across the plains, even though they found them "frightful for other occasions." In 1860, the English traveler Richard Burton spoke of a meeting west of Fort Laramie with two ladies, "one a Bloomer, 'an uncouth being,' in a dress and pants of brown glazed calico." Two reform-minded Oberlin College graduates, Sarah Pellet, a lecturer on temperance, and Mart Atkins, who later established a female academy, wore brown linen Bloomers on the trip from New York to California via Panama in 1854. Their chronicler was Major Sherman, a fellow passenger on the trip.[54]

While the number of women who actually wore Bloomers for travel is unchronicled, late in the century feminists again challenged prevailing folkways and encouraged women to wear a trousered outfit for train travel to Chicago and to continue to wear such reform styles while attending the Columbian Exposition in 1893. The World's Fair occurred at the time when women were beginning to take up bicycling and adopting a trousered garment for the activity.[55]

Trousers at the World's Fair. Although many feminists ceased wearing the Bloomer, they continued to support the concept of dress reform. In the 1870s, both the National Woman Suffrage Association, headed by Mrs. Stanton, and the American Women Suffrage Association, dominated by Lucy Stone, promoted dress reform in their publications, the *Revolution* and the *Woman's Journal.*

Yet, it was not until the 1890s that women's organizations collectively took up the cause of dress reform. In 1891, at its first meeting, the Board of the National Council of Women established a dress committee to recommend specific

Fig. 34 Syrian Costume, *Arena* 6 (1892): 642.

Fig. 35 Gymnasium and exercise dress, *Arena* 6 (1892): 643.

styles to use as an "every-day dress," one that would be "suitable for business hours, for shopping, for marketing, house work, and other forms of exercise." Not surprisingly, the styles they chose were similar to the earlier Bloomer-trouser design, styles that were by then acceptable for women engaged in physical activities and sports.[56]

That dress reform became a prominent women's issue at the Chicago World's Fair was not by chance. For in February 1891, at the first convention of the National Council of Women in Washington, D.C., Frances E. Willard, first president, spoke on the subject of dress reform. At that meeting when the council established a framework for carrying out a crusade for rational dress, many prominent women signed the committee's petition for "freedom and common sense" in clothes. Chairman of the Dress Committee was Mrs. Frances E. Russell of St. Paul, Minnesota. The other members were Mrs. Annie Jenness Miller, Mrs. Frank Stuart Parker, Miss Octavia Bates, and Dr. Mary E. Emery. The report on everyday business dress drawn up by the Dress Committee was unanimously adopted by the National Council. The brief report dealt only in essentials and offered three styles to serve as basic patterns that individuals could then vary according to their own tastes. These three styles were the Syrian Costume (Fig. 34), the gymnasium suit (Fig. 35), and the American Costume (Fig.

Fig. 36 The outfit on the right is Annie Jenness-Miller's American Costume. *Jenness Miller Magazine* 5, no. 11 (1891): 528.

36). The Syrian Costume had a "divided skirt" (actually trousers), with the fullness of each leg gathered at the ankle and allowed to bag over. Butterick's pattern for the second style, the gymnasium suit, was quite acceptable according to the committee. The trouser part of the gymnasium suit, made much narrower than the pattern and worn with extra high shoes, was suitable to wear with the American Costume in place of the usual buttoned leggings. The American Costume could be made from any dress, especially a princess style if cut short, or it could be a short skirt/shirtwaist and jacket worn with either leggings to match or with straight-cut trousers.[57]

The National Council of Women advised women to wear one of these costumes while traveling to and from and when visiting the Columbian Exposition in Chicago. Most women who spoke on dress reform at the fair wore one of the suggested styles. Mrs. Sewall, chair of the meeting and current president of the council, wore a "close fitting dark blue serge dress, the full skirts . . . stopped eighteen inches above the floor. Mrs. Avery, Mrs. Jenness-Miller, Mrs. Ecob, and Mrs. Morris-Smith all wore reform dress. Mrs. Avery wore a Syrian style and Annie Jenness Miller wore her version of an American costume with an Eton jacket, short divided skirt and gaiters."[58]

Others who wore reform dress were Professor Hayes of Wellesley College, who read a paper on "Dress and Sociology." Hayes wore a short blue serge dress with ten pockets, enough to satisfy Frances Willard, who advocated pockets on women's dresses. Mrs. B. O. Flower wore a Syrian Costume, as did Emily A. Bruce, M.D., of Boston (see figure 34 above), who stated that with "physical culture, careful diet and correct dress the American woman may attain to consummate beauty, grace and strength." Laura Lee, an artist from Boston, also wore the Syrian Costume. She believed that "women need no other one thing so much as freedom in dress." Miss H. J. Wescott, another Bostonian, noted that she was asked many times for the pattern of the dress she wore. Isis B. Martin, of Wichita, Kansas, who regularly wore reform dress, observed that it was getting to be an old thing, that people stared less. With so many Boston women wearing it, the Syrian Costume became known as "Boston Rational Dress." In an article titled "Dress for the Columbian Exposition, What Shall I Wear?" *Harper's Bazar* offered only a "sensible dress with a skirt clearing the ground by one inch, and sensible under clothes—no petticoats—only knitted cotton and light wool and silk underthings," to avoid laundry bills.[59]

While the World's Fair awakened the world to the need for dress reform and proved that women could change, and while women were adopting sensible, artistic, comfortable, and healthful dress, many did not openly wear trousers as a substitute for fashionable dress. For the most part, trousers remained restricted to the privacy of home or gymnasiums and for sports, games, outings, bicycling, and any other activities that would be difficult to carry out in skirts and that took place in a more or less private setting. Most women could not bear for long the conspicuousness they experienced while wearing trousers in public, especially for events that, in terms of current social expectations, did not warrant them.

Notwithstanding the reluctance of many women to adopt trousers as reform dress, and perhaps in light of the publicity given their efforts during the Chicago World's Fair, reformers continued to argue the practicality of short skirts and trousers, denoting their appropriateness not only for outings but for business and for rainy days. The practical business dress had a short skirt worn over short knee-length trousers with matching leggings (gaiters). It also required boots. It was much like the variation of the American Costume suggested by the Dress Committee of the National Council of Women in 1893. Indeed, the committee members; the authors Annie Jenness-Miller, Frances Parker, and Helen Gilbert Ecob; as well as reformers at the Battle Creek Sanitarium, consistently promoted this style throughout the 1890s. Ecob saw the practicality of the shortened skirt and trousers even though she believed that the costume ignored the laws of beauty; it was necessary and practical for some situations.[60]

As is clear from the efforts of the National Council of Women, earlier attempts to convince women to wear a comfortable trousered outer garment as their normal "mode" had not been successful; trousers had not been wholeheartedly accepted by American women for fashionable dress, although many clearly wore the garment for specific occasions—work, travel, sports—for which trousers were deemed appropriate. The reform activities developed by the National Council of Women, with support from the *Arena* in publishing their message, were a clear and bold effort to bring about change. Nonetheless, resistance to trousers was still strong, for in the same issues of the *Arena* (1892), advocates were still offering suggestions on how to accustom women and their husbands to the garment.

Writing in the *Arena* in 1892, Alice Stone Blackwell supported the suggestion made by Celia B. Whitehead that women adopt the gymnasium outfit as a "house gown." One advantage would be in allowing women to recognize the "immense increase in ease, comfort, and convenience to be obtained by the change." The second advantage would be that men would become accustomed to the costume and would no longer consider it *outré*. She believed that "whenever the reformed dress becomes customary, it will seem perfectly correct; and one may hope that from the house its use will gradually spread to the street."[61]

THE TROUSERED WOMEN OF EUROPE

While trousers or what came to be called Bloomers were eventually promoted in America as a suitable garment for women to wear for business and travel, clearly their greatest degree of acceptance was for recreational activities and as a means to promote healthful living. Europeans held a somewhat different view of trousers for women. The medical profession and feminist clothing reformers in Germany, Austria, France, Scandinavia, and the Netherlands did little to promote their adoption. It was in England that dress reform saw considerable support, even for women's adoption of a form of trousers to wear with their dresses on a daily basis.

Divided Skirts, Trousers, and Knickerbockers in England

In England, the issue of dress reform created enough concern to generate interest in establishing a number of societies devoted to the subject (Fig. 37). These organizations endeavored to educate the public about the evils of corsets and

MEETING OF THE "BLOOMER" COMMITTEE. The *Lady's Newspaper*, 1851

Fig. 37 "Meeting of the Bloomer Committee, London, 1851," *The Lady's Newspaper* (1851). Courtesy National Museum of American History, Smithsonian Institution.

other items of apparel that they considered injurious and unhealthful as well as unaesthetic. Three English societies specifically interested in clothing reform were the Rational Dress Society and its offshoot, the Rational Dress Association; the Rational Dress League; and the Healthy and Artistic Dress Union, a society largely concerned with the aesthetic aspects of dress. Other societies such as the National Health Association also took an interest in reform of women's dress, though this was not their sole concern. These societies, however, did not come into being until the 1880s, many years after the Bloomer costume was first introduced in the 1850s in America.[62] The promotion of trousers centered on efforts of various groups interested in improving health and having practical, comfortable clothing for physical education and sports.

The reception in England of the new American trouser style of 1851, the Bloomer, seemed at first to be favorable, for women soon formed an association of Bloomers in support of the new style. Women wearing bloomers gathered on the stage as the American Mrs. C. H. Dexter lectured on the advantages of the new dress. The *Illustrated London News* for September 27, 1851, reprinted an article by a Boston physician and carried an engraving of Mrs. Bloomer wearing the new costume. But while English newspapers for the most part commented favorably on the costume, magazines advised young women against wearing it.

Musicians, songwriters, and artists responded, and ballrooms echoed to the sounds of the Bloomer Schottische, the Bloomer Quadrille, the Bloomer Waltz, and the Bloomer Polka. The covers of sheet music presented exotic versions of the Bloomer costume. The many caricatures of the new costume that appeared in English magazines, such as *Punch,* ridiculed the garment long after the furor died down. George Cruikshank's illustrations suggested the many objections that nineteenth-century society had to women wanting to wear trousers in public.[63]

In October 1851, the year American women first started wearing the Bloomer, *Chamber's Edinburgh Journal* noted the limited reception it had in Scotland. Yet the journal observed that the Bloomer was "common sense itself in comparison with the monstrous error and evil which it seeks to correct." *Bartley's Miscellany* had this to say: "Hitherto [the Bloomer] has made little or no progress in this country. . . . It has produced Bloomer lectures and Bloomer balls; both signal failures. It has furnished a subject for one or two pretty engravings on the title pages of polkas . . . and many ludicrous caricatures. We deprecate this novel costume . . . yet demonstrate against the coarse and vulgar attacks that are generally made on those who dare to exhibit it in public."[64]

In 1871 *Chamber's Edinburgh Journal* offered a retrospective view on the success of Bloomerizing efforts, noting that "there was some good in Bloomerism. It might have answered for female doctors and lecturers who are determined, . . . to assert the rights of women." But it was not until the 1880s that a rational dress and a trouserlike alternative regained public notice. This occurred through the efforts of two women, Lady F. W. Harberton and Mrs. E. M. King. Indeed, dress reform did not have a well-organized forum until the Rational Dress Society came into existence in 1881, with Harberton as president and King as secretary. Both women had published articles on the need for reform in dress. The object of the society, as stated in every issue of their *Gazette,* was: "to promote the adoption, according to individual taste and convenience, of a style of dress based upon considerations of health, comfort, and beauty, and to deprecate constant changes of fashion that cannot be recommended on any of these grounds."[65]

In March 1882, at the Exhibition of the National Health Society, the Rational Dress Society placed its "divided skirt" on view. This new departure in dress was the invention of the Viscountess Harberton and may be described as a skirt "so divided in twain down the front and back as to clothe each leg separately," in essence a bifurcated garment. The public received the divided skirt with divided opinions; the *Lancet* declared it decidedly injurious, others considered it an improvement.[66] G. Armytage, writing in *Littell's Living Age,* thought Lady Harberton's divided skirt was unfeminine and concluded that "it is morally impossible that it can ever be made popular." The author further observed that "the principles which underlie the Rational Dress Association are false to nature. Here again the female sex is asked to accept ugliness for the questionable privilege of being the more able to practice athletic sports." "The supporters," as Armytage noted, "almost sealed its fate when they were persuaded into exhibiting publicly the clothing they advocated."[67]

The October 16, 1885, issue of *Knowledge* described the costume of the Rational Dress Society for readers who might have some misapprehensions, especially respecting the "dual skirt," which was the only garment in their program that departed from "normal" clothing: "The divided skirt should quite clear the ground. Each half of the dual skirt should be a yard or three quarters of a yard at the ankle. Our Society recommends that the skirt and the underclothing be fastened to a broad band fitting round the hips, so avoiding pressure of any sort round the waist, or, if preferred, hooks or buttons can be sewn on a bodice to correspond with buttonholes on the skirt." The society chose this arrangement because they believed a skirt hung from the waist would cause displacement of the internal organs.[68]

For the top part of the dress, the society favored any loose body or jacket but forbade bands, ligatures, or pressure of any sort, from below the fixed ribs to the top of the hips. They argued that in their system the weight of the clothing was minimized because the dual skirts clothed the body thoroughly and evenly, fewer garments were needed, and each garment was a simpler form. The essay stated that while the garment was not perfect, it did not injure any internal organs, cramp any muscles, or impede movement of the body.[69]

The society offered two forms of the "divided skirt": the Harberton, a narrow skirt (one-half yard wide at the ankle) with a narrow box pleat around it; and the Wilson, a yard and a half wide at the ankle with pleats carried up nearly to the waist. The latter design was derived from traditional Japanese men's trousers. In trying to make the fashionable dress rational, it appears that the Rational Dress Society was somewhat successful. In *The Science of Dress* (1885), Ada S. Ballin observed that the divided skirts might be made so artfully that an outsider would not know the difference between them and an ordinary skirt. That is, they could be made so they did not appear to be trousers. The arrangement of the materials, Ballin stated, prevented the division from being obvious: the pleated bands of the two skirts looked like a single flounce at the hemline.[70]

The divided skirt could also be worn as an undergarment, to replace the petticoat when an outer skirt was worn. A more thorough discussion of the Rational Dress Society's efforts to reform underwear appears in chapter 3.

The Rational Dress Association, a somewhat radical offshoot of the original society, presented an exhibition of reform dress in Prince's Hall, Piccadilly, in May 1883. The object of the exhibition, as stated by the association's honorary secretary, Mrs. E. M. King, was to "teach a lesson,—a lesson with illustrations,—a lesson to those who make dresses, and to those who wear them." King noted that the "Exhibition has been got up entirely at my own personal cost and responsibility." The bifurcated garments that the association showed at this exhibit were no doubt similar to the trousered garments that it placed on display at the International Health Exhibition a year later. The "Reports of the Judges," which appears in the 1883 exhibition catalog, includes a section titled "Remarks, No. 2" in which the author declares: "Every true woman who is anxious for the freedom of her sex from the trammels of present-day dress will rejoice at the decision of the judges of the Rational Dress Exhibition. I, for one, am very thankful that they have been unanimous in awarding every one of the prizes to trousers of knickerbocker costumes, medical men, artists, and ladies agreeing that these best fulfill the requirements of a perfect dress . . . . One of the fashionable dressmakers exhibiting has already had a large number of orders for a prize dress . . . [with] trousers."

Reform garments could be purchased from many of the exhibitors. Many exhibitors came from London—Messrs. Liberty & Co. occupied Stand No. 1 to exhibit their "Art Fabrics." Others came from outside London: Cornwall, Kew, Kent, Surrey, Bristol, Northampton, Guildford, and Manchester; still others came from abroad: America, Italy, France, and Switzerland.[71]

The catalog gave information about the Rational Dress Association, including its "Requirements of a Perfect Dress," which were:

1. Freedom of movement.
2. Absence of pressure over any part of the body.
3. Not more weight than is necessary for warmth, and both weight and warmth evenly distributed.
4. Grace and beauty combined with comfort and convenience.
5. Not departing too conspicuously from the ordinary dress of the time.

The association offered a list of firms willing to make dresses according to these requirements. The London firms were: Mrs. Beck, Hyde Park; Madame Brownjohn, Belgravia; Mrs. Cutler, Osnaburgh Street; Madame Ainslie Cook, Westbourne Grove; Messrs. Denbenham & Freebody, Wigmore Street. And should anyone insist on having their dresses Paris-made, the list also included Mlle. Vital of Champs-Elysées, Paris.

The Rational Dress Association apparently had more extreme views on every subject than the original association, the Rational Dress Society. The exhibition included reform dresses for many occasions, to be worn with various types of trousers. There were tea gowns and outfits for sport but also dresses with trousers for walking, traveling, and evening wear. The exhibitors used the term "trousers" to refer to their bifurcated garments, but they also labeled them as wide or narrow, narrow or full Turkish trousers, or narrow knickerbocker trousers. Sometimes they combined the styles. The fifty-pound first prize went to Mme. Brownjohn, No. 28, for a "dress with trousers," which was praised highly in the "Remarks by Lady Judges" for meeting the five criteria of the association but also for being made with great skill, avoiding clumsiness in the trousers, and fitting well without the aid of a corset. No. 45, "A Dress of the Future" (Fig. 38), was a knickerbocker (trouser) costume "with hardly any skirt and no draperies of any kind." Mrs. King had Worth et Cie. design the Dress of the Future for her. One commentator noted the similarity of this costume to the Bloomer dress in America, which the commentator further noted was distasteful to American women, who had now chosen to reform underclothing rather than outer clothing.[72]

Fig. 38 "A Dress of the Future. Made for Mrs. King by Worth et Cie." *Exhibition of the Rational Dress Association. Catalogue of Exhibits and List of Exhibitors.*

Trousers for Exercise. Although the press played on public reaction to the American Bloomer in the 1850s and the English "divided skirt" and trousers in the 1880s, it paid scant attention to the earliest use of trousers by young women for exercise classes. Depictions of young girls engaged in physical exercises in 1832 portrayed them in calisthenics classes, which were part of a "genteel curriculum thought appropriate for English school girls." English physicians promoted exercise for girls and young women to develop strength they would need for adequate reproductive health. Elizabeth Blackwell, the first regular (allopathic) female doctor in America and England, wrote several treatises on the need for physical education of females, averring that "exercise is the grand necessity which everything else should aid." Blackwell delivered her first lectures on health to a group of American Quaker women, who were her first patients, and in 1858 presented similar lectures in London. Blackwell believed that English traditions saved women in that country from being totally deprived of exercise because they "had more home education, more fresh air, more parks and fields, simpler food, more riding and archery, more education, later marriage and no central heating." She argued that girls should care for their bodies so they would be "ideal vessels for motherhood." In her major health treatise for women, *Laws of Life,* Blackwell's first law was "she should exercise regularly."[73]

In 1858, before Blackwell settled permanently in England, she helped Elizabeth Garrett Anderson prepare for entrance to an English medical school. By the time Blackwell returned to settle in England, Anderson had been practicing medicine and promoting physical training for women for four years. Anderson's efforts paid off, for in 1878 the London School Board hired Madame Bergman-Osterberg to introduce the Ling gymnastic program to the English elementary schools. The new gymnastics, which were quite unlike calisthenics, originated with Per Henrik Ling and were taken up by men and women in Sweden through the Royal Central Gymnastic Institute, which Ling founded in 1814. Ling based his system on physiology and anatomy. Interestingly, until the post–World War II years (1950s), the Ling Association was the sole province of women physical educators. Prior to the introduction of the Ling system, calisthenics could include almost any form of exercise. Some schools based classes on Dio Lewis's rhythmics.[74]

All teachers of gymnastics ultimately had to deal with the question of appropriate attire for women while exercising. Some parents balked at their daughters wearing the gym tunic. The gym suit worn at Bedford College consisted of a blue serge tunic that reached to the knee, white blouse, yellow tie, thick blue woolen knickers (like Bloomers), and black woolen stockings. Since women played field hockey outdoors in areas open to public view, their uniforms were skirts cut six inches off the ground. As was the case in America, Englishwomen wore skirts for activities that took place in public. Indeed, when women ventured from their playing fields into public areas, they were expected to put a skirt over their knickerbockers. In the early years at Bedford College, this extended to walking from one building to another. At Hampstead College, the women were resigned to being called "those dreadful girls" for wearing gym suits that could be viewed by passersby.[75]

In comparing American women to their English counterparts, Dora de Blaquière tells us that "the healthy country life and love for out-of-door sports in England, have been the safeguards of English women in the matter of dress." Englishwomen adopted clothing suitable for the outdoor life: "Norfolk jackets," "Newmarket" coat and jacket, "Ulster" and "Ulster hat," "Billycock" and hard felt hat, high boots and gaiters, leather petticoats, and shooting and mountaineering costumes. Many of these styles were borrowed from the types of garments worn by men when engaged in rambling through the highlands and treading in downs and moors. This style of clothing was worn by women and girls described by De Blaquière as the "athletics," women who differed in their approach to life from the "aesthetes," who wore artistic dress. Such comfortable clothing also was worn by women who did not necessarily fit one of these two groups but who were becoming aware of the need to form their own opinions about dress and select suitable and sensible clothing as an expression of individuality.[76]

Fig. 39 Award-winning skating costume designed by Mrs. C. B. Whitehead and an alpine climbing costume. *The Exhibition of the Rational Dress Association. Catalogue of Exhibits and List of Exhibitors.*

Fig. 40 Ladies' cricketing costume and calisthenic dress. *The Exhibition of the Rational Dress Association. Catalogue of Exhibits and List of Exhibitors.*

In *The Science of Dress,* Ballin also discussed proper attire for women while engaged in sports, which by 1885 was no longer an unusual occurrence. Ballin believed that sports were far more beneficial than gymnastics because the latter were confined to the indoors. (She excluded football from the sports she thought were appropriate for young women.) She based her clothing suggestions on the amount of running required. For active sports such as tennis and cricket, she suggested a divided skirt and a blouse with loose-fitting sleeves. Jersey knit was recommended for comfort. She also suggested the "expanding dress" designed by the London-based Mrs. Beck, with gathers in the front that could expand as the body moved. For cricket, Ballin recommended a protected pad for the bodice front. For horseback riding, she thought a light skirt worn over knickers was adequate and suggested an elastic band in place of stays. For tricycling she also favored a skirt worn over knickers. Her favorite skirts were ones that were quite ordinary looking but that could be unbuttoned while riding. With all of these clothes, Ballin recommended woolen combinations for underwear, and in place of stays or a corset, a simple flannel bodice to which the knickers could be attached.[77]

The Rational Dress Association Exhibition in 1883 had a number of garments for sports, including mountain climbing, skating, cricket, boating, tricycling, lawn tennis, boating, bathing, riding, and calisthenics. Most of them included some sort of knickerbockers or trousers. Prizes for athletic costumes went to

Mrs. Louisa Beck, ten pounds for a lawn-tennis dress; Mrs. E. M. King, for a tricycling dress; the American Mrs. C. B. Whitehead, ten pounds for a skating outfit (Fig. 39). Silver medals went to Mrs. Beck and Mr. J. T. W. Goodman for tricycling dresses, and the judges commended the calisthenics dress exhibited by Mrs. Fowler. No prizes were awarded for the exhibited boating dresses, cricketing wear (Fig. 40), or riding habits, although the judges did commend the riding habit shown by Harris Jones & Co.[78]

The International Health Exhibition, held in 1884, also included several garments appropriate for athletic endeavors. The ladies' cycling dress was worthy of being illustrated, since, as the author noted, "that form of exercise and amusement is gaining ground so much amongst us." It consisted of a "jacket bodice and small draped over-skirt, a plain skirt with a kilted flounce, heavy enough to keep down." The skirt was bowed out in front to allow the knee to move more freely. "When desired as an ordinary walking dress this part is buttoned over under the bows of ribbon." Mrs. Fleming Baxter's Highland or "mountaineering costume" was perhaps the most extreme example of a masculine-looking style shown in the Health Exhibition. It included a "short coat, petticoat plain in front with kilts [pleats] at the back, knickerbockers [Bloomers], and cloth gaiters to match the costume, and a hat of the same cloth."[79]

In the 1890s, the fashion magazine *Queen* regularly reported on sports—golf and tennis tournaments, hunting (hounds), bicycling, etc.—and carried announcements of events such as cycling trips for women. It carried illustrations of trousered garments for bicycling and mountaineering. During the heyday of the bicycling craze, a supplement to the *Queen* featured Parisian fashions that included an illustration of a bicycle costume consisting of full knickers worn with spats. Indeed, the *Arena* reported that the "divided bicycle dress is so common in Paris as to excite no remark."[80]

While some men may have thought that "a woman in knickers possesses infinitely less sex attraction to a man than a woman does when costumed in skirts," women were ecstatic about the "delightful sense of independence and power" felt while bicycling in knickers.[81]

Women in Trousers on the Continent of Europe

In writing about the development of dress reform in Germany, Brigitte Stamm observed that the movement was part of "life reform," a social-reform movement that developed after the first phase of industrialization in mid-century. Life reform embraced "natural healing" methods, which included water massage and exercise treatments; air and light cures; and, most important, a rational way of dressing, especially the improvement of undergarments. This movement is discussed in chapter 3. It must be noted, however, that advocates of "life reform" supported women's adoption of trousers. While many advocates, such as the artists Fidus (Hugo Köppener) and Heinrich Scham, who had been influenced by Karl Wilhelm Offenbach, first designed clothing for themselves and other men, then soon created rational clothing for their wives. Trousers were part of the garment Fidus recommended as a work dress for housemaids, noting that the knickerbockers would prevent seeing "under her skirts from the street." Heinrich Lahmann, one of the early promoters of life reform and director of a natural healing center, saw the revolution in female dress as a significant liberation for women because "the fashion-slave is useless for the resurrection of mankind."[82]

In France, it appears, the bicycle provided entrée for women to wear trousers in public. Several writers have commented on the "craze." Sarah Levitt quoted one Englishwoman's comments on seeing quite fashionable women in Dieppe wearing wide breeches while strolling around the casino grounds.[83] This occurred apparently despite the prohibition against cross-dressing. Permission for women to wear trousers was granted only to a few, usually for reasons of health. Writer George Sand sometimes wore trousers in order to accompany her male friends into the pit of a theater. Sarah Bernhardt also occasionally adopted them for stage and private life. Neither were given permission to do so. Trousers also were worn by women who worked in coal mines and fisheries and other occupations. This clothing, however, was unrelated to fashionable dress or efforts toward reform. As in America and other parts of Europe, there were clubs for the emancipation of women that sought to improve women's dress. In some cases these "revolutionaries" adopted a masculine costume. For the most part, the French effort toward reform is recognizable in artistic garments created by the Paris couture in the early twentieth century.[84] Much of the effort to reform women's clothing in Germany, Austria, Scandinavia, and the Netherlands was concerned with improvements in undergarments and in making fashion more artistic, topics discussed in chapters 3 and 6.

Nevertheless, trousers worn under a skirt had seemed to be a practical solution for many dress reform advocates. The bifurcated garment would have provided modesty, comfort, and ease of movement and would not drag on the ground. Yet, social forces saw it differently—men viewed the trousers as a threat to their exclusive right to wear pants. It was their symbol of masculinity. Besides, women in Bloomers demanding their rights were a new threat to men. Despite the opposition, the Bloomer did not die; it became the preferred garment for women engaged in all sorts of athletic endeavors. And even after midcentury, the trousers continued to be worn by health reformers and occasionally by women making a political point in public regarding their rights. That trousers were promoted by the National Council of Women as the preferred garment for travel to the Columbian Exposition in 1893 suggests that restrictive social barriers were breaking down.

While it appeared that progress was taking place, critics roundly denounced women for wearing trousers in public, especially in America. Such behavior was too blatant. Therefore it did not take women long to devise a more subtle means to eliminate the health problems that they believed were caused by fashionable dress. The reformers soon began to alter their underclothes. For them it was a direct attack on the garments that were the cause of their discomfort.

CHAPTER THREE

The Invisibles

Hygienic Underwear, "Dress Systems,"
and Making Fashion Rational

At least we can begin with the invisibilities and reform ourselves from within. . . . If we succeed . . . the rest will follow.
—*Rational Dress Society's Gazette,* April 1888.

While the adoption of trousers clearly eliminated the need for petticoats and reduced the problem of skirts dragging on the ground, not all women were comfortable wearing what they perceived to be a radical form of dress. Except for athletic endeavors, many women felt that trousers were *outré,* too extreme for everyday dress. There was, nonetheless, a large number of dress-reform enthusiasts who promoted a change in women's clothing that was both hygienic and rational but that did not greatly alter their outward, fashionable appearance. Such changes might be termed the "invisibles." These changes were a subtle if not subversive means of letting women appear "as usual," that is, in outer clothing considered fashionable and appropriate. Some advocates, such as Annie Jenness-Miller, saw improvements in women's dress as evolutionary, not revolutionary.

This new look was not associated with men's clothing and did not expose the body or create an uncomfortable situation by drawing unwanted attention to the wearer. Some promoters of more healthful clothing for women wanted to "make fashion rational" through subtle changes, such as shortening the shirt and loosening corsets. However, most women achieved this rational and invisible reform of their clothing by altering the way in which their gowns were supported on the body and through changes in the style and amount of underclothing. Thus, one of the essential features of making fashion rational was the new underwear, which, while it released women from the bonds of the corset and heavy petticoats, could not be seen. Since many objections to fashionable dress were directly related to abuses caused by undergarments, it is not remarkable that reformers found a way to alter them. Fashionable women of the nineteenth century generally wore too much underwear; it restricted them and weighed them down. It could be too hot in the summer and not warm enough in the winter. Certainly, the hoop of the 1860s allowed air to blow around a woman's legs. The corset often was worn too tight. The many skirt layers created excess bulk at the waist, which in turn encouraged women to resort to tight lacing, a practice that many believed greatly damaged women's internal organs and caused disease.[1]

The creators of reform underclothing devised new styles of undergarments to replace the heavy and bulky combination of corsets, corset covers, petticoats, bustles, and other paraphernalia worn under fashionable dress. They also desired to eliminate problems of uneven distribution of the weight of the clothing on the body. Some promoters of reform devised what they termed "dress systems," whole sets of rational underclothing, which reduced the number of garments worn. Many completely eliminated the corset. Health and hygiene were an underlying concern that continued to generate improvements in dress. The new underwear was meant to be worn over a body that had been revitalized through appropriate exercise.

❧ AMERICA

One of the earliest writers to offer a rational, invisible alternative to trousers was Mrs. M. M. Jones. At the World's Health Convention in New York in 1864, Mrs. Jones, who also lectured on health and dress reform, suggested that health reformers achieve their goals by: "mak[ing] the long dress hygienic." Jones advised women to "let out your dresses . . . and never wear a tight dress again. . . . Make all your waists [bodices] precisely as you would for the reform dress, leaving them a little looser . . . [and] shorten your skirts till they swing free entirely from the floor." More significantly, in the matter of underwear, she advised women to wear drawers instead of petticoats under their hoops, and reform-style "underdrawers" underneath the drawers, two for extra warmth if needed. To support their skirts, Mrs. Jones suggested wearing suspenders. The underwear would look like figure 41.[2]

In a speech before the New England Women's Club in 1873, Elizabeth Stuart Phelps argued for a change in current women's fashion, which she thought debilitating. "Something of the nature of the American costume—the gymnasium dress, the beach suit, the Bloomer, call it what you will—must take the place of our present style of dress, before the higher life—moral, intellectual, political, social, or domestic—can ever begin for women." However, she went on to note

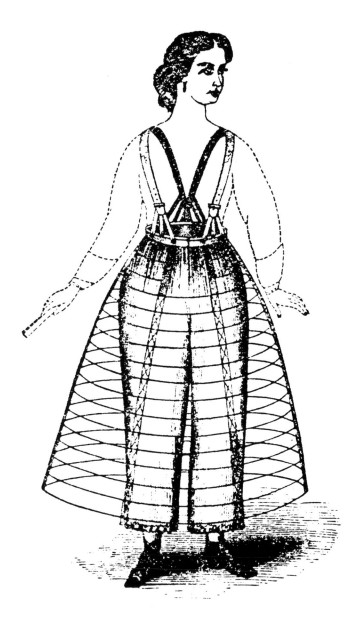

Fig. 41 The suspenders include braces to support the drawers and hoop skirt. From M. M. Jones, *Woman's Dress: Its Moral and Physical Relations* (New York: Miller Wood Pub., 1865), 25.

garment app
"The First U
Thomas Car
a women's s

Various l
at improvin
signer of a u
wore a man
appearing ir
to freeing w
she infuriat
masculine-s
her service i
sets, tight ga
and called a
proved fema
Taylor Conv
the union su

that "we cannot at one fell swoop impose such a style of dress upon the prejudices of the public. Here, I fancy, has been our most serious mistake." Phelps offered one more way to make fashion rational. She suggested that women begin first by shortening skirts to a regulation distance of from four to six inches from the ground; that "we dispense with the biassed [*sic*] waist and corset, and retain the plaited gamp, or little jacket . . . that we hang every thing from the shoulders; and that we set ourselves humbly to study the 'grammar of ornament.'"[3]

In her discussion of how she would dress a young woman Phelps added that she "would also reduce the number of skirts to two—the dress and underskirt, and these should be of as light material as possible." She suggested that women could gradually loosen the corset until they no longer needed it. Without the

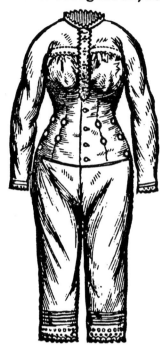

The Emancipation Suit.

Patented August 3d, 1875.

The suit consists of the waist and drawers, either in one continuous garment, or made separate and buttoned together at the hips.

Since this suit was actually a corset and corset cover all in one, it reduced the number of undergarments. It had a gathered section across the bodice that freed the breasts from compression and had sets of buttons at the waist and hips for suspending several layers of skirts. The Emancipation Suit also could be purchased as two separate parts that buttoned together at the hips.[10]

The dress-reform committee of the New England Women's Club held an exhibition of reform garments in 1874 and then gave a seal of approval to those garments, particularly the undergarments, that met their standards. It was here that Converse first displayed her Emancipation Suit, which had the official endorsement of the New England Women's Club. Many of the approved undergarments were manufactured by George Frost and Co., of Boston. The club also offered patterns and set up its own shop in Boston, presided over by Mrs. H. S. Hutchinson and Mrs. E. R. Horton, where they sold patterns of their chemiloon (a union suit), gabrielle skirt, and other approved garments for twenty-five cents each. It was not long before other shops offering reform garments appeared in large cities across the country.[11]

At the Centennial Exhibition in Philadelphia there were many exhibits of hygienic undergarments for women that were meant to improve health and comfort. Manufacturers also marketed these through advertisements in newspapers and magazines. Although the Bloomer costume was not to be seen at the Exhibition, the movement for dress reform was very much in evidence. Prominent among the innovators was Mrs. H. S. Hutchinson, who had moved to New York from Boston. Her rooms in New York City served as national headquarters for the wholesale and retail trade of garments approved by the dress-reform committee of the New England Women's Club. These garments were constructed on four basic hygienic principles: no ligatures, uniform temperature, lightness of weight, and suspension from the shoulders.[12]

At the exposition, Madame Demorest, who with her husband ran one of the most successful fashion houses in America, received commendation for her corsets, stocking suspenders, and skirt supporters. The centennial judges praised their "'utility, form and fashion, and high degree of excellence in workmanship.'"[13] It was not surprising that the Demorests received such awards, for Ellen Demorest and Jane C. Croly ("Jennie June"), editor of *Demorest's Monthly Magazine*, supported the dress-reform movement in New York. Both were founding members of Sorosis, the women's club of New York City, and were equally active in a number of feminist causes. *Demorest's Monthly Magazine* insisted that the only way that American women could achieve beauty was to preserve their health. These women did not condemn corsets; indeed, they believed corsets were absolutely essential during many periods of a woman's life. However, they did insist on health corsets, especially the Demorest designs, which, they stated, were constructed on scientific principles.[14]

By the 1870s hygienic principles had been clearly defined, encouraged, and taught in public schools. Therefore, designers and manufacturers all over America quickly began marketing a great variety of healthful garments. At the Centennial Miss Emmeline Philbrook showed her patented "Equipoise Waist." The Worcester Corset Company won an award for Madame Griswold's abdominal skirt supporting corsets, which were covered by patents awarded to Catherine A. Griswold of New York. Olivia P. Flynt of Boston—who had been designing, patenting, and selling reform undergarments long before the dress-reform committee took up the cause—won an award for improved underwear for women and children.[15]

In a very real sense, the reformers did succeed in raising public consciousness. After the 1876 exhibition, corset advertising almost invariably stressed comfort and health even though many of the garments did not always live up to their promise. Almost twenty years later, the judges of corsets at the Columbian Exposition in 1893 noted the great progress made in improving undergarments, pointing out that "every woman if she so desires can have a good form and be comfortable." The reform elements of the Ferris-patented "good sense" corset included "button fronts instead of clasps, cords instead of bones [leaving the corset pliable], adjustable shoulder straps which support the skirt and stockings from the shoulders, and shaping to conform to the natural figure, not made after 'French Patterns.'" Other corset manufacturers making sincere claims regarding the reform aspects of their corsets still used whalebone.[16]

Dress Systems

The cause of underwear reform gained much impetus from the commitment of the New England Women's Club, particularly through the efforts of Abba Goold Woolson. While promoting new designs for improvements in underwear, they made it clear exactly what should be worn. Indeed, the appendix to Woolson's *Dress Reform* offers an underwear system for improving women's health and illustrates it as well (Fig. 44). One of the most prolific reformers of the late nineteenth century was Annie Jenness-Miller, who clearly supported the efforts of the New England Women's Club. Indeed, Jenness-Miller also developed an underwear "dress system" and became one of the best-known promoters of hygienic dressing. Jenness-Miller was a lecturer, author of several advice books, including *Physical Beauty, How to Obtain and How to Preserve It,* and publisher of *Dress,* a journal that focused on educating women about the need for correct dress and physical culture. As Jenness-Miller stated in the first issue, the magazine was to become the "authority on the subject of healthful, beautiful clothing for women and children" and to "secure health and beauty to the race."[17] In its first years (1887–88) she referred to the magazine as *Dress, a Monthly Magazine.* By volume 2 it became *Dress, The Jenness Miller Magazine.* By 1893 it was known as the *Jenness Miller Monthly,* and in 1896 it became the *Woman's World and Jenness Miller Monthly,* then in 1898 the title changed to *Gentlewoman,* with a declining emphasis on correct dress and physical culture until it reached its final year of publication in 1900.

The term "dress reform" was not acceptable to Jenness-Miller, who preferred to use the term "correct dress." She stressed that their object was the adaptation of healthful and artistic principles to life and dress:

> [A]ccepting the human figure in its divine beauty and purity, it will be and remain our idea to so adapt essential clothing as to preserve the unity of the whole figure, and not call attention to the details of anatomy, as fashion is so prone to do. We shall lead so gently that the sting of sarcasm directed against our efforts as a "dress-reform" work will necessarily recoil upon the author and glance harmless from off our armor. Freedom from pressure, weight, and deformity will be our aim—dresses adapted to the natural body undefiled by the appliances of death that compress the vital organs and paralyze mental and bodily energy; freedom for the exercise of all God-given faculties; the right to the use of every member unimpeded by dress respected; life and health exalted above all considerations of fashion and sacrificed never to the mandates of ignorant customs which defy physical law.[18]

Fig. 44 The figures in this illustration represent the dress reform system presented by Abba Goold Woolson in the appendix of *Dress Reform: A Series of Lectures Delivered in Boston, On Dress as It Affects the Health of Women* (Boston: Roberts Brothers, 1874).

In both *Physical Beauty* and her journal *Dress* Jenness-Miller promoted the ideas of physical culture and the Greek ideal promoted by François Delsarte, a French singing teacher who invented a system of expressive body movements and offered readers articles on the aesthetic effect of fabrics and colors. Editorial policy was clear in that there were persistent instructions to readers on how to go at the work of "emancipating themselves from the discomforts, dangers, and crudities of fashions which have no other reason for challenging popular favor than daring and novelty." Jenness-Miller invited correspondence on the subject of "How, What, When, and Where" regarding dress and offered the following advice concerning the aesthetics of clothing: "The question of what to wear can be answered by the analysis of what constitutes art and utility with beauty."[19]

More important, the magazine featured the Jenness-Miller System of Dress (Fig. 45). This system included a variety of undergarments for women that were to be worn in place of fashionable chemise and drawers, corset, corset cover, and petticoats. As first described and illustrated in *Dress,* in 1887, the system of undergarments included beginning with, first, a "union suit" worn next to the body; second, a "bosom support," or stiffer, and more supportive "model bodice"; third, a combination of cotton or linen called a "chemilette," which was a perfect substitute for corset cover, drawers, and chemise; and fourth, the replacement for the petticoat, the "leglettes," straight-legged or in the full Turkish style. The outer dress would be formed over a foundation called the "gown form," which served as the lining for the skirt. As further described by Jenness-Miller the garments were:

Union Suit. A jersey-fitting garment of woolen or silk. Annie Jenness-Miller often suggested the Ypsilanti Union Suit made in Michigan or those made by Mrs. Converse in Massachusetts.

Chemilette. A combination garment of cotton or linen worn over the union suit. This garment, like the woolen union suit, put no pressure on the body.

Leglettes. These took the place of petticoats and were worn over the chemilette. Leglettes garment caused the most alarm because they were most like trousers. But unlike the divided skirt promoted by the English reformers in the Rational Dress Society, leglettes were not meant to be seen.

Gown Form. The gown form was a foundation dress on which all drapery could be designed. It was a waist (bodice) and skirt combined, fitting the body smoothly.

Bosom Support or Model Bodice. The bosom support was available for stout women who needed more support. It was not recommended unless necessary. This garment most resembled the corset but without the objectionable features. The model bodice was a boned version of the bosom support and meant to be worn in place of a corset.

Fig. 45 (opposite) The Jenness-Miller underwear system included (clockwise from top left) a union suit; a chemilette, a union garment to replace the petticoat and chemise; leglettes (or divided skirt and waist), and to replace the petticoat; a bosom support or model bodice (the latter had some stiffening). A gown form provided a foundation for the outer dress, as a lining, and could also be a substitute for a bodice. There were several variations of the divided skirt, which replaced the petticoat. *Jenness Miller Monthly* 7 (November 1894): 28.

Combination Skirt and Waist. The divided skirt and waist could be purchased as two pieces or combined and was a favorite of Annie Jenness-Miller.[20]

The system itself was available as patterns that could be purchased through the Jenness-Miller offices in New York City or through their *Pattern Illustrator,* a separate publication. Prices for patterns ranged from $.20 to $.30 each. Patterns also were available at various "dress reform depots," which were retail agents, usually dressmakers or stores, which purchased patterns wholesale from the Jenness-Miller System Co., East Orange, New Jersey. Although it was not an undergarment per se, the "gown form" promoted by Jenness-Miller (and later by J. H. Kellogg) was crucial to her system and the new "invisible" reform, or as Jenness-Miller would state, "correct dress." The Jenness-Miller gown form was cut in the princess style and served to replace the lining of a fashionable bodice and skirt. The outer "dress" would be formed over this "lining." Jenness-Miller boasted that the gown form would distribute weight equally over the body and thus avoid the pressure of heavy skirts. It eliminated "tie backs" and had no constricting band at the waist.[21]

In an article titled "What Others Are Doing for Improved Dress," published in 1887 Jenness-Miller reviewed the dress-reform activities in other American cities, noting especially that "Boston took the lead in [the] so-called 'dress-reform' movement . . . and it may be said that it boasts at present more establishments devoted to this branch than any one other city." The best known, perhaps, was George Frost and Co., at 287 Devonshire Street. However, as Jenness-Miller observed, "Mrs. Flynt and Miss Fogg—the former at 319 Columbus Avenue, the latter on Hamilton Place," both "have extended reputations for good and faithful service in the cause of improved underwear. Mrs. Flynt has pushed her business until it reaches every State in the Union. She has the good fortune to have been the originator of a very desirable nursing and extension waist. Holmes & Co., at 17 Kingston Street, hold a patent on a union suit which is simply perfect in quality, workmanship, and price." Jenness-Miller continued noting that "outside of Boston, at Woburn, Mass., can be found the veteran union-suit maker, Mrs. Susan Converse, whose combination garment was the first to attract public attention. Here in New York, besides ourselves can be found the old stand, at 6 East Fourteenth Street, of Mrs. A. Fletcher, whose long and faithful efforts in behalf of healthful dress have given her a national reputation." Jenness-Miller went on to note the flourishing establishment in Philadelphia managed by Madame Smith on Walnut Street and farther west, in Battle Creek, Michigan, the Sanitary and Electrical Supply Co., doing a very large business in hygienic goods, both as manufacturers and retailers. She recognized the efforts of an enthusiastic worker, Mrs. Rosinah H. Tonge, 8 Clayton Block in Denver, Colorado; Mrs. Ober, of 332 Sutter Street in San Francisco had built up an enviable business and reputation in the line of improved dress specialties.[22]

Another reformer who promoted a dress system was one of America's best-known health advocates, J. H. Kellogg. Kellogg argued that the common mode of dress produced widespread and marked physical deterioration of women and frequently lectured on the subject before the Michigan State Medical Society. While he was the director, the Battle Creek Sanitarium developed a "Dress System" which was "practical, healthful and artistic." The fundamental point of this system, like that of Jenness-Miller, was to avoid any appreciable sense of weight on the hips, shoulders, or any other part of the body. According to the

Fig. 46 (opposite) The underwear system offered by the Battle Creek Sanitarium in Battle Creek, Michigan, is quite similar to the Jenness-Miller System. Clockwise from top left: union underwear, combinatin suit, tights gown form, freedom waist, back and front. In the center, three arrangements of the divided skirt. *The Battle Creek Sanitarium Dress System* (Battle Creek, Mich.: Sanitary and Electrical Supply Co., [1890]), 41–53.

sanitarium pamphlet, women could purchase patterns ($.35–$.75) and cambric models ($.75–$1.50), or else dressmakers at the sanitarium would make up garments for customers at prices commensurate to the amount of work done. The general plan for the "system" included 1) union underwear, 2) tights, for cold weather, 3) combination suit to replace the drawers and chemise, and 4) a divided skirt with attached or detachable freedom waist (Fig. 46). While not an undergarment, a gown form would provide a lining for the outer dress. Fashionably styled draperies placed over the gown form could be made to suit the individual tastes of the wearer. According to the pamphlet, corsets and tight waists (bodices) were meant to be discarded so that perfect freedom could be obtained.[23]

Possibilities with the Battle Creek system were endless. In addition to the gown form, there was a princess dress and varieties of waists (bodices, without whalebone) and jackets. Although this system appears to be more practical than aesthetic, the classical ideal of beauty was adopted as a standard by the sanitarium. The pamphlet that described the system offered advice to women on how to correct the faults created by corset wearing. Kellogg believed that any young woman who had not permanently ruined her body by badly constructed apparel could learn to stand like the Venus Genetrix.[24]

The ideas promoted by Jenness-Miller and Kellogg concerning rational underwear, hygiene, and exercise for women became popular, and they appear in advice books written in the 1890s by Frances Mary Steele and Elizabeth Livingston Steele Adams, Helen G. Ecob, and Frances Parker. They all offer systems for underwear reform, but, in fact, their goal, like Jenness-Miller's, was to return the body to its natural form. They promoted exercises for women that would allow them to achieve a more natural body, and they recommended replacing restrictive undergarments with new, loose-fitting, lightweight underwear. They believed that women could reach true ideal beauty by following their advice.

In *Beauty of Form and Grace of Vesture* (1892), Frances Mary Steele and Elizabeth Livingston Steele Adams were largely concerned with the application of the principles of art to dress. Yet they also observed the importance of bathing, exercise, and proper diet, and they expanded on the necessity of discarding the corset. Foremost, they focused on the importance of the condition of the physical body and good health in general, advocating physical conditioning to attain body symmetry. This they noted could be obtained at a gymnasium, which would prescribe proper general exercise. The whole physique could then be further beautified using Delsarte principles of expression. The result would be grace and elegance through the achievement of harmony of mind and body. They also recommend "health-lifts," rowing machines, and other devices. Their goal was the beauty of classic models rather than the protuberances of the athlete. They saw exercise as a way of reducing fat, believing that corpulence destroys beauty of form and grace of motion. They recommended Mr. Edwin Checkley's *A Natural System of Physical Culture*. One good year of exercise, they believed, would "do more for a woman's good looks than all the cosmetics that were ever invented."[25]

They also recommended a healthful diet of grains, fruits, and vegetables and frequent bathing. In addition to the above, Steele and Adams professed that in order to achieve the "ideal body," a woman should immediately procure healthful underwear. "Not an hour should be spent in the faulty garments." A suitable garment would be a union suit: "one piece from neck to foot, hung from the shoulders, without whalebones or bands, and loose enough to allow the fullest breathing." The union suit was the first garment in their system of rational underwear. They also suggested a good bust supporter that was light, adjustable, elastic, with no horizontal bands around the body; it "is a most valuable adjunct to underwear for women" desiring to discard corsets. It could be worn with a corset cover over it or a knitted vest underneath. The next item they recommended was a waist, with or without an attached petticoat, and with no whalebones. They advised against health waists, which "are as pernicious as any corset," and recommended only the Equipoise Waist or Mrs. Flynt's True Corset, suggesting changes to each. Equestrian tights (footless knit leggings) are the next item suggested in silk, wool, or cotton. Finally, they suggested a petticoat with attached waist. They offered an illustration of what they thought would be appropriate.[26]

In *The Well-Dressed Woman: A Study in the Practical Application to Dress of the Laws of Health, Art, and Morals* (1892), Helen Gilbert Ecob also discussed the problem with heavy skirts and petticoats, corsets, and the so-called health waists. As with the efforts of these other reformers, her system of underwear tried to eliminate all of the weight hanging from the shoulders, which was a departure from the stance taken by the earlier reformers such as Oscar Wilde and Mrs. M. M. Jones. The garments Ecob suggested would distribute the weight evenly, "by having nether garments continuous with upper garments." Therefore, in addition to the reform union underwear, she stated, when "the need for firmer support was felt . . . we have the Flynt, Bates, Equipoise, and Emancipation Waists," all to be worn without whalebones. Other women, Ecob observed, wore the combination waist and drawers, either the Bates "chemiloon" or the Jenness-Miller "chemilette." For a petticoat, Ecob recommended a divided skirt. Other suggestions were to adopt the Jenness-Miller "gown form," a lining consisting of a skirt attached to a sleeveless bodice (waist). All of these garments, Ecob declared, should be made from a lightweight material, and the outer dress should be one piece; otherwise the outer skirt should be sewn to a sleeveless lining.[27]

The Chicagoan Frances Stuart Parker was active in establishing a dress-reform club called the Chicago Society for the Promotion of Physical Culture and Correct Dress. She stated that Annie Jenness-Miller had influenced her own efforts, and, like her mentor, she promoted physical exercise as provided by the Delsartean system of physical culture, a method of French gymnastics. In her book *Dress, and How to Improve It* (1897), she also provided information on correct undergarments. Frances Parker was an active lecturer and spoke on the subject of dress at Chautauqua programs, a popular lecture circuit. In order to show the advantages of reform garments, she illustrated the number of undergarments normally worn as part of "fashion" and contrasted them with drawings of reform garments.[28]

Parker's underwear system (Fig. 47) included a combination garment like those manufactured by the Jaros Company and the Ypsilanti Manufacturing

Fig. 47 Frances Stuart Parker's new system of undergarments. From *Dress, and How to Improve It* (1897), 32–33. Shown with the appropriate outer dress (4), the garments include (1) an Ypsilanti union suit, which takes the place of under vest and under drawers, and (2) tights worn for extra warmth in winter (also shown is a lisle under vest [3] often worn with the tights). Over this Parker advocated a silk petticoat sewn to the waist. She noted that a woman inclined to "embonpoint," or who had a full bust, would also want to wear a bust supporter. In cold weather, equestrian tights, lower right, might also have been worn.

Company. For warmth in winter she recommended equestrian tights (which were as warm as "two additional [under]skirts"). Over this Parker recommended that women wear a thin silk, cotton, or linen underdress, with a petticoat attached to a waist. She suggested making one by cutting off an under shirt just below the waist and gathering to it five breadths of material to form a skirt. For large-breasted women she felt a bust supporter would be needed and suggested Mrs. Newell's Perfection Bust Supporter. In order to reform their dress, she observed, all women needed were two combination suits, "two pairs of tights, three pairs of socks, three under vests, two pairs of equestrian tights, and two silk petticoats (made with a waist), one black, one white."[29]

The new reform underwear systems that included union suits, knit chemises and drawers, and even corsets with a few whalebones and elastic inserts (such as the Flynt and Ferris waists), and especially the Kellogg and Jenness-Miller boneless bodices would have given women more comfort. Eliminating the excessive bulk and weight of fashionable undergarments and the heavily boned corset allowed more ease of movement. The divided underskirt, worn in place of the petticoat, the union suit, and the equestrian tights provided needed warmth. All these reform undergarments no doubt could be worn without being readily noticed, and from a reformer's point of view were a great improvement over the more fashionable heavy, bulky, and body-distorting undergarments. The bust supporter recommended for heavily endowed or stout women is similar to a brassiere, thus giving the modern bra the status of being one of the earliest of reform garments. Women wore the bust supporter under the simple boneless bodice (waist), gown form, or vest.

For most underwear reformers, the idea was to return the body to its natural shape unfettered and undeformed by constrictions caused by tight corsets or appliances such as bustles. The care of the body through good hygiene and exercise was essential to their ideas of how women could achieve beauty. In *Physical Beauty* Jenness-Miller includes chapters on the care of skin, eyes, teeth, hair, and hands, as well as one on food, sleep, and the effects of fabric.

While a large number of women worked at reforming their dress in the 1890s, fashion still retained a hold on many women. *Needlecraft* magazine offers insight into undergarments worn in 1911 when the ideal fashionable style was one based on the natural figure. Despite the "naturalness" of the look, fashion still called for women to wear a corset, one that "molds the hips, flattens the abdomen and raises the bust, while all the time preserving the natural lines." (In the summer months women had the option of wearing only hip confiners of ribbon elastic sometimes worn with a brassiere or bust supporter if one were heavily built above the waist.) Underwear did follow the reformers' suggestions about combinations of corset covers and drawers, with drawers taking the place of petticoats. As it happened, these styles worked best with the slim silhouette.[30]

Advocates for the reformation of women's dress in England also believed that fashionable dress could be made to conform to hygienic principles, and, indeed, many reformers were adamant that the outer dress should not differ from what was in fashion. The idea to improve undergarments had many supporters in England and was greatly encouraged by health and hygiene reformers whose theories had taken hold in Britain. The success of numerous health exhibits that took place in the early 1880s in South Kensington attests to a growing public interest and awareness in personal hygiene and health at that time.

Even Wilde, while perhaps best known in this respect for his promotion of artistic dress while on an American tour, held a health promoter's view of the problems with women's dress. He was concerned about the proper cut of garments as well as the harmful effect of corsets. For Wilde, the ideal dress should be "shaped more or less to the figure, but in no case should it be confined at the waist by any straight band or belt. . . . It should fall from the shoulder . . . in fine curves and vertical lines, giving more freedom and consequently more grace." Remarks by Wilde that appeared in the *Pall Mall Gazette* in 1884 clearly reveal his attitude regarding the corset and other articles of dress prescribed by fashion. "Indeed all the most ungainly and uncomfortable articles of dress that fashion has ever in her folly prescribed, not the tight corset merely, but the farthingale, the *vertugard*, the hoop, the crinoline, and the modern monstrosity, the so-called 'dress improver' also, all of them have owed their origin to the same error, the error of not seeing that it is from the shoulders . . . that all garments should be hung."[31]

Dora de Blaquière expressed the reformers' point of view in an essay titled "Modern Dress Reformers," which appeared in the magazine *Leisure Hour.* She observed that the true evil that needed to be rectified was not the "outward dress . . . but the faults of the underclothing, and weight." As is clear from reading mid-nineteenth-century British magazines and journals, the English also considered tight lacing of the corset to be an evil supported by "Dame Fashion." As was the case in America, many English producers of corsets advertised somewhat false claims for their "health corsets"; nonetheless, real efforts were made to design more healthy corsets. For example, in response to a need to develop a corset that would not distort the body and be ruinous to health, W. Thomas and Brothers of London offered a "rational corset" made of India rubber, a corset that was "made for la dame, not, as hitherto, la dame for the corset." The medical journal *Lancet*, recommended this new elastic corset, which, it noted, would "obviate and supersede the close armor of the ordinary stay, and would do away with tight lacing."[32]

While individual corset and underwear manufacturers in England developed "new" reform undergarments—corsets and knit union suits, it was the dress-reform associations that effectively promoted reform of clothing as part of the general physiological and hygienic movements. These associations drew on arguments that took on a "scientific air" and were clearly distinguishable from the rhetoric of artists and individuals swept up in the aesthetic movement of the 1870s and 1880s.

Indeed, in a letter in response to the many comments on women's use of corsets and clothing reform that appeared in *Knowledge*, Richmond Leigh recommended the Rational Dress Association to every intelligent lady "to combat the stupid vagaries of fashion, to show how to dress rationally, and to restore the pristine beauty of the human figure." "Reason and science, he optimistically noted . . . must eventually succeed."[33]

One of the requirements of dressing rationally was the need to have hygienic dress made so that it appeared to be fashionable but in fact be designed so it gave freedom to the wearer. This point was made in print by leaders of the rational dress movement on many occasions. Indeed, in an essay titled "Principles of Dress Reform," which appeared in *Knowledge*, Mrs. E. M. King, who along with Lady F. W. Harberton led the society, offered readers the requirements for the perfect dress. These requirements became the motto of King's new association, the Rational Dress Association, and were used as criteria in judging reform garments at their exhibition in 1883. King's fifth requirement, upon which she "specially desired to write," was that reform wear must not depart too conspicuously from the ordinary dress of the time. She later noted that this fifth requirement meant that "we must depart a little conspicuously."[34] King observed that two things are necessary—reform of the individual and reform of the social medium in which the individual lived. The latter might put the reformer out of harmony with her surroundings. It was King's hope, since dress appeals to the eye, that society would become accustomed to rational dress just as they became adjusted to the more tasteless forays of fashion.[35] Her reasons for having an exhibition were valid.

The exhibition of the Rational Dress Association in 1883 included some reform undergarments. In some cases explanations of outer reform garments state specifically that they should be " worn without a corset." Some descriptions mention a union suit, a "flannel combination . . . for extra warmth," as part of the reform dress. Mr. G. Patten exhibited two quilted bodices "designed to replace the ordinary corset, and the skirt must be suspended from them." He noted also that they were "admirably adapted for tricycling, lawn-tennis, and other out-door amusements." Mrs. J. Wright showed "boneless stays," and Worth et Cie., "Boneless corsets . . . constructed so as not to give undue pressure to any part of the body." There were also knitted vests, working dresses, hygienic boots, and hosiery.[36]

The Rational Dress Society is clear about the need for altering undergarments. The title page of their *Gazette* reads, "The maximum weight of underclothing (without shoes), approved of by the Rational Dress Society, does not exceed seven pounds." The society was aware of efforts made in America: they include a quotation from Mary Tillotson in the first number of the *Gazette* in April 1888. The *Gazette* was full of commentary on the need for reform and the progress being made in England and America. It reported on events of interest to society members such as a lecture by Mrs. Oscar Wilde titled "Clothed and in Our Right Minds," presented at the Somerville Club, chaired by the honorary secretary of the society, Lady Harberton. Most important the society maintained a depot where they sold patterns for their system of underwear reform.[37]

The society's "A Rational System of Underclothing" included several garments: "Vest and drawers (or combinations) of wool, silk, or the material called 'Cellular cloth'"; a bodice of some firm material cut high to the throat, to support the breasts and also enable "such garments as fasten round the waist to be buttoned to it"; a chemise of their own design (sometimes called the "Survival"); and a "divided skirt made in whatever shape or material the individual may prefer. The ordinary dress is worn over this." They noted that as "the common dress skirt is indefensible on any grounds of common sense, it should be regarded as mere concession to an ignorant public, and be as light and short as possible. It should never weigh more than two pounds, all needful warmth being supplied by the underclothing." Apparently the original divided skirt, initially worn as a garment to be seen, such as the Bloomer, began to be worn in place of a petticoat under long dresses. In 1889 the *Gazette* reported on a tennis costume designed for a young woman who planned to spend the summer at Newport. It noted that she planned to wear it with a divided skirt, which the *Gazette* considered a replacement for a petticoat. The outfit consisted of a gray-green silk divided petticoat with ruffles up to the waist, worn with a little low-necked silk bodice. The tennis dress proper was gray-green serge embroidered with buttercups about the hem. The skirt was cut full and hung to just below the ankles, and there was a Garibaldi loose blouse of white serge. A yellow silk sash and silk scarf completed the outfit. A green serge sleeveless jacket was worn over it. It is interesting that just one year earlier, in 1888, the *Gazette* had observed: "Though they may not yet see their way to have their over skirts made dual, the time is not very far off when dressmakers will . . . drape dual foundations instead of single ones."[38]

Ada S. Ballin

Ada S. Ballin, lecturer to the National Health Society, was perhaps one of the few women to publish a book on the subject of dress reform in England. She thought that the majority of books on the subject of dress in relation to health had indifferent success because, as she believed, "they have been written for women by men." Her views on the subject of beauty of the human figure is immediately apparent in the frontispiece of her work, *The Science of Dress in Theory and Practice*, which has an illustration of a normal female figure with no distortions caused by tight lacing or stays (Fig. 48). Ballin observed that "what we want is reform, not revolution. We want in dress to obtain the maximum of health with the maximum of beauty." Drawing on classical standards of beauty and art, she further declared, "If our girls were taught the laws of health and a few of the principles of art as known to the ancient Greeks, they would soon see 'what a reformed thief

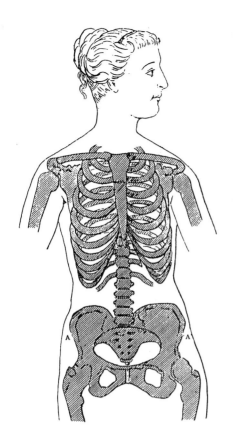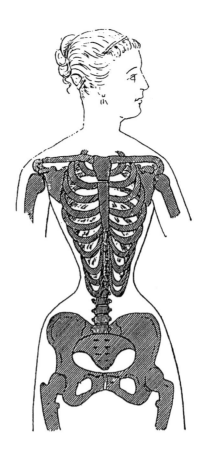

Fig. 48 "Normal figure."
From Ada S. Ballin, *The Science of Dress in Theory and Practice* (London: Sampson Low, Marston, Searle & Rivington, 1885), frontispiece.

Fig. 49 "Distorted figure."
From Ada S. Ballin, *The Science of Dress in Theory and Practice* (London: Sampson Low, Marston, Searle & Rivington, 1885), 148.

this fashion is.'" Continuing her argument, Ballin stated that if everyone were so educated they would "laugh at the squeezed-in waist, the crinolette, and the foot mangled and crushed by the high-heeled and pointed boots of recent times."[39]

Ballin further noted that "Fashion's sins against health are well understood by sanitarians." She had much to say about underwear and surprisingly did not totally denounce the corset. In chapters titled "The Use and Abuse of Corsets" and "A New System of Dress for Women," she discussed the abuses of the corset and substitutions for it that would be healthful, beautiful, and fashionable. Furthermore, in her conclusion she offered broad principles. Many of her arguments and suggestions reflect the beliefs of the Rational Dress Society, which supported the trousered dress, or divided skirt as the society euphemistically called it, as an alternate to fashionable dress.[40]

Ballin argued that women should teach their children the principles of dress reform so they would become accustomed to dressing rationally. She came to this conclusion after realizing that men and women could not understand the contentions of the reformers because they were so accustomed to the painful effect of fashionable dress that it no longer registered as an inconvenience or pain.[41]

Many authors of reform literature liked to illustrate the "evil" and detrimental effect of tight lacing on the female body, and Ballin was no exception. She illustrates not just the effect on the ribs but displacement of organs of the body when women laced the corsets too tight (Fig. 49).[42] While she abhorred corsets, she did not denounce them completely. She thought women who were stout needed stays, and she designed a corset made of woven fabric, woolen preferably, with full-length elasticized inserts along each side, as few bones as possible, and only a thin, narrow busk placed down the center front. Ballin recommended the new method of lacing that used pulleys, which was an award-winning invention at the International Health Exhibition in 1884.[43]

Ballin likewise recommended the "Girton stays" sold by the Rational Dress Society for women who tended toward corpulence. It was believed that the stiffer, tighter stays could help check an increase in fat. Her opinion regarding corset-wearing was that the need for stays was peculiar to each individual: some needed no stays, others a light corset, and still others those of a more substantial kind.[44]

She also thought that the chemise could be wholly dispensed with. Many people, Ballin noted, quit the chemise because it was bulky, not for sanitary reasons. Chemises should not be worn, she thought, because they were made from cotton or linen, both of which, compared to wool, were good conductors of heat, bad absorbers of moisture, and bad ventilators. When it was wet, she observed, wool might feel dry or merely damp, whereas cotton would be wringing wet. Ballin also objected to chemises because they were poorly cut: armholes were cut round, and the sleeves were cut in one piece with the garment itself, preventing arms from being raised. According to most reformers, any garment that impaired free movement was objectionable because such movement is necessary for development of the chest. Ballin recommended that chemises be made of thin materials with an open weave so they could ventilate, with gussets added at the armpit to ensure movement.[45]

Ballin also urged the use of woolen combinations. To the question, "What garments ought to be worn over these?" her answer was, "as few as possible." Knit combinations would be stretchy and so would fit quite close to the body and reveal the symmetry of the figure. Combinations, she noted, helped support the outer garments. For when stays were not worn it became more difficult to hold up the clothing so that the weight would be distributed evenly. The union undergarment or other combination suits could be fastened to separate outer skirts and bodices, or the skirt and drawers could be fastened to the bodice. Braces, Ballin concluded, were objectionable because they supported clothing only from the shoulders, weighing them down and causing women to stoop.[46]

Ballin's system for rational dress included the following: A high-necked and long-sleeved woolen combination vest and drawers should be worn next to the skin. Over this women should wear a closely fitting flannel bodice, on to which the suspenders of the stockings should be buttoned and to which the drawers could be fastened if made separate from the vest. The divided skirt also should fasten onto the bodice. (When worn as an outer garment, these loose trousers should be made of the material of the dress, the bottom of each leg being finished with a kilting.) These garments then form the whole of the underclothing, although in very cold weather an extra pair of woolen drawers might be worn under the divided skirt. The advantages of this system of dress, Ballin observed, were manifold. The system clothed every part of the body evenly and warmly, permitted perfect freedom of movement, gave the maximum of warmth with the minimum of weight, and, as none of the garments fastened round the waist, avoided injurious pressure on the abdominal and pelvic organs. Besides the advantage to health in adopting this plan, as the thickness of the clothing was removed from the waist, its natural outline was shown; and if the figure was beautiful, "its light is not hidden under a bushel, as in the former case."[47]

Ballin's recommendations for using knits and wool fibers for reform underclothing reflects the influence of German health reformers who promoted new clothing for better health. One of the best-known reformers of underwear was the German Dr. Gustav Jaeger, who in his writings on dress and health advocated wearing wool next to the skin. Jaeger's knit union suits were particularly popular with reformers in England after they were featured at the International Health Exhibition in 1884. A depot also was set up on Fore Street in London for its sale. In an essay in *Leisure Hour* de Blaquière included a description of Jaeger's "normal" clothing and briefly discussed the scientific dress movement in Germany.[48]

❧ Undergarments and Health Waists in Germany and Scandinavia

Dr. Jaeger, a professor at the Royal Polytechnic School of Stuttgart, was one of the most prominent health reformers in Europe. He began his investigations in 1872 and reached the conclusion that health was dependent on the materials and the form of clothing. His theories were widely accepted in England; in Germany they supposedly revolutionized trade, and many leading men, Count Van Moltke and others, adopted his clothing. Jaeger's reform clothing was also sold in the Swiss cities of Berne, Lucerne, and Vevy. Jaeger's reform for "normal clothing" consisted of using wool that was specially arranged to keep the front midsection of the body warm. "The general object is to prevent accumulation of fat and water in the system; the author's leading principle being that the greater the specific gravity of the human body the more it is able to resist epidemic diseases."[49]

Professor Jaeger made a curious addition to the well-known properties of wool. He desired to prove that there are certain volatile gaseous substances—*Dufstoffe* (odorous substances)—that we expel in the acts of breathing and perspiring, which have important relations to our mental state. He distinguished two distinct groups: those of *Lust* and *Unlust Stoffe* (substances of pleasure and disliking). The first group is exhaled during a joyful and pleasant state of mind and produces a state with heightened vitality if inhaled. The second group has the opposite effect. It may be readily verified, Jaeger argued, that during joy and happiness the odor of perspiration is not disagreeable, while during anguish and great nervous excitement the odor is offensive. The substances of disliking must then have bad odors and in an atmosphere full of them the vitality is lowered. Therefore, in a state of anguish and fear the body is more susceptible to contagious diseases. Professor

Jaeger believed that sheep's wool attracts the substances of pleasure while clothing made of plant-fiber favors the accumulation of the offensive substances. He gathered a large amount of experimental evidence in support of these views. He claimed that the many persons who adopted his "normal" clothing, both for summer and for winter, had a very satisfactory experience.[50]

The clothing recommended for women was not too different from that advised for men. The night dress was the same, except for a slight trimming of lace at the neck. The union, or "combination," garment, a pair of woolen stays (corset), and a petticoat of knitted dyed wool, with another, if desired, of woven stockinette, constitute all the clothing needed in addition to the outward dress, which also should be made of wool, high in the neck. By living in a more "normal" environment of animal fibers, Dr. Jaeger believed people would have improved immunity from disease.[51]

Prior to Dr. Jaeger's scientific studies becoming well known, the need for clothing reform in Germany was presented to the public by Dr. Max Pettenkofer, Professor of Hygiene at the University of Munich. At the request of the crown princess of Saxony, Pettenkofer gave several popular lectures on the "relations of the air to the clothes we wear, the houses we live in, and the soil we dwell on."[52]

In writing about the development of dress reform in Germany, Brigitte Stamm observed that the movement was part of a "life reform," a social reform that occurred after the first phase of industrialization in the mid-nineteenth century. Life reform advocated by numerous physicians embraced nudist culture and "natural healing" methods that excluded medication and instead embraced water-massage and exercise treatment, air and light cures, and, most important, a rational way of dressing. Private natural healing centers were very popular and had increasing numbers of visitors. Healing experiments started around 1820 and continued in popularity for much of the century. As discussed in chapter 1, these early experiments with water cure in Germany greatly influenced the development of hydropathic medicine in America.[53]

Heinrich Lahmann was one of the early promoters of life reform and director of a natural healing center. Like Gustav Jaeger, he attempted to provide a scientific foundation for women's dress. Lahmann, however, promoted linen and cotton rather than wool. He saw the revolution in female dress as a significant liberation for women because "the fashion-stage is useless for the resurrection of mankind." He was, perhaps, expressing views shared by many American advocates of hydropathic therapy.[54]

It is not surprising that the German dress-reform movement also was connected to the feminist movement. The German women's liberation movement started in 1848–1849 as a liberal association for women through the effort of Louise Otto-Peters. The movement was largely concerned with women's right to work and gain an education. Clothing reform was not greatly discussed until the first International Congress for Women's Work and Women's Endeavors held in Berlin in 1896. Delegates at that gathering came to realize the need for clothing reform for working women. They needed clothing "which would not affect [their] health nor be too tight fitting."[55] The congress drew seventeen hundred people from Germany, America, Belgium, Denmark, England, Finland, Russia, Sweden, Switzerland, and Hungary. Dr. Spener, a well-known advocate of clothing reform, was the main speaker on the need to dispense with harmful fashions for practical and health reasons.[56]

Following the congress, the Club for the Improvement of Women's Clothing came into being in Berlin in February 1897. The Berlin club soon published an informative booklet, held workshops, and organized exhibitions of reform clothes. The first exhibition was held April 11–24, 1897, with thirty-five firms taking part and eighty-five hundred visitors in attendance. A second exhibit was held in 1898. Its concern was to develop women's clothing that was healthy, practical, and beautiful at the same time, and its booklet noted that the club detested any kind of uniformity. They welcomed cooperation from doctors and artists. Most of the designs were improvements in undergarments, the use of a combination garment, and an improved corset. The movement for reforming undergarments was effective, for Stamm found thirty-four establishments offering rational undergarments in Germany.[57]

The Berlin organization for improving women's clothing had branches in several other German cities, but both Dresden and Düsseldorf formed their own distinct societies. In 1902 the Berlin organization joined with the German Organization for Popular Hygiene. These organizations existed largely to publish magazines devoted to reform dress and health. However, in 1906 the Dresden organization joined forces with the artists in putting on a dress-reform exhibition of fourteen reform dresses, Liberty and Co., of London "art" fabrics, reform underwear, and accessories. By 1912 the organizations all merged into one, the German Association for New Female Dress and Female Culture, with a publication titled *New Female Dress and Female Culture*.[58]

In 1907, Minna Cauer observed that the corset was on the "black list"; even with many new and improved models, manufacturers were complaining that their profits were falling off. In Paris, she noted, designers were inventing new styles to do away with the old rigid lines. Cauer thought that the medical profession did not support the dress-reform movement as it should. The exception, of course, was the sensible dress prescribed for women during visits to health resorts. Hygienic underclothing, however, had a tremendous following with women. Women were able to reduce the number of petticoats by wearing lightweight tights or Bloomers in their place.[59]

Cauer noted that the early development of women's dress reform in Germany was practical and utilitarian, more attention being paid to the mandates of health than to the dictates of form. She commented on the invention of the Mother Hubbard dress, which she observed, "transformed the average woman" into a "human caricature of a marsupial." The style, she noted, was transitory and was later improved. Cauer did not object to the style noting that "if the material is soft and hangs well and the figure well proportioned and slender, this style of gown may be made most attractive."[60]

Minna Cauer edited a German paper titled *Die Frauenbewegung* (*The Women's Movement*), the best paper in Germany for the education of women in the fields of politics, business, and the home. Cauer was a leader in the so-called *Party of the Left,* in the woman's suffrage movement in Germany. The aim of the party was the practical advancement of the cause of women in all its various forms.[61]

Cauer concluded that "it must be admitted that reform dress is more suited to the house than to the street." She further observed, "I think I have never yet seen a successful walking gown on the reform plan. The most suitable are simply straight-cut English tailor suits worn without a corset." Cauer believed that the reform dresses only fulfilled hygienic and practical demands and that the reform movement lost many adherents and prestige owing to what she termed its ugly and clumsy creations that failed to appeal to popular taste. Many women had a horror of reform dress, regarding it as nothing more than a flabby, badly fitting bag made of cheap material and depriving the wearer of the very last vestige of gracefulness and elegance.[62] The reform of the "invisibles" was more successful.

Sweden

In 1887 Oscara von Sydow, secretary for the Reform Dress Society of Sweden, apparently corresponded with Annie Jenness-Miller, editor of *Dress,* the American clothing reform magazine. In an extract of the correspondence Von Sydow commented on the advances made in reforming women's and children's clothing, especially that of schoolgirls. She noted that the Swedish reform society sent circulars to schools and physicians that included a drawing of a hygienic costume for girls. The garments, illustrated in *Dress,* included a jersey knit union suit, a bodice to which a skirt could be buttoned, and a pair of leglettes or knickerbockers that came just below the knee (Fig. 50). The outer dress was a simple sailor dress with a natural waist and short, pleated skirt. The society also established a museum of hygienic clothing and a shop, and it set up exhibits throughout the country. Von Sydow noted that dress reform had spread from the society to Denmark, Norway, and Finland.[63]

In commenting about the Swedish efforts toward clothing reform, the author, probably Jenness-Miller, declared that however different in detail the hygienic garments may be, generous waist proportions and freedom for the vital organs were recognized as essential to health by thinking people and students of anatomy everywhere.[64]

In her discussion of dress reform in Scandinavia, Brigitte Stamm noted the efforts of Christine Dahl, who had studied reform dress worn in America. Dahl's reform dress focused on placing the weight of the dress on the shoulders. The basic style that she promoted was the princess line. She designed dresses so that the dress lay on the outer curve of the hips. Dahl patented the pattern for this dress and sold it through the company Steen & Stromm in Christiana, Sweden. A doctor from Copenhagen wore this dress in 1896 to the International Congress for Women's Work and Women's Endeavors in Berlin.[65]

Fig. 50 Swedish reform garments were illustrated in the first volume of *Dress, a Monthly Magazine* (1887). The secretary of the Reform Dress Society of Sweden noted in her report that the movement had spread from Sweden to Denmark, Norway, and Finland.

The efforts toward underwear reform carried out throughout Europe and America were persuasive. The early "scientific" studies by Lahmann and Jaeger had great appeal, especially in England. The systems of underwear devised by Americans in the late 1880s and 1890s were practical and easily achieved, with the invisibles being an accepted way to reform women's clothing. The most practical garment, however—the Mother Hubbard—was viewed by many as comfortable but unattractive on most women and unsuitable to wear in public. Seeing the need for a more attractive, yet comfortable alternative fashion, it was not surprising that artists and designers involved with the modern design movement created what we now come to know as aesthetic dress or that they, like the reformers Jenness-Miller, Mary Haweis (an important writer on artistic dress), Wilde, and Steele, promoted the idea that art principles should be applied to dress.

The next three chapters consider the efforts of reformers in Europe and America to create artistic dress.

CHAPTER FOUR

Artistic Dress in England

Visions of Beauty and Health

Trousers and reform underwear offered practical, if controversial, relief for women who believed that fashionable dress was unhealthful and impractical. In addition to dress reform in the name of comfort, health, and practicality, however, there were also many people who believed that beauty and aesthetics were not being considered by dress designers. It is not surprising, then, that "artistic" dress came into being. Artists, designers, and other proponents of applying principles of art to dress—many of whom were associated with the aesthetic movement in England and comparable movements on the Continent and in America—encouraged women to adopt artistic dress. Not only did they design artistic dress, these reformers held exhibitions and wrote articles and books on the subject. Like reformers before them, they believed that their new styles of dress would improve women's health and that in turn women would regain their "natural beauty." Artistic dress is associated with historicism; often it was deemed exotic, and thus appropriate for fantasy dress, fancy dress, masquerade, fêtes, and intimate clothing. In its manifestation as tea gowns, all women could wear it in their homes; the more daring and avant-garde wore it in public. In the end, its many variations greatly influenced the changing styles of fashion in the early decades of the twentieth century.

What we call aesthetic or artistic dress had its origins in England. The source of this dress is most often attributed to the artists and designers associated with the British Aesthetic and Arts and Crafts Movements. Therefore, any discussion of artistic dress adopted to improve beauty and health must first consider the general reform in art that occurred in Britain during the second half of the nineteenth century. For, indeed, it was in England that the roots of the Aesthetic Movement, "that great creative upsurge which took place in Britain in the second half of the nineteenth century," developed and ultimately spread to other parts of the world.[1] There were many underlying cultural and artistic developments that both triggered and gave fuel to the movement. William Gaunt suggests that the beginnings were not only fostered by a reaction to the impoverishment of beauty created by the rise of industrialization but also influenced by a new inspiration from the art of Japan, as well as historical romanticism, which generated renewed interest in classical and medieval aesthetics and art.[2]

Perhaps two of the best-known and most widely read philosophers of the modern art movements of the nineteenth century were John Ruskin and William Morris. While Morris was a major innovator, it was Ruskin who inspired the group of young artists and writers who created the Pre-Raphaelite Brotherhood in 1848. This brotherhood of artists, formed by students at the Academy of Art in London, was the force behind the development of what is termed the Aesthetic Movement, which was at its height in the 1870s and 1880s. This group of artists also may be viewed as the parent of the Arts and Crafts Movement of the late nineteenth and early twentieth centuries. Artists involved in both the Aesthetic and Arts and Crafts movements, their friends and associates, not only advocated reform in the visual arts but also recognized the need to improve taste in all aspects of life, including women's dress.

It was not unusual for artists to have an interest in clothing. Indeed, there was a long-standing theoretical basis for their interest in decorum in paintings, which meant depicting dress that was appropriate to each character depicted, such as age, social class, occupation, and nationality. The ideas communicated by dress had long been a concern and continued to interest artists from the early years of the Pre-Raphaelites in the 1850s and 1860s through the period associated with the Arts and Crafts Movement. The artists who advocated the importance of dress included, among others, William Morris, Dante Gabriel Rossetti, William Holman Hunt, John Everett Millais, and Walter Crane.

Artistic-clothing reform extended beyond the depiction of dress in art. Many associates of the artistic community supported reform through their writings and lectures, and a number of women connected to the group began to wear artistic clothes that served to identify them with the cause. The community consisted of writers, critics, actresses, and others with aesthetic interests who associated with the artists, and included such well-known individuals of the time as the author Oscar Wilde, the store owner Arthur Lasenby Liberty, the author Mary Haweis, the actress Ellen Terry, and the architect and designer Edward William Godwin, as well as regular attendees at galleries where aesthetic art was exhibited. Outside of the artistic community, there were many individuals in England and abroad who continued efforts toward reforming women's clothing. These included sanitary reformers, physicians, feminists, physical culturists, clothing designers, and retail merchants, as well as groups devoted solely to rational dress reform. They not only argued for reform in women's clothes but recognized that a logical argument and perfectly sound way to achieve a positive change in what they believed were debilitating garments would be best achieved through artistic means and by applying aesthetic ideas to dress. This chapter examines chronologically from 1848 to 1914 the efforts in Britain to create acceptable artistic reform dress.

PRE-RAPHAELITE ARTISTS AND THEIR FOLLOWERS

In his *Modern Painters,* John Ruskin advocated the study of nature and art as an elevating pursuit. In 1848 three young artists associated with the Royal Academy, William Holman Hunt, Dante Gabriel Rossetti, and John Everett Millais, formed the Pre-Raphaelite Brotherhood. The three adopted John Ruskin's precepts as the underlying philosophy for their art. Ruskin became not only the apostle for the Pre-Raphaelites but their defender as well. He preached a gospel of beauty where nature was to be adhered to at all costs. Ruskin's advice extended to a concern for costume, for as he observed: "True nobleness in dress [is] . . . to be an important means of education. . . . No good historical painting ever yet existed, or ever can exist, where the dress of the people of the time are not beautiful; and had it not been for the lovely and fantastic dressing of the thirteenth to the sixteenth centuries, neither French, nor Florentine, nor Venetian art could have risen to anything like the rank it reached. Still even then the best dressing was never the costliest; and its effect depended much on its beautiful . . . arrangement and on simple and lovely masses of color, than on gorgeousness of clasp or embroidery."[3]

Indeed, William Holman Hunt noted that Ruskin's criticisms of "contemporary furniture, to which I drew Rossetti's attention on his first visit to me, encouraged visions of reform in these particulars, and we speculated on improvement in all household objects, furniture, fabrics, and other interior decorations. Nor did we pause till Rossetti enlarged upon the devising of ladies' dresses and the improvement of man's costume, determining to follow the example of early artists not in one branch of taste only, but in all."[4] The paintings of the members of the Pre-Raphaelite Brotherhood, especially those of its founders Holman Hunt, Rossetti, and Millais, clearly reflect an interest in depicting clothing so that it reveals a more natural human form. They achieved this largely by avoiding contemporary fashions and using instead historic costumes and drapery.

The founders of the Pre-Raphaelite Brotherhood as well as many artists who were associated with them, such as Ford Madox Brown and Edward Burne-Jones, chose the costumes they depicted in their paintings with great care and attention to detail. A number of artists designed and made their own costumes, while others had their models or relatives sew up garments to their specifications. It was not unusual for an artist to keep a large wardrobe of clothing from which the most appropriate drapery could be selected. Artists painting in the Pre-Raphaelite style turned to medieval and Renaissance subjects for their paintings, which

Fig. 51 Dante Gabriel
Rossetti's study for the
figure of Guenevere in *Sir
Launcelot's Vision on the
Sane Grail,* part of the
decoration in the Oxford
Union Debating Society,
now the library (1857).
Courtesy Birmingham
Museums and Art Gallery.

Fig. 52 (opposite) *Found,*
by Dante Gabriel Rosset-
ti, begun in 1854. Oil on
canvas 36 x 31 1/ x 2 in.
Courtesy Delaware Art
Museum, Wilmington;
Samuel and Mary R.
Bancroft Memorial Col-
lection.

allowed them to depict figures in the picturesque garments of the fourteenth through the seventeenth centuries. They chose these earlier styles rather than struggle with contemporary nineteenth-century dress, which to them was not aesthetic, beautiful, or even appropriate. The artists also knew that clothing worn during earlier periods was rich in color and when placed on a figure would easily reveal the shape of the human form underneath (Fig. 51).

In his Pre-Raphaelite period, according to Leonée Ormond, Dante Gabriel Rossetti painted tight, precise costumes that reflected a medieval subject matter chosen partly because "of his dislike of painting formal nineteenth-century costume." Ormond noted that Rossetti felt at home painting medieval and Renaissance subject matter taken largely from literature in which he could employ rich colors in garments that, unlike contemporary dress, were not of an "unnatural" shape and truer to the female form.[5]

According to Ormond, Rossetti copied the fourteenth-century styles from the reign of Edward III (1327–77) fairly carefully, using costume books, effigies, or brasses. The close-fitting cotehardie and kirtle, the dress and underdress worn by women, and the short tunic of men "attracted Rossetti because of [their] simple body-revealing style[s] and possibilities for contrasting colours." Documentation

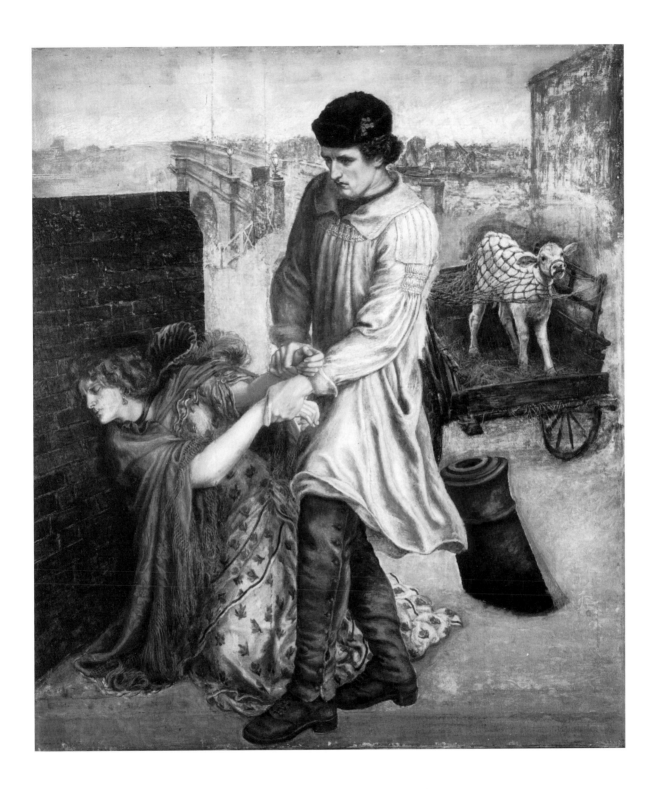

reveals that Fanny Cornforth, one of Rossetti's models, made up some of his costumes. Our knowledge of Rossetti's interest in costumes comes from letters he wrote to his assistant, Treffry Dunn, requesting him to send specific garments from his studio collection. (Rossetti at one point was distressed to discover several medieval dresses missing from his studio collection. It is not clear why or how they disappeared.)[6]

The source of some of Rossetti's ideas regarding dress may have been the eighteenth-century illustrator Camille Bonnard. Rossetti owned the original illustrations that appeared in Bonnard's *Costume Historique* (1829–30), a copy of which he loaned to Millais. Other available sources for information about early costume were Joseph Strutt's *A Complete View of the Dress and Habits of the People of England* (1796) and F. W. Fairholt's *Costume in England* (1846).[7]

Rossetti clearly enjoyed experimenting with unusual costume. In his later works, largely in portraits of women, he began to replace the colorful, crisp medieval clothing with opulent brocades and silk fabrics incorporating silver and gold yarns. The artist often draped cloth on his models to make it appear like clothing, giving the effect of loose folds and graceful drapery that could lend a degree of "nobleness" to his figures. A painting of which he was most proud, *Venus Veneta* (1867), depicts a Venetian woman draped in a rich "dress" of white and gold. This figure was Rossetti's ideal of female beauty. He used the same drapery in *Mona Rossa* (1867). Rossetti also experimented with Japanese and Chinese clothing, examples of which were in his collection. However, as noted by Ormond, when Rossetti chose contemporary dress for a subject, as in the painting *Found*, he tried to avoid a specific fashion by using shawls and a man's smock, but he was less successful in capturing the ideal grace he so admired (Fig.52).[8]

William Holman Hunt likewise took great care to have his studio properties reveal characteristics appropriate to individual paintings. In his book *Pre-Raphaelitism and the Pre-Raphaelite Brotherhood* (1905–1906), Hunt noted that he designed the clothing that appears in several of his paintings. "The dress of Julia . . . I made out of materials bought at a modern Mercer's, and I embroidered the sleeve in gold thread with my own hand. The hat also I made myself, and the dress of Proteus was painted from my own tailoring."[9]

Ford Madox Brown and John Everett Millais both took caution in selecting appropriate historical garments for paintings. Brown noted that for his painting, *Lear and Cordelia*, he chose to be in harmony with the mental characteristics of Shakespeare's work and had therefore adopted the costume prevalent in Europe about the sixth century. In M. H. Spielman's small volume on Millais (1878), attention is drawn to Millais's painting *Isabella* (1849), in which the figure and dress of Isabella is taken from an illustration by Mercuri of Beatrix D'Est found in Bonnard's *Costume Historique*.[10]

The Pre-Raphaelites' concern with accuracy and beauty of costume for their historical paintings may well have come from their admiration for William Hogarth, who is often cited as the father of modern English art. At the suggestion of Ford Madox Brown, a group of Pre-Raphaelite artists and their friends named their exhibition and social club the "Hogarth Club." This club was in existence from 1858 to 1861. As is clear from his treatise on art, *An Analysis of Beauty* (1753), Hogarth espoused "nature" as the true source of beauty and promoted the educational virtue and power of paintings. Hogarth's views certainly were shared by members of the Hogarth Club. Moreover, like the Pre-Raphaelites and those painters who expressed similar concerns throughout the second half of the nineteenth century, Hogarth sought to improve the taste of the English public, especially through the publication of the *Analysis of Beauty*.[11]

What might have been a greater influence on these painters than the idea of nature as a true source of beauty was Hogarth's own theory of beauty. For, like art theorists since the Renaissance, Hogarth delineated his principles of painting and was greatly concerned with the need for "decorum," or fitness, in a painting. That is, he believed that all the characteristics of a person, including the clothing, should be appropriate to age, gender, social position, rank, profession, and time period. Hogarth observed that "in every dress convenience and fitness and propriety should first [be] complied with, but it is also fit it should be pleasing." Propriety, or fitness, was only one of Hogarth's formal principles; the others were uniformity, variety, simplicity, intricacy, and quantity.[12]

Art principles continued to be adopted as arguments for beauty in dress. Indeed, Hogarth reflects his own attitude toward morals in dress in the illustrations for *An Analysis of Beauty* and more specifically in his painting *Taste in High Life*. In these works, Hogarth's criticism of prevailing eighteenth-century fashion may well have given nineteenth-century painters, especially the Pre-Raphaelites, support and encouragement to reject contemporary nineteenth-century dress for their paintings. Although the Pre-Raphaelite Brotherhood lasted only until 1861, its members continued to paint and influence a larger artistic circle, which identified with the new aesthetic that glorified nature, beauty, truth, and the classical principles of art. For it was ancient Greek aesthetics and the classical principles of art that the proponents of aesthetic dress drew on to argue for the reform of women's dress. These principles also had informed Hogarth's theories.

Aesthetic Females in Art and Life

The paintings of the Pre-Raphaelites and other artists who shared their beliefs became known to the public through exhibitions in London at the Royal Academy, Grosvenor Gallery, and the previously mentioned Hogarth Club. It is clear that clothing depicted in Pre-Raphaelite paintings served as one source for women who desired to dress in an aesthetic manner in the late 1870s and the 1880s. These women adhered to the ideals of what writer and caricaturist Max Beerbohm termed the "Cult of Beauty," referring to the aesthetic lifestyle of the Pre-Raphaelite artists who had settled in Chelsea. This "cult" had as its goal not merely reform in dress but a reformation in all the fine and decorative arts. A Pre-Raphaelite beauty thus would find the current fashionable dress unappealing. As noted in chapter 1, the fashionable mode in the 1870s and 1880s generally consisted of a tight corseted bodice with restrictive sleeves and draped skirt worn with a bustle and several petticoats.

Rossetti's drawings (sketches for paintings) of his wife and model, Elizabeth Siddal, show her in what has become the archetypal Pre-Raphaelite costume, a

Fig. 53 *Elizabeth Siddal,*
by Dante Gabriel Ros-
setti, June 1854. Pencil
and pen and ink on pa-
per, 41/16 x 7 in. Cour-
tesy Fitzwilliam
Museum, Cambridge,
England.

dress with a loose bodice, sleeves set in high on the shoulder so they would not
restrict movement, and a full skirt worn without extending petticoats or crinoline (Fig. 53). Rossetti also posed Jane Morris, the wife of William Morris, in a
dress with full sleeves and a normal but unrestricted waistline (Fig. 54). To what
extent these looser, freer-fitting garments were worn by these women on a daily
basis is not known. However, as Stella Mary Newton observed in *Health, Art, and
Reason,* "The circle of women who actually wore Pre-Raphaelite dress during

the period of the Brotherhood's existence was not confined to Rossetti's models—Elizabeth Siddal, Fanny Cornforth and Jane Morris—for Effie Ruskin on holiday in the Highlands in the 1860s appears in sketches by Millais wearing picturesquely comfortable clothing."[13]

In *The Aesthetic Movement in England* (1882), Walter Hamilton described the aesthetic female who adhered to the "Cult of Beauty" as "a pale distraught body with matted dark auburn hair falling in masses over the brow, and shading eyes full of love-lorn languor, or feverish despair; emaciated cheeks and somewhat heavy jaws; protruding upper lips, the lower lip being undrawn, long craned neck, flat breasts, and long thin nervous hands." The dress of the Pre-Raphaelite woman, according to Walter Crane, drew inspiration "from the purer and simple lines, forms and colours of early medieval art . . . it became spread abroad until in the 1870s and 1880s we saw the fashionable world aping it with more or less grotesque vulgarity."[14]

There is ample evidence to support the idea that aesthetic concerns for dress reached beyond the Pre-Raphaelite circle and were an acceptable alternative to fashionable dress. To be called a Pre-Raphaelite beauty was a notable achievement. The dresses were inspired not only by Pre-Raphaelite paintings but also by later painters such as Frederick Leighton, Lawrence Alma-Tadema, and Albert Moore, who adopted loose-fitting Greek-style chitons to express an ideal beauty. In the 1870s and 1880s the Aesthetic circle included women who were themselves active in theater, music, or the arts or else indirectly associated with contemporary artists, poets, playwrights, and intellectuals. Many of these enthusiasts no doubt also continued to support the views of the Pre-Raphaelites and the philosophies of Ruskin and Morris.[15] Our knowledge of English aesthetic dress of the 1870s and 1880s comes from a variety of sources. In addition to George DuMaurier's cartoons for *Punch* (Fig. 55), sources include extant photographs,

AN IMPARTIAL STATEMENT IN BLACK AND WHITE.

ÆSTHETIC LADY AND WOMAN OF FASHION.

WOMAN OF FASHION AND ÆSTHETIC LADY.

paintings, and written descriptions in diaries, novels, essays, and extant garments.

As contemporary visual sources reveal, especially *Punch* cartoons and W. P. Frith's painting *A Private View at the Royal Academy of Art* (1881), aesthetic dresses were designed using fabrics that appeared soft and drapable and in colors that were considered unconventional, such as odd reds, amber yellows, peacock blue, and dull green. An apparent absence of corsetry was one feature of aesthetic dress. Another was the full, puffed sleeve reminiscent of Pre-Raphaelite and Renaissance paintings. The dresses were worn without petticoat or bustle and, by contrast to fashionable dress, seemed limp and drooping. The waist was either high or in a natural placement, evoking Wilkie Collins's comment, "her waist, perfection in the eyes of man, for it occupied its natural circle, it was visibly and delightfully undeformed by stays." One of the best examples, perhaps, is Walter Crane's illustration of the princess weeping over the loss of the golden ball for *The Frog*

Prince (figure 56). Crane's publisher, Routledge, at one time asked Crane to avoid making his heroines look like "Pre-Raphaelite girls."[16]

Leonée Ormond has noted that many aesthetic dresses featured art embroidery or smocking. A loose garment smocked at the neck, wrist, and waist offered considerably more ease and flexibility than the fashionable stiff, heavily boned dresses, which also required a stiffened corset. By 1884, the fashions and designs for such art dresses could be procured from the Mssrs. Liberty & Company on Regent Street. Liberty silks, especially, became associated with aesthetic dress. Another source of healthful and aesthetic dress in London was Miss Louise Barry, a fashionable dressmaker at 152 Regent Street who offered artistic tea gowns and house gowns. Other London establishments offering artistic reform dress were Grace et Cie., on Vauxhall Bridge Road, and Worth et Cie., in London and Brighton. The *Rational Dress Society's Gazette* in 1888 also mentions Miss Franks, 23 Mortimer Street, and Mrs. Piddington-Horwood Aston Rowant, Tetsworth, Oxon.[17]

In many respects the gowns called artistic dresses and tea gowns were similar in style to house gowns, which were variously named wrappers or morning gowns and meant for use only in the privacy of the home, especially the private areas of the home. As noted in chapter 1, the difference between gowns worn out of the home and those worn only at home often depended on the quality of the fabric, degree of lining, and amount of decoration. The real difference was that artistic-dress styles were worn in public, though perhaps only by the more daring aesthetic types.

While it appears that the aesthetic women had their dressmakers copy the gowns depicted in Pre-Raphaelite paintings to wear to public functions, it is also true that professional designers such as Worth et Cie., and Grace et Cie., picked up on the idea and adopted the Pre-Raphaelite style for the tea gown, which by the late nineteenth century had become a very fashionable item. In this respect, fashion did copy art. The tea gown became an acceptable gown for entertaining at home in the afternoon and evening but not necessarily just for tea. In its early development, few women would have worn the tea gown in public, outside the home. The exception was avant-garde women who wore the artistic styles for gatherings of "aesthetes" at art openings and parties. After tea gowns became an acceptable fashion in the 1870s and 1880s, apparently more designers and dressmakers were willing to create them for their clients. This meant that women of an artistic nature had more places to purchase clothing for their appearances at aesthetic functions—the openings at the Grosvenor Gallery, "at homes," and balls.

That aesthetic gowns were actually worn for events outside the home in public is given great support by entries in diaries kept by a young Londoner, Jeannette Marshall (1855–1935), whose father was an important London surgeon and a professor of anatomy at the Royal Academy. He was also a lifelong friend and adviser to the painters Ford Madox Brown and Dante G. Rossetti. In the process of ridiculing the dress of the members of her family's aesthetic circle of friends, Miss Marshall's entries clearly indicated not only the nature of the dress but the numbers of young women who wore aesthetic costume. After an "at home" at the Ford Madox Browns she commented, "The flood of 'artistics' in everything hideous in the way of costume was appalling." In describing the dress of several women seen "at homes" she frequently resorted to using the expression "sloppy," as in her description of William Morris's wife, Jane, and her two daughters at a ball given by Aglaia Coronio in 1883. On visiting the Holman Hunts Miss Marshall noted that "the three Morris women looked more witch-like than ever" and that the hostess was in "an awful embroidered garment of doubtful cleanliness" looking untidy and gaunt. Zuzanna Shonfield observed that Mrs. Henry Adams's sketch of Mrs. Lawrence Alma-Tadema, whom she had seen at a Royal Academy soirée in 1873, reveals a true aesthetic image. Alma-Tadema was described as "a lymphatic tigress draped in yellow Japanese embroidered silk, bracelets at the top of her arms, hair the colour of tiger lilies and that fiery flower hanging in bunches from it."[18]

Miss Marshall's own aesthetic fashion was somewhat subdued. But she did wear a boneless bodice and only light padding when large bustles became the fashion. She wore amber jewelry, the preferred beads of the aesthetic crowd, and owned a green sage dress, a decidedly aesthetic color. Indeed, as observed by Shonfield, many of Miss Marshall's dresses were artistic in style and color and made from Liberty silks.[19]

Further evidence of dress worn by the "artistics" occurs in reports of exhibitions at the Grosvenor Gallery that appeared in the London fashion journal Queen. "Here might be seen Mr. Holman Hunt with Mrs. Holman Hunt in a quaintly made gown of pale violet plush. . . . Black was worn by Mrs. Pfeiffer, whose peplum-shaped tunic of lace and jet was classically dropped over a simple black silk underdress." The essay continues to tell who was there, naming "a number of ladies known in art." At four o'clock Mr. and Mrs. Oscar Wilde arrived, the latter wearing "a fawn-gray woolen gown, the short waist bound by a wide salmon-pink sash . . . [with] a large Vandyke lace collar," a quaint necklace and a "cluster of daffodils." Later Lily Langtry showed up. James Abbott McNeill Whistler was among other notable artists in attendance. In addition to describing the garments worn by the aesthetic women, the article observed that "green continues to be a color much in vogue with 'picturesque dressers.'"[20]

It is clear, then, that Frith's painting of aesthetes attending an exhibition, A Private View at the Royal Academy of Art, and DuMaurier's cartoons in Punch reveal a somewhat accurate picture of aesthetic dress. Frith's images are perhaps idealized while DuMaurier's, as an expression of humor, no doubt are exaggerated. Yet there may be truth in both. That Gilbert and Sullivan chose to parody the Aesthetic circle in the operetta Patience suggests not only an awareness of the fashion on their part but also an acute sensitivity to a subject that would have great appeal for an audience. The public would have had a natural curiosity about the world of artists, those groups who dared to go against the norm. Indeed, while Gilbert and Sullivan's operetta pokes fun at the cult, it shows much respect for some of their ideas. By using Liberty fashions for D'Oyly Carte's production of *Patience*, they were, in fact, giving great publicity to a company whose efforts at reforming English taste had never ceased.[21]

ℰ PRINCIPLES OF ART IN SUPPORT OF ARTISTIC DRESS REFORM

The popularity of artistic dress was not strictly based on its meaning as a sign of an individual's conversion and acceptance of aesthetic thought or even on its fashionability. Indeed, the adoption of aesthetic dress found philosophic support in theories regarding traditional ideals of beauty. During the nineteenth century within the Aesthetic circle in London, and especially among the writers on art and beauty, one of the dominantly held arguments regarding what constituted ideal beauty was based on the classical ideal. Objects most often used as a standard for beauty were Greek sculptures, especially of the Venus de Milo and the Venus de Medici. Beauty for the aesthetes was apparent in the figures of these classical female sculptures whose bodies, while an ideal, suggested a more natural, or undeformed, shape than contemporary women's bodies.

"Aesthetes" shared the artistic and rational approach to dress that had been addressed by the Pre-Raphaelite artists. This is made clear through the writings of such diverse writers as William Morris and his daughter May; Mrs. Haweis; Oscar Wilde and his wife, Lucy Wilde; Walter Crane; Lucy Crane; Lord Leighton; G. F. Watts; W. Pajet; and Edward William Godwin. They shared the beliefs that reform was needed in all the arts and that "nature" was the true source of beauty. They admired classical Greek ideals and recognized that Greek statuary exemplified these ideals and could be drawn on as standards for beauty and proportion. But, most important, they were convinced that aesthetic principles and concepts of art ought to be applied to dress. A summary of the prevailing thought regarding dress could be stated as follows: First, the current modes and corset-wearing distorted the human form, which was most beautiful in its natural state, and were not beautiful in line or color; second, Greek statuary was a perfect example of an unaltered natural and beautiful figure; third, earlier styles of dress such as classical and medieval could reveal the natural beauty of the human figure; fourth, the principles of art should be applied to clothing, such as ideas of beauty in simplicity, fitness (appropriateness), and utility; fifth, the colors adopted by the Pre-Raphaelite painters were more beautiful than colors found in current fashion in dress; sixth, there was a need to reform British taste in dress and it was possible for art to educate and teach good taste; and seventh, Japanese designs had a beautiful simplicity.

One of the earliest writers to point out the appeal of Pre-Raphaelite dress was Mary Haweis, author of *The Art of Decoration* (1881), *The Art of Beauty* (1878), and *The Art of Dress* (1879). In 1878 the Englishwomen's journal *Queen* invited Haweis to write three articles on "Pre-Raphaelite Dress." As Stella Mary Newton notes, Haweis had just completed her *Art of Beauty* the previous year and the editor "must have decided that she was the right person to discuss the particular kind of dress that was seen to be increasingly worn by women of a minority group in society at the time."[22] Yet it was a previous article published in the journal *Saint Pauls* in 1873 that established Mrs. Haweis as an authority on dress. In an article simply titled "Dress, Hints to Ladies," Haweis elaborated on the importance of dress as an art object and set forth several laws regarding its use, which she termed its "morality," dealing with questions of decency, with how we wear dress, and with the independent morality of the fashion itself.

The so-called morality of the garment itself revealed Haweis's concern for the artistic integrity of the garment. Haweis believed that the noble principles of art are moral and should be applied to a building as well as to clothing. "Imbecile ornament," she believed, created a universal artificiality and false effect on all objects. Trimming, she declared, that has no *raison d'être* is generally ungraceful. "Peasants, fishwives and such folk look picturesque and beautiful," she noted, because the motive is apparent in all they wear. She further observed that "Ruskin preached to us the motive of all good art," and "Charles Eastlake . . . taught us the practical dangers of debased art."[23]

Indeed, Haweis's philosophy reflects Rossetti's statement regarding the need to reform all the decorative arts. For in the same essay she discusses the importance of simplicity of attire, the reduction of stays that create a grotesque outline of the body, and the possibilities for creating naturalness in all parts of women's dress—sleeves, bodice, skirts, sandals, capes, etcetera. Her aesthetic leanings and support for reform in all the arts are evident in her writings. In "The Two D's or; Decoration and Dress," Haweis states, "A dress whether in life or on canvas, in order to be considered as a beautiful one, must be regarded in two lights: first, in its relation to the wearer, and second, in its relation to the surroundings. . . . You must not buy dresses which in fashion or colour are unsuitable to your room, and you must not have rooms which disagree with your dress."[24]

Haweis developed seven dress rules for an article titled "The Aesthetics of Dress," which appeared in the *Art Journal*. These rules reveal a similarity to the art principles espoused by the Pre-Raphaelite artists and their followers:

1. Retain the human form under all circumstances.
2. Allow the human form to determine the folds and the trimmings.
3. See that the proportions of the dress obey the proportions of the body.
4. Allow the dress to reasonably express the character of the wearer.
5. Consider the fitness of times and seasons.
6. Avoid discomfort, and weight sufficient to cramp and disable either really or apparently.
7. Avoid colours too pure, or brilliant enough to overpower the features of the face.[25]

In her lectures on art published in *Art and the Foundation of Taste,* Lucy Crane likewise revealed her belief that art principles should be applied to dress. She observed that in order to have reform in dress, that is, to "modify and improve the form and construction of our garments," we need to observe reason and "simplicity in moderately fashionable attire to gradually lead the way to improvement." Regarding the form of garments, she believed that soft, long flowing lines must always be the most graceful. "Any tightness *across* any part of the form is a discord, and must destroy the gracefulness of the whole." Any shape that seems to confine or "that *really* does so, is defective." She also noted that any trimming that had no function—that is, that did not button or fasten or tie—could have no beauty.[26]

Oscar Wilde also believed that beauty lies in the "exquisite play of light and line that one gets from rich and rippling folds." He was proposing, not an antiquarian revival of ancient dress but rather the right laws of dress "dictated by art and not by archeology, by science and not by fashion." He proposed combining the Greek principles of beauty with the German principles of health to form the costume of the future.[27]

In a discussion of reform for men's dress, Wilde drew on art principles as he observed the differences between ugliness and beauty: "An ugly thing is merely a thing that is badly made, or a thing that does not serve it[s] purpose; that ugliness is want of fitness . . . while beauty "is the purgation of all superfluities. There is a divine economy about beauty, it gives us just what is needed and no more, whereas ugliness is always extravagant. . . . Ugliness is always a sign that something has been impractical." Therefore, if "the costume . . . is founded on the true laws of freedom, comfort and adaptability to circumstances, [it] cannot fail to be most beautiful."[28]

Further declarations regarding the importance of art principles occur in the writings of G. F. Watts, who noted "that good taste is violated when natural conditions are entirely lost sight of. . . . That it cannot be in good taste to outrage the laws of proportion, or to ignore in cut and arrangements of dress all reference to natural form." He wrote further that according to the Greek canons human proportion may be taken as established law.[29]

In "On Taste in Dress," which appeared in the magazine *Nineteenth Century,* Watts commented further that sudden bulges and violent amplitudes that are the consequence of unnatural restrictions (such as created by the corset) are distressing to the sense of beauty and modesty. Recalling perhaps Hogarth's comment that quantity adds dignity and grace to a figure, Watts observed that "general amplitude is indeed far from ungracious, but on the contrary carries a dignity that is pleasant to look upon; but short violent curves are eminently ugly."[30]

In another essay in *Nineteenth Century,* W. Pajet supported art principles in his declaration that the principle of simplicity is the basis of grace. Observing the psychology of dress, Pajet quoted Polonius "for the apparel oft proclaims the mind of man [woman]" and subsequently suggested that "we should remember how the world judges by appearances and that a harmonious exterior inclines one to presume a well balanced mind."[31]

Along with supporting the notion that the principles of art should be applied to dress, many writers of the time pointed to the classical Venus statues as perfect examples of beauty. A number of promoters of reform took this one step further and argued for the adoption of classically inspired garments as a means to achieve reform in women's dress. They created garments inspired by the Greek chiton and himation.

The Adoption of Classical Greek Dress

In an essay titled "Slaves of Fashion" that appeared in *Art and Decoration,* Oscar Wilde lauded "the most charming women in Paris" for "returning to the idea of the Directoire style of dress." He noted that the style was not perfect but "at least it has the merit of indicating the proper position of the waist." Wilde was most ecstatic about the Greek style of dress because it could be suspended from the shoulders, rather than from the waist. Further, Wilde disagreed with theorists who believed Greek dress to be inappropriate to the English climate. He proposed that a substructure of pure wool, such as supplied by Dr. Jaeger's system, would make the Greek costume "perfectly applicable to our climate, our country and our century."[32]

Mrs. Haweis was one who believed that Greek dress was truly beautiful, especially where it revealed the natural figure, but she could not reconcile its use in nineteenth-century England. "The Greek dress," she noted, "is wholly unsuited for our climate, habits, tastes, and complicated trade interests. It is adaptable to [only] a few soft clingy materials, making it unsuitable for the large numbers of people who subsist on changing fashions. And it is inconsistent with stays, which have become a necessity to a race naturally small-waisted."[33]

Indeed, when Haweis argued for simplicity in attire she was not looking for the classic mania associated with Jacques-Louis David's imitation of Greeks toward the end of the eighteenth century. Rather, she meant for women to curb their "unsatiable passion for sticking everything . . . feathers, flowers, beads . . . tinsel and tails all over us."[34] The imitative Greek dress, according to Haweis, did not suit or become everyone and therefore could not universally hide women's defects and accentuate good points or protect them from the elements.

Percy Fitzgerald, like Wilde, believed that the Greek idea of suspending clothing from the shoulders was the most natural as well as graceful manner to give support to the dress. He stated, "Now, according to the classical ideal, the dress, from the shoulder to the heels, 'is one and indivisible'; the waist is formed by simply confining the dress, which would otherwise fall away from the figure, by a belt. Here is the solution, and the beginning of grace and of elegance."[35]

Reflecting a belief in the rightness of the aesthetics of the ancient world, the author of "Eccentricities of Costume" in the magazine *All the Year Round* argued that the "costume of the ancient Greeks was indeed the perfection of utility and elegance, considered with reference to the climate and the surrounding accessories. They were 'exemplars of genius.'"[36]

The Aesthetic Body and Greek Statuary

Aesthetic dress incorporating the dress of the ancient Greeks was thought to be truly beautiful and was viewed by a number of reformers as the ideal solution to problematic women's dress. It is clear that in arguing against the current fashions, writers drew on the aesthetics of ancient Greece. The artistic reformers, of course, went beyond the wish to apply art principles; health was an issue as well. Many artists as well as others in the artistic community believed first that the natural figure of the human body was the most beautiful (and therefore should not be distorted) and, second, that the standard example of what was natural and beautiful could be found in art. Their point, of course, was that fashion-dictated corsets created distortions of the body. Indeed, in order to evoke an emotional response the artistic reformers provided illustrations that compared the distorting effects of the fashionable corset to the "natural" figures found in Greek sculpture, especially the statues of Venus de Milo and Venus de Medici. (See Fig. 16.)

The connection between Pre-Raphaelite dress and the classical Greek ideal as these ideals are revealed in ancient works of art clearly was not lost by writers for the *American Agriculturist*. For in 1878, the journal observed that "there is a band of artists, poets, and others of their set . . . who refuse to be led about in costume [created] by every whim . . . of the fashion leaders in Paris." The Pre-Raphaelite style of dress had as its "aim . . . to have a thick waist—'Thick like the Venus de Medici, thick like that for Nobler Venus de Milo.'" The author continued by stating that the artists declared that tight-laced waists were unartistic and vulgar and "that the natural beauty of the female figure is lost by destroying its proper healthy proportions" and noted further that the sleeves of the Pre-Raphaelite dress were cut high and full on the shoulders so women would have ease in moving their arms when dressed. However, the author observed, the Pre-Raphaelites had said nothing about freedom of the "lower limbs, . . . except that skirts must never be tied about the legs."[37]

Venus vs. the Corset: The Aesthetes and Health

The charm and attraction of a small waist had long captivated British men and women. It had been prized and admired by men and sought after by women since the fourteenth century. Since not all women have a naturally slender waist, many women had sought the artificial means of a corset to achieve the waspish look and to maintain it. For almost the same length of time other people had rallied against its use. For, as noted in *Chamber's Edinburgh Journal*, "This instrument of torture is [not] of modern invention. More than one part of antiquity has reproached his country women with its employment." The writer further noted that "some women had discontinued this article of dress . . . without sustaining any inconvenience. It is the long habit of wearing it which deceives most."[38]

G. F. Watts pointed out that the perverse state of taste and good sense was best observed in what was considered desirable in the female form. The ancient

Greeks, he noted, would be amazed especially by "a well draped young body" with "a waist like a pipe, having scarcely any natural reference to the form above or below—in reality hideous!" He continued by stating that "the deeply-rooted preference for this deformity must surely be a mark of retrogression."[39]

Mrs. Haweis was equally appalled by the "tyrant—that, aspiring to embrace, hugs like a bear—crushing in the ribs, and injuring the lungs and heart, the stomach, and, indeed, all internal organs. For what end? The end of looking like a wasp, and getting rid of the whole charm of graceful movement and easy carriage, the end of communicating our over-allish sensation of deformity to the spectator."[40] Doctors, feminists, and educators all sought to improve not only women's health but also their position in society by improving their clothing. And they, too, saw that aesthetic principles were lacking, and they called on artistic arguments to bring about change. Many of the essayists, of course, drew on the classical standard of beauty, and they, too, offered the visual comparison—a drawing of a woman in a contemporary tight-laced dress placed next to a Venus statue. For example, William Fowler, professor of anatomy at the Royal College of Surgeons, asked the reader to compare the two figures, "one acknowledged by all the artistic and anatomical world to be a perfect example of the natural female form."[41] (See Figs. 48 and 49.)

There is no doubt that physicians writing on the subject of health and the principles of hygiene charged the women who tight-laced with threatening their health. Clearly they rallied against those who supported the practice. And almost universally they, too, seemed particularly drawn to arguing for the beauty of nature and lauded Greek sculpture as the ideal standard for the female form. Indeed, as noted by Stella Mary Newton, "Doctors no less than artists had found in Greek art a continuing source of inspiration." Dr. Andrew Combe observed in 1834 that "the statue of Venus exhibits the natural shape, which is recognized by artists and persons of cultivated taste as the most beautiful which the female figure can assume: accordingly it is aimed at in all the finest statutes of ancient and modern times. Misled, however, by ignorance, and a false and most preposterous taste, women of fashion, and their countless flocks of imitators, down even to the lowest ranks of life, have gradually come to regard a narrow or spider-waist as an ornament worthy of attainment at any cost or sacrifice."[42]

Stella Mary Newton also noted the observations of Dr. George Wilson of Edinburgh, who stated in his *Healthy Life and Healthy Dwellings* (1880) that young girls must be taught "not merely to understand the Greek tongue, but to copy somewhat of the Greek physical training." He further observed that "on physiological grounds, the classic mode was incomparably superior to the modern style of dress, because the whole weight of the garments was borne by the shoulders, and not from a waist constricted by strings and bands, if not by tight-laced stays. It may be true that the style of garments worn by Greek and Roman women may not be suited to our colder climate, but the closer the adaptation of modern apparel is to that style, so much more artistic taste will be displayed, and the better will be the health enjoyed."[43]

In his *Madre Natura versus the Moloch of Fashion* (1874), John Leighton (Luke Limner) quoted many medical authors, such as Combe, whose book he recommended, as well as philosophers and writers on aesthetics—Georges Buffon, Friedrich Schlegel, Hogarth, and Edmund Burke. In the usual comparison of the skeleton of a corseted woman with that of one who never wore stays (the Venus de Medici) he offered a list of ninety-seven diseases that medical authorities ascribed to corset-wearing. Yet for all of "Limner's" persuasive rhetoric, he never advised young women on an alternative to fashionable dress.[44]

In a letter to the editor of *Knowledge,* Richmond Leigh responded to earlier remarks by two correspondents who favored the corset. He, too, made the comparison of the distorted fashionable figure with the elegant "Venus of the art galleries," averring that "with the mass of coverage enveloping the body in the present day the true natural and artistic form has been lost." He observed that "the ancient Greeks, who knew not the corset, had a true knowledge of the beauty of figure and their lighter and simpler vestments covered, without distorting, the human form."[45]

Tight Lacing vs. Artistic Dress: A Dialogue

There is no doubt that tight lacing was the greatest outrage in the eyes of aesthetes as well as in those of health advocates, physicians, and feminists concerned with the health of women. In her lectures on art, Lucy Crane observed that those who were victims of the epidemic of tight lacing "must have strongly incredulous minds; they disbelieve all doctors, as a matter of course, and what is more to my purpose, they disbelieve artists; and the verdict of all the ages as to the beauty of antique statues has, for them, been given in vain. The Venus of Milos and all the goddesses of Olympus are to them as nothing."[46]

The question of corseting apparently reached its peak during the 1880s, for numerous popular magazines proclaimed the evils of the corset, especially the detrimental effect of tight lacing, which apparently was practiced enough to cause some degree of alarm. Indeed, *Knowledge* published a discussion of the issue of tight lacing between two individuals: R. A. Proctor, who abhorred tight lacing, and "An Observer," who favored tight lacing. Proctor clearly made his case from an artistic point of view where the argument was "all against the straightly-laced, and all in favor of the curves of beauty." He argued that "the corset-spoiled waist does not err in being out of proportion, but in being deformed. It is not merely the ellipticity of the natural waist that is wanting, but all the curves which a well-shaped waist possesses . . . a corset-made waist is sheer discord to the artistic mind."[47]

The Observer's response to Proctor's artistic argument was that he should dress one of the statues of Venus in modern dress to see how ridiculous it would look. Also, the Observer noted that although one would assume that binding realigns, no one had yet proven that corset-wearing weakened, and, furthermore, testimony from "a multitude of people have proved just the contrary to their own satisfaction." Indeed, the Observer commented, the wearers of corsets "have found tight-lacing in stiff stays pleasant, useful and beneficial in a variety of ways. . . . It preserves and improves their figure and carriage [and] makes their dress fit and look better." He obviously believed that the statements of personal experience with all their variations in detail were worth infinitely more for practical purposes than all the talk about lungs and diaphragms and capacity of chests, nature, and anatomy, Greek women in flesh and marble, and the unquestioned bad effects of unduly tight-lacing. He further noted that "it is quite clear from history that corsets and tight lacing in one form or another have been the windmills of dress-reforming Quixotes for 1,500 years at least. 'While the wind has sometimes lulled, it has risen again' so they may as well save their preaching for something more amendable, or at any rate preach more rationally than they do."[48]

Unfazed by the Observer's rhetoric, Proctor continued to argue his artistic point and observed that letters he had received on the subject of corsets indicated very clearly that "very few hold the views which have been so strongly maintained by 'An Observer.'" He then commented that he would let doctors speak on the health side of the question, noting that 99 out of 100 opposed tight lacing with whatever form of stays. Likewise, and with great candor, Proctor offered evidence of his own unfortunate experience in wearing stays as a means to reduce corpulence, as well as the experience of a young American lady who discarded her corset because it impeded movement.[49]

Health and Art

While there were two camps regarding reform in dress, the aesthetes, who advocated artistic dress, and the athletics, or philistines as they were sometimes called, who advocated a bifurcated garment, both drew on aesthetic arguments. Indeed, it was E. W. Godwin, in a lecture given during a health exhibition in 1884, who upheld the notion that Greek dress was most appealing. He advocated wearing Dr. Jaeger's woolen combinations underneath the garment. Such a garment would have the effect of negating the Rational Dress Society's, especially Lady Harberton's, objection to Greek dress. For while Harberton recognized that others believed that Greek dress was beautiful, she, like Mrs. Haweis, found it to be unsuitable to the English climate and English ways. The Secretary of the Dress Reform Society, Mrs. Carpenter, however, while she wore the divided petticoat, admitted "a drapery over it á la Greque."[50]

The Healtheries, as the various London health exhibitions came to be called, had as their purpose to illustrate the most advanced knowledge regarding sanitary practices, health, food, and dress. Yet they also had the intention to illustrate all of these from an artistic and useful character—that is, to combine both art and hygiene, which proved a difficult task to carry out. However, the Official Guide to the 1883 exhibition sponsored by the Rational Dress Association noted that "if the aesthetic side of the question of dress reform were kept more in view, the difficulties now experienced by dress reformers would to a great extent vanish."[51]

While neither the Rational Dress Society nor its offshoot, the Rational Dress Association, advocated dress that is now associated with the concept of artistic dress, they did believe in the beauty of nature and the importance of aesthetics in dress. As stated in their *Gazette,* which began publication in 1888:

> The Rational Dress Society protests against the introduction of any fashion in dress that either deforms the figure, impedes the movement of the body, or in any way tends to injure health. It protests against the wearing of tightly-fitting corsets, of high-heeled or narrow-toed boots and shoes; of heavily weighted skirts, as rendering healthy exercise almost impossible; and of all tie-downs, cloaks or other garments impeding the movement of the arms. It protests against crinolines or crinolettes of any kind as ugly and deforming. The object of the R.D.S. is to promote the adoption, according to individual taste and convenience, of a style of dress based upon considerations of health, comfort, and beauty, and to deprecate constant changes of fashion that cannot be recommended on any of these grounds."[52]

Furthermore, Mrs. E. M. King, who broke away from the Rational Dress Society to organize the Rational Dress Association, believed that "the requirements of the perfect dress which combined health and art are similar to those of the group of reform-minded artists who founded the Healthy and Artistic Dress Union in London in the 1890s."[53]

The Healthy and Artistic Dress Union. By the 1890s the link between health and beauty became the established philosophy for dress reformers. A society that took a decidedly aesthetic point of view was the Healthy and Artistic Dress Union, established in 1890. The purpose of this society was for the "propagation of sound ideas on the subject of dress." Between 1893 and 1894 the Union published *Aglaia,* a journal devoted to their concerns for grace in dress. In Greek mythology Aglaia was the "grace of adornment," one of the three graces who presided over the beauty of life. The objectives of the Union were educational. As stated in the journal, their desire was "to inculcate sound principles [for] devising and executing beautiful and healthy garments; to familiarize our readers with the structure of the human figure . . . that they may learn to understand the difference between adornment and distortion; and . . . suggest others for the future." They intended to critically examine existing forms and point out defects and suggest modifications, but also occasionally to offer designs for dresses.[54]

Although they insisted that *Aglaia* was not a "fashion book," in 1893 they illustrated Empire fashions, which they thought could be commended. Many of the styles they suggested reflected antique Greek dress, which, they believed, would provide individual ease for the health. In 1894 they offered alternatives to the exaggerated sleeves then in fashion (Fig. 57). Other practical suggestions in-

Fig. 57 *Aglaia*, 1894. A drawing of aesthetic dress.

cluded improving not just women's dress but children's and men's as well. The members of the union who cared about health and the beauty of dress included the physicians Sir Spence Wells, J. G. Garson, and Wilberforce Smith, as well as the artists Hamio Thorycroft, G. F. Watts, and Henry Holiday. Holiday, best known as a designer of stained glass, joined the Healthy and Artistic Dress Union after attending a debate on dress reform at Hampstead Town Hall. His service to the organization was significant; he served as president of the organization and contributed to *Aglaia*. His support for the journal included the cover design and several persuasive articles on reform: "The Artistic Aspect of Dress," "Men's Dress," and "A Suggestion for Evening Dress for Men." He also illustrated articles written by other writers on the subject of dress reform.[55]

Aglaia was not a commercial success but apparently it was widely read among the artistic elite, many of whom were Holiday's friends in the aristocracy. The journal may have inspired and helped to popularize artistic styles of dress, especially Liberty gowns, which became associated with progressive thinkers in the 1890s. Certainly, members such as Holiday, Walter Crane, G. F. Watts, and Arthur Lasenby Liberty were in the forefront of the modern design and artistic dress reform movements.[56]

The philosophy of the Healthy and Artistic Dress Union clearly was that of Arthur Lasenby Liberty, founder of the Liberty Company, which was a major purveyor of artistic (or aesthetic) fabrics and gowns. In an article in *Aglaia* (1894), Liberty discussed the progress of taste in dress in relation to manufacture. (In the same issue, Walter Crane related the subject to art education.) In his article, Liberty traced the development of taste in dress, noting the mid-nineteenth-century interest in Japanese costume and the demand for softer draperies and daintier fabrics between 1870 and 1880. But he also observed that there were crude copies made of both fabrics and dresses in which grace and simplicity were confused with negligent eccentricity. He felt that the new aesthetic movement was a "fashion" in which all canons of taste were forgotten or ignored. The year he referred to was 1881, so his references were to aesthetes who wore their artistic dress in public. By the turn of the century, however, Liberty felt that his ideas were taking hold and making an impact on fashionable dress.[57]

Liberty's ideas about dress were similar to other reformers. He believed that clothing should not distort the natural form of the body with corsets but rather should be in harmony with natural and individual characteristics and should reflect independent personal opinion. That is, women should be able to reject novelty and select clothing that was suitable to their individuality as well as to use. Liberty strongly advocated adopting or modifying old designs, especially the Empire mode, because he felt that it reflected artistic truth and had the graceful dignity of ancient Greek draperies.

Yet for Liberty, the clothing should not be eccentric or bizarre. He rejected the fashionable aesthetes, those Pre-Raphaelite beauties who followed the "Cult of Beauty," as being too eccentric. Most important, he believed in using beautiful fabrics. He was celebrated for his ability to manufacture textiles in England equal to those from Asia. He chose to control manufacturing to produce these, although he disliked the effects of mass production as much as did his friends in the Arts and Crafts Movement.

Our knowledge of Liberty and his ideas regarding dress reform comes from catalogs published by the Liberty Company and from *Aglaia*, the journal of the Healthy and Artistic Dress Union, as well as from contemporary commentary by individuals involved in the various reform movements in England and, of course, from the writings of Arthur Lasenby Liberty himself.

The Liberty Company. In 1875, after serving 12 years as manager of Farmer and Roger's Oriental Warehouse in London, Arthur Lasenby Liberty established his own company, which he called East India House. Liberty specialized in "art fabrics from the Orient" and carried in addition other exotic wares that appealed to his artistic friends—Lord Leighton, Burne-Jones, Rossetti, Whistler, Crane, Godwin, and others. From this beginning sprang the famous Regent Street firm of Liberty and Co., well known to both Europeans and Americans. The Liberty company had long provided Oriental silks for the clothing favored by his artistically inclined customers. The soft, drapable Liberty dress fabrics also appealed to the artistic dress reformers of the day. Thus, it was not surprising that in 1884 E. W. Godwin, a well-known architect, antiquary, and advocate of dress reform, agreed to become the first director of the costume department.[58]

The Liberty costume department was arranged for the study and execution of costumes embracing all periods of historic dress, together with such modifications of really beautiful examples as might be adapted to the conventionalities of modern life without rendering them eccentric or bizarre. The useful and informative store catalogs encouraged women to visit the shop so they could inspect and study the folios of colored manuscript drawings, make up stock examples, and work with the assistants. For those not able to visit the London or other shops, on receipt of a letter or telegram an experienced dressmaker would attend ladies at their country residences with special selections of materials and sketches. This was the advised method of ordering for important orders; lesser orders would be taken through the post.[59]

One Liberty catalog stated that "what is good in current art is the outcome of earlier experiments and that there is nothing that is absolutely new—it is all a matter of evolution." The text continued by noting that "the designs presented reflect the influence of Ancient Greece, Italian Renaissance and 18th Century France which reflect Artistic Truth—designs which were good and true in principle."[60]

Although Liberty sold imported fabrics, he also manufactured his own silks and cashmere—"UMRITZA cashmere/thick & thin." He desired to offer to the public fabrics that were excellent and pure and beyond the influence of the fleeting vagaries of mere fashion. He protested against copies of his fabric and desired to prove that industry, mechanized industry, could produce tasteful and artistic goods. Apparently, Liberty intended to establish an Educational School of Personal Adornment, where "shall be secured such forms, draperies, colours and ornaments as harmonized most perfectly with the natural characteristics of the wearer; and where shall be provided, for amateurs, artists and the stage, the most beautiful types of modern dresses, and the best reliable reproductions of ancient costume, plain or rich, according to the requirements of the person or the character."[61]

While the death of Godwin in 1886 may have dampened the idea of creating a school, the Liberty catalogs and special issues, such as *Dress and Decoration* (1905), offered advice to customers on how to dress with taste, much of it an effort toward dress reform. These efforts pre-date the organization of the Health and Artistic Dress Union. *Libertys Art Fabrics, Liberty & Co Ltd. Catalogue No. 9*, published in 1886, included extracts from the work of one M. Chevreul that provided suggestions for choosing colors of dresses based on individual skin, eye, and hair color. A catalog dated circa 1890 titled *Liberty Developments in Form and Colour* offered patrons a formula to guide them in choosing "colour-harmonies" appropriate for "artistic garb."[62]

The importance of the individual is apparent in all Liberty publications. *Catalogue* No. 25 (1893) offered "The essentials in the Selection of becoming Costume": "(1) *Self-reliance*. The exercise of independent personal opinion on rulings of fashion; (2) *Discrimation*. (a) The acceptance of fashions in vogue; subject to rejection . . . of novelty and . . . avoidance of exaggeration. (b) Recognition of the fact that it may be an advantage to ignore . . . fashion . . . and adopt as an alternative modifications of a more slowly perfected earlier model; (3) *Regard to individual characteristics*. (a) A clear appreciation of infinite diversities of personal characteristics . . . [which] if ignored, no grace nor dignity can . . . be secured. (b) The *gaucheries* of orders *à la mode*, enforced without regard to age, figure, or complexion . . . are painful . . . examples of forgetfulness of this rule."[63]

Until the 1920s the Liberty catalogs offered fashions that "will never go out of style," such as the classically inspired Directoire or Empire high-waisted gown

Fig. 58 Illustration from a Liberty & Co. catalog comparing a new Liberty style with its inspiration, a gown from the Empire period.

of the early 1790s, which they described as having a "quaint short waist, a supple contour freed from contorting basque or other rigidities, and a graceful dignity of flowing classic draperies." Furthermore, one catalog stated that "a prominent feature of the adoption of the Empire mode is the assurance that, so long as it holds sway, the tightly-laced corset cannot be the grim essential it has been deemed erstwhile."[64] The illustrations of Empire gowns in the 1893 catalog included a fashion plate from an earlier period and a contemporary Liberty modification, both of which could be custom-made in a variety of fabrics (Fig. 58). A 1905 catalog included "Josephine," an Empire-styled evening dress (Fig. 59), and "Hera," a silk evening gown designed like a dress of ancient Greece, "with crisscross bands hand-embroidered in pearls and silver (Fig. 60). Also included were "Amelia," an Empire evening gown with embroidered satin robe; "Marian," a Directoire visiting cloak, which had embroidered collar and cuffs; and "Helen," an Empire tea gown of flowered crepe-de-chine (or gauze). The catalog also presented other historical styles, such as "Jacqueline," an indoor gown fashioned after a fifteenth-century French gown of velveteen and silk crepe.[65] The classical styles remained popular, for in autumn 1915 Liberty's offered a gown very close in style to a classical Greek chiton (Fig. 61).[66]

Fig. 59 (left) "Josephine," from *Liberty & Co. Catalogue*, no. 98, 1905.

Fig. 60 (right) "Hera," from *Liberty & Co. Catalogue*, no. 98, 1905.

Fig. 61 A gown offered in a 1915 Liberty catalog strongly suggests a Greek chiton yet bows to fashion with elements of the fashionable hobble skirt and a train.

The advice and commentary in Liberty's catalogs reflected ideas regarding dress reform shared by Arthur Lasenby Liberty and E. W. Godwin, the director of the costume department, as well as Henry Holiday and Walter Crane. Godwin's opinions regarding the need for dress reform appeared in essay form in the catalog for the 1884 International Health Exhibition. Oscar Wilde drew on Godwin's essay to support his own views on dress reform. Apparently, reform efforts were effective, for the preface to the 1905 Liberty catalog stated that the question of dress "has nowadays become one of individual settlement." The catalog observed that women reserved the right to adopt the current fashion to their particular tastes and requirements; "This emancipation from slavish subjection to passing fashions is a feature of the new century. . . . The resultant general effect is that women's dress is more graceful, more refined, and more suited to its requirements than at any previous age." The catalog continued by noting that "the science of hygiene (of Jaeger) asserted its right to consideration, but the extended knowledge of the laws of decorative art has refined the taste of the nation." It was this refinement of taste in dress, the catalog concluded, that had created "the discerning power of selection and rejection—election of what is good, rejection of the bad and offensive."[67]

The Liberty dress department grew over the years. In a reminiscence that appeared in the *Liberty Lamp*, the employee publication of the Liberty Company, one former employee of the department remarked that

> the establishment [of the dress department] was considered a distinct break with the traditions of the Firm, and many felt uneasy at the introduction of Ladies' Costumes, with its concomitants millinery and other phases of female adornment, into a business which was laying itself out for artistic decoration and the manufacture of articles and fabrics which could educate the public taste; it was felt it would be difficult to keep out of the current of the whirling changes of fashion, and some doubted the wisdom of expecting men to extend their patronage for furniture decoration to an establishment where the feminine side of personal requirements was much in evidence.

The fears were not warranted, for Liberty-style dresses soon "became the 'mode' for special occasions among artistic people and their imitators; it [the Liberty style] was recognizable at a glance."[68]

The question often arises: What influence did the Liberty Company have on fashion? The Liberty Company itself offered a response in *Liberty Developments in Form and Colour*, stating that its aim was to "re-establish the craft of dressmaking upon some hygienic, intelligible, progressive basis." The company surveyed past fashions for practical and beautiful sources to adopt to present-day needs and extended these researches to design and color of fabrics. It introduced "soft-draping" fabrics prior to establishing a dress department. Indeed, it was because "modistes" of the day were prejudiced against the fabrics that Messrs. Liberty undertook "Dressmaking . . . in order to defend and support their new fabric inventions." The catalog stated that "colour-reform is perhaps the most important among the varied efforts towards artistic decorative progress, inaugurated or stimulated by Messrs. Liberty." Its authors declared that the public worldwide had benefited; the company had revolutionized public taste in regard to both form and color and its "'Liberty'-fashions, and 'Liberty'-colours . . . are now universally adopted."[69]

Immediately following the publication of *Form and Colour* in 1890, detailed dress models and adaptations of the Empire mode were made up by Messrs. Liberty and exhibited in their new Paris showroom at 38 Avenue de l'Opéra. In *Catalogue* No. 25 Messrs. Liberty inserted a notice titled, "How Was the Empire Mode Reintroduced." The notice indicates that Empire-styled gowns were sold in Paris by Liberty prior to the fashion for the Empire mode being reintroduced from Paris into England. Messrs. Liberty did not want Paris to have credit for the initiative in stimulating an interest in artistic dress that was rightly the effort of the Liberty Company.

The popularity of Liberty gowns and fabrics is apparent from the many references made to them. B. O. Flower, a prominent American publisher and advocate of reform in women's dress, observed that "an encouraging sign of the times is the increasing demand on the great and fashionable house of Liberty and Co. of London, for the Greek and other simple costumes by fashionable ladies, who are using them largely for home wear."[70]

ℰ Conveying the Message of Reform at Home and Abroad

One cannot underestimate the popularity of the soft drapable Liberty fabrics or the artistic reform styles of dress promoted by the Liberty Company. Nor can the efforts of the various writers on reform and organizations, such as the Healthy and Artistic Dress Union, be considered inconsequential. All the available media at one time or another published illustrations and articles about the artistic reform of women's dress. By the turn of the century, the modern design movement embracing reform in architecture, the decorative arts, and home interiors had made its mark on the landscape. The aesthetic reform in women's clothing, based on the same artistic principles, likewise could be seen in fashionable modes of the day.

In looking back on the progress of taste in dress, Walter Crane observed that "commerce . . . was not slow to flood the market with what were labelled 'art-colours' and 'aesthetic' fabrics." Likewise, he concluded that the "aesthetic movement . . . did indicate a general desire for greater beauty in ordinary life, and gave us many charming materials and colours, which, in combination with genuine taste, produced some very beautiful as well as simple dresses." Still later, in 1911, Crane contended that among the undisputed rights of a woman "the liberty to dress as she pleases even under recognized types for set occasions, and with contrast, variety, and change of style, is not a little important." He further noted that "it is a liberty that has very striking effects upon the aspects of modern life we are considering." While this liberty might be checked by modistes, the trades, etcetera, it was "too important . . . to be ignored or under valued in any way."[71]

The Healthy and Artistic Dress Union actively promoted artistic dress as a way to reform women's clothing. At its meetings numerous members of the organization—Dr. Sophie Bryant, Henry Holiday, Walter Crane, and Arthur Lasenby Liberty—spoke on such subjects as aesthetics in dress and the progress of taste in dress. Perhaps the dress union's most impressive public achievement was the presentation, at St. George's Hall in May 1896, of a series of "Living Pictures" illustrating dress in the past, present, and future. Henry Holiday noted that the hall was crowded and the tableaux deemed a great success. Among the tableaux were "Aglaia— the Three Graces," with three women in classical dress, and an "Evening Scene," arranged by Arthur Lasenby Liberty and Louise Jopling. In the latter eight women were dressed in Empire dresses and seven men in velvet suits with knee breeches and silk stockings.[72]

While all these efforts were perhaps making an impact at home, it was outside England that the Liberty Company was most influential in conveying to a broader public ideas regarding artistic dress. There were a number of outlets for Liberty styles. First, there were the catalogs. But more important perhaps were the depots, or shops, in cities throughout Europe and America.

Liberty started to place depots, as the company called them, in other cities in the late 1800s, with a Paris shop opening in 1890. Other early depots were in Bristol (1904–10) and Manchester (1905–12). Liberty also arranged to place depots in specialty shops in North America: in New York at Messrs. Johnson & Faulker, Union Square; in Boston at Messrs. W. H. Devis & Co., Summer St.; in Chicago at Messrs. Colby & Son; and in Toronto at Messrs. J. Kay & Son. Liberty also located depots in all of the major cities in England, Scotland, and Ireland.[73]

The Paris shop was in existence between 1890 and 1932, and Liberty fabrics no doubt made quite an impression at the Paris Exhibitions of 1889 and 1900. Fashion periodicals such as the *Queen* carried illustrations of the artistic styles. The artistic community and wealthy patrons continued to desire the Liberty fabrics as well as the company's styles well into the twentieth century. However, after the First World War and into the twenties, the Liberty style became an anachronism. The Paris *Exposition des Arts Decoratif* saw the new style of Art Deco gain enough attention to direct the world toward a new era in design. The Messrs. Liberty and Company were not a part of this movement. The costume department in Paris maintained a traditional look, and Liberty's still produced catalogs in two sections, "Gowns Never Out of Fashion," made in the same Grecian and Empire style of fifty years earlier, and "Gowns of the New Season," which did not reflect the new designs promoted by Chanel, who had discovered a new simplicity, freedom, and comfort. Still, intellectuals, artists, and would-be "artistics" clung to their Liberty fabrics.[74]

The influence and reach of the Liberty Company were indeed vast and international in scope. In Glasgow, Scotland, seemingly beyond the immediate reach of the artistic circle, Jessie Newbery knew about Liberty fabrics. According to Newbery's daughter, Mary Newbery Sturrock, "My mother's motto was 'warmth without weight.' . . . Liberty's materials were to be her main source for many years." Some of the silks she purchased in the 1920s were the same as she had bought as a student. Liberty's was "the only place where she [Jessie] could find pure light woollens in the soft blues and greens which were our only wear." Mrs. Newbery, who taught embroidery at the Glasgow School of Art, where her husband, Francis H. (Fra) Newbery was headmaster, had a distinct style of dress that incorporated the principles of the Healthy and Artistic Dress Union. According to Margaret Swain, "She never wore a corset in her life" and deplored the tight lacing imposed by fashion.[75]

Jessie Newbery generally made her own clothing, using no darts; "everything was gathered and tied," for a comfortable fit was essential. When busy teaching and entertaining, Mrs. Newbery hired a visiting dressmaker for five shillings a day with meals. She desired materials that were "light, supple and warm; silks and light wools." She often made her own cords and "bobbles," and took delight in Russian peasant crafts, textiles, jewelry, and metal buttons and clasps, which she also found in London.[76] Margaret Swain makes it clear that Jessie Newbery was not a propagandist; her dress "was a wholly personal style meant only to satisfy her exacting standards of comfort and beauty." Nonetheless, many of her students copied her look.[77]

While Jessie Newbery was not part of the aesthetic circle found in London in the 1870s and 1880s, she would have had access to information about artistic reform dress in magazines from contacts at the Glasgow School of Art and most certainly through her dealings with Liberty's.

Liberty fabrics and styles of dress had quickly spread beyond Britain. With a Liberty shop in the center of the fashion world, Paris, it is not surprising that Liberty fabrics were easily adopted for artistic dress in Austria, Germany, and other countries of Europe. The Viennese made direct contact with Scottish artists involved with the Arts and Crafts Movement when Fra and Jessie Newbery and Charles Rennie Macintosh and his wife, Margaret Macdonald, exhibited their furniture and textiles at the Vienna "Secession" in 1900. This is an important encounter, for it reveals the interest in reforming all of the decorative arts, which included women's dress, on like-minded designers and artists in Europe. A similar aesthetic awakening occurred in America as well, where followers of the Arts and Crafts Movement also renounced the effects of industrialization on design and good taste. A major influence in America was through Oscar Wilde and his tour of the operetta *Patience*. Not only were costumes for the production built with Liberty fabrics but Wilde lectured on the subject of women's dress. He continually argued for applying the principles of art to dress, an idea that began to appear in popular arts literature and one picked up and promoted by a number of America supporters of artistic dress.

CHAPTER FIVE

Artistic Dress in America

It did not take long for Americans to embrace the reforming ideas and precepts of the British aesthetes. In the second half of the nineteenth century, as in many parts of the world, American artists, architects, designers, and like-minded citizens were leaning toward cultural reform, especially of the visual, decorative, and practical arts. They were reacting to extremes of industrialization as well as to what they viewed were stultifying traditions. For those so inclined, it became necessary to dress in clothing that reflected new artistic sensibilities and reforming sentiments. The earliest aesthetic ideas regarding dress came to America from England through a number of sources, including essays on artistic taste and fiction in periodical literature, especially in *Peterson's Magazine*; the writings of the English promoter of good taste Mary Haweis; and, of course, from Oscar Wilde's enormously successful lectures and tour of America with the comic operetta *Patience* in 1882.

Americans were receptive to the new aesthetic dress. Even in the late 1870s the press observed that American women had begun to dress like the quaint figures in Pre-Raphaelite paintings. By affecting the aesthetic, or artistic, styles of dress worn by the Londoners who participated in what was described as the "Cult of Beauty," American women were expressing their own feelings of modernity. Since wearing aesthetic dress in public meant breaking the rules of etiquette and customary standards established by American society, many women in the late nineteenth century confined their aesthetic expression to tea gowns worn in the home. Yet the new artistic dress had a growing public appeal, because it had exotic qualities and connections to historic dress. Indeed, ultimate acceptance of the artistic garment known as a tea gown followed the process by which almost any new style becomes a fashionable mode.[1]

While the tea gown (see Fig. 6) became all the rage as a fashionable garment during the 1880s, the gown did have cachet as a rational garment. Artistic dress for Americans was more than an outpouring of sentiment for a new fashion. It represented the substance of a new way of thinking. For many women it was a means to achieve freedom in dress, a unique approach to clothing reform. It was relatively subtle and had few, if any, feminist overtones. Along with being romantic, one of its appealing features was that women could choose to wear it without a corset. Aesthetic dress provided dress reformers with a fresh approach to continue their battle to free women from restrictive dress, one that linked beauty more than ever to physical well-being.

Supporters of freedom in dress for women viewed the aesthetic styles as acceptable alternatives to restrictive women's fashion. Trousers, although appropriate for physical activities, would not become a viable alternative to skirts worn in the public sphere until the late twentieth century. Although women began to adopt reform underwear in the 1870s, corseted gowns remained a fashion well into the twentieth century. At first, only the more daring women wore aesthetic dress in public. Others wore it only as a tea gown in the secure home environment, but soon the tea-gown styles were seen in dresses meant for many different public occasions, such as dinner, visiting, and the theater.

When reformers advocated applying the principles of art to clothing in the late 1880s, they meant all clothing, not just tea gowns. They wanted to create artistic dress meant for wearing in public, and they sought alternatives to constricting and uncomfortable styles of dress then in fashion. In the new artistic dress they offered women a means to make fashion sensible without appropriating men's dress. They did so by applying art principles to both garment design and by thoughtful selection of garments based on the needs of individual women. The successful reformers suggested accommodating fashion, not changing it. Their goal was to make fashion rational, hygienic, beautiful, and as Annie Jenness Miller might have said, correct.

BRITISH INFLUENCE ON AMERICAN DRESS

The general social exchange between America and Europe created a desire by Americans for what was new from abroad. The information about the British aesthetic movement that came through essays and reports in journals and popular magazines, imported theatrical productions, and public lectures by British aesthetes had a clear message regarding dress. American women should look to the classical world for a standard of beauty. That is, they should strive to achieve the natural beauty of the Venus de Milo; they should cease wearing restrictive clothing that went against nature; and they should apply the classical principles of art to their dress. Some even suggested that women wear classically inspired garments. Such was the message of Oscar Wilde as he traveled across America.

Almost all of the available media followed the travels of Oscar Wilde while he was on a year's sojourn in America in 1882, partly to serve as advance man for D'Oyly Carte's production of Gilbert and Sullivan's aesthetic comic operetta *Patience*, which parodied the British aesthetes. American fashion periodicals detailed the aesthetic costumes portrayed in these productions. Americans were overwhelmed with Wilde's personality. Art circles in every major city in America entertained him "aesthetically," with women dressed in the latest artistic styles as interpreted by their dressmakers.[2]

During his travels, Wilde had opportunities to explain the spirit of aestheticism. He lectured on many art subjects, including fashion. In one lecture regarding women's clothing titled "Slaves of Fashion," Wilde deplored the evils of corsetry. In another, "Women's Dress," he advised women to make their dress hygienic by suspending the weight of clothing from the shoulders and reducing the number of layers of clothing. Through his lectures Wilde dispersed the aesthetes' ideas regarding the inspiration artists could gather from Japanese and classical art. He advised women to look to antique dress of any kind in order to create beautiful and healthful garments. As previously discussed in chapter 4, Wilde and other modern reformers desired to legitimize the art of dress through the application of art principles to their design.[3]

Excerpts from *The Art of Dress* by Mary Haweis, one of the best-known supporters of aesthetic dress in England, were published in America in *Cassell's Journal of Art*. Haweis encouraged readers to apply the principles of art to dress. Women, she advised, should consider color, line, and fabric when designing and selecting clothing. For Haweis, the source of ideal beauty was none other than the classical standard, the female Greek statue. These art principles were the only way for a woman to alter her appearance from being an obvious slave to fashion to become a natural, aesthetic beauty. It is clear from reading American reform literature on ways to improve women's dress that the authors share sentiments put forth in the writings of Mary Haweis, Oscar Wilde, and other aesthetes.[4]

The press also commented on famous actresses who dressed in the aesthetic style. Most notable was the English actress Ellen Terry, who often appeared on stage in artistic dress. As the wife of the versatile artist and architect Edward William Godwin and a member of the Aesthetic circle in London, Terry was perhaps one of the more visible aesthetic women. Ellen Terry did not restrict the wearing of artistic dress to gatherings of aesthetes such as might take place in private salons or public art galleries. For Terry, aesthetic dress was the only style; it was her everyday dress. She therefore pushed the boundaries of propriety, which she could do simply because she was an actress with artistic sensibilities.[5]

While many American magazines reported on the travels of individuals like Wilde and Terry in America, *Demorest's Monthly Magazine* frequently reported on major aesthetic events that occurred in England, especially openings at private galleries that exhibited the new works of the artists in the Aesthetic circle. For instance, in an article taken from the London *Queen* titled "Dress at the Private View Day at the Grosvenor Gallery" readers could learn what various members of the Aesthetic circle wore to the event or simply that "green continues to be a color much in vogue with 'picturesque dressers.'"[6]

In addition to reporting on the artistic lifestyle, the editors of *Demorest's Monthly Magazine* often displayed aesthetic symbols such as sunflowers and Japanese designs on the cover. And while they illustrated fashionable dress, they also extolled the virtues of artistic styles in the text. *Demorest's Monthly Magazine* (1866–89), and *The Delineator* (1873–1937), published by the Butterick Pattern Company, and to a lesser degree *Harper's Bazar* (1867 to the present) published essays advocating artistic dress. Articles with titles like "Artistic Methods in Dress," "The Esthetic in Dress," and "Artistic Dress," which found their way into these magazines, usually encouraged women to follow art principles in designing gowns and selecting clothing for themselves.[7]

In the 1890s the magazine *Arena* frequently published articles on dress reform. In addition to reporting on the history of dress-reform movements in America and the reform activities that took place before and during the Chicago World's Fair, it espoused the virtues of wearing artistic dress. B. O. Flower noted that "another encouraging sign of the times is the increasing demand on the great and fashionable house of Liberty & Co., of London, for the Greek and other simple costumes by fashionable ladies, who are using them largely for home wear." Most important, Flower continued, was the "effect or influence which is sure to follow this breaking away from the ruling fashions in wealthy circles. When conventionalism in dress is fully discredited, practical reform is certain to follow."[8]

This is not to suggest that there was wholesale advocacy of the artistic style. Judith Ann Fuller has noted that *Godey's Lady's Book* and *Peterson's Magazine* rarely commented on aesthetic dress. Certainly, not all authors supported the aesthetic lifestyle. Indeed, some writers, such as William Dean Howells in *The Coast of Bohemia*, revealed an opposing point of view and viewed the aesthetic woman a threat. Nonetheless, the authors who did support women wearing aesthetic dress were, in fact, continuing to promote the dress-reform philosophy of the English aesthetes, such as John Ruskin, Haweis, and Wilde.[9]

ℰ WOMEN TAKE CHARGE: ADVICE ON HOW TO DRESS ARTISTICALLY

The idea that taste could be improved through education permeated American literature. More than simply reporting on the English aesthetes, women's magazines, reform magazines, pamphlets published by women's clubs, and fiction began to carry messages for Americans that were seeped in the rhetoric of the artistic reformer. Furthermore, a number of national leaders of the reform movement published monographs in the 1890s. One of the earliest promoters was Mary Abigail Dodge, writing under the nom de plume Gail Hamilton, who produced a series of essays in the early 1870s entitled *Twelve Miles from a Lemon*, which was devoted to ways in which women could reform their clothing and lifestyles.[10]

It is not surprising that the connections of hygiene and health to dress, art, and beauty were the focus of a number of advice books devoted to women. Abba Goold Woolson, of course, was one of the most well known of a number of female Boston educators and physicians who advocated a reform in underwear for women in the 1870s. Woolson, along with her colleagues in the New England

Women's Club, not only recommended reform underwear but frequently argued for aesthetics in dress as well. Advice on how to improve women's dress using artistic principles proliferated in the 1880s and 1890s. Many advice authors who advocated reform underwear, exercise, and improved health in general also promoted artistic dress. As noted in chapter 3, the one magazine most devoted to correcting women's dress was Annie Jenness-Miller's *Dress, a Monthly Magazine* (also known as the *Jenness Miller Magazine* and *Jenness Miller Monthly*). Annie Jenness-Miller and her sister, Mabel Jenness, were devoted to freeing women from constricting clothing and improving health through exercise. Both published books on the subject. Other writers who actively promoted artistic dress were Frances M. Steele and Elizabeth L. Steele Adams, in *Beauty of Form and Grace of Vesture* (1892); Frances S. Parker, *Dress, and How to Improve It* (1897); and Helen Gilbert Ecob, *The Well-Dressed Woman: A Study in the Practical Application to Dress of the Laws of Health, Art, and Morals* (1892).[11]

The Classical Ideal, Health, and Beauty

The advocates for improving women's dress no doubt had picked up many aesthetic ideas from the English reformers. It would be redundant, however, to reiterate in detail the aesthetic ideas put forth by the British promoters of the Aesthetic Movement. Yet it must be made clear that American writers extolled Ruskin's philosophy regarding the beauty of the natural body. American reformers argued that a woman's body was beautiful only if it was undeformed by corsets, hoops, bustles, and other distorting attachments. As Woolson observed in 1874, "What opposes Nature can never be beautiful." Nearly all of the writers on women's dress reform drew on the classical ideal as a standard for beauty. Hence, there was a predetermined ideal, with specified proportions such as those embodied in the Venus de Milo and other sculptural Venus portraits. Natural, for these Victorians, apparently did not really mean "as found in nature"; rather, it meant unrestricted and in proportion, "like a Greek goddess," neither too fat nor too thin, with legs not too long or too short.[12]

That the Venus de Milo (Fig. 62) and other classical female sculpture became the standard for female proportions in the belief that they represented the most natural form cannot be questioned. Numerous examples support this view. The board of trustees at Vassar College announced that the graduates would go forth "'physically well-developed, vigorous, and graceful women . . . with enlightened views and wholesome habits as regards the use and care of their bodies.'" The trustees therefore provided instruction in physiology and physical training. The exercises were performed "'without stays and in loose dress'" and a "'cast of the Venus of Melos was set up in the room. . . . The professor of art helped by up-holding the classic ideals of beauty.'" The idea of an educated woman never wearing stays was an important issue for Volney S. Fulham of Ludlow, Vermont. Fulham bequeathed a sum of money to Tufts College in the form of a scholarship for any woman entering Tuft's women's division, Jackson

Fig. 62 A statue of Venus de Milo.

College, or some other college for women. However, the recipient "must never have worn a corset" and she must have the proportions "equal to that of the statues of the 'Venus de Medicis' or the 'Venus of Milo.'" At the time of probate $908.43 was due Tufts College.[13]

The connection of health, exercise, beauty, and the Greek ideal became accepted educational policy early in the development of higher-education institutions for women. Indeed, American reformers believed that physical beauty could be achieved only through good health. Since one of the keys to good health was exercise, they concluded that exercise was necessary to achieve true beauty. Exercise programs such as sports and calisthenics in schools and colleges and the Delsartean system of movement provided opportunities for women to improve their health and thus become more beautiful.

The addition of the Delsartean system and other exercise programs to the reformers' list of ways to achieve the ideal classical standard was a distinctly American phenomenon. Indeed, the Americanized version of François Delsarte's aesthetic system for movement in America supported the artistic dress-reform movement in that it paralleled the enlightened aesthetic sensibility that occurred in all of the arts, including dress. The Delsarte exercises were promoted by many educators who supported the view that movement could develop beauty and grace in individuals. The Delsarte-system movement was particularly popular in the 1880s during the time when there was high interest in artistic dress.[14]

Yet the reformers were realistic. They did not expect women to rely solely on a physically fit body for a correct natural form. They saw a need to apply art principles to dress. That is, they suggested ways to improve imperfections in the natural form and line of the body through selection of clothing to create the "correct" balance and proportion of the figure. The idea was not to reshape the body with undergarments, but rather to use clothing to create an illusion of the ideal proportions of a Venus de Milo. There would be no distortions of women's bodies through corsetry or bustles to create a singular fashioned look that would last for a short period of time. Each individual woman could look her most beautiful through classic proportions that would lend the most amount of grace to a figure. Also, artistic dress draped on the body could give a woman freedom to move gracefully, which would be enhanced by training in the "new" Delsarte techniques. Since all bodies are different, reformers placed emphasis on the individual. The artistic reformers thus created a new ideal. For them the fashioned ideal was transformed into the classical ideal. Unlike fashion, this new ideal was not expected to change, because it was adapted to each individual woman.[15]

The theorists who promoted applying the principles of art to dress discussed the importance of color, as well as line and form. In essence, these writers were arguing that the clothing should be designed on artistic or aesthetic principles and that women should consider these principles when they selected clothing for their specific body types. The artistic reformers also drew on classical principles when they disavowed excessive ornamentation in dress. Indeed, simplicity and fitness to purpose were well-known aesthetic precepts that writers often drew on when offering advice to women on how to dress. Etiquette books from early in the nineteenth century had railed against ostentatious dress, so it is clear that these principles were already present in the minds of women. It just happened that during periods when fashionable dress was not simple (which was most of the time), women simply ignored the advice rather than go against the mode. For women fashion was reality; it meant more to them than abstract ideas.[16]

The Jenness Sisters on Artistic Dress

A broader understanding of the efforts toward freeing women from restrictive and constrictive clothing may be gleaned by examining the activities of Annie Jenness-Miller and her sister, Mabel Jenness. In the 1880s and 1890s these two women tirelessly offered women advice on beauty. They believed that the only way for women to attain true beauty was to apply artistic principles to their dress and to adopt the exercise system of François Delsarte. They were New Englanders by birth, received their education in Boston, and are perhaps best known for their association with *Dress,* the monthly magazine devoted to the practical and beautiful in women's and children's clothing that was published in New York City between 1887 and 1900, under various titles. Annie Jenness-Miller also published *Physical Beauty, How to Obtain and How to Preserve It* (1892), as well as several novels and informational pamphlets related to rational dress and physical culture. She and her sister, Mabel Jenness, who wrote *Comprehensive Physical Culture* (1891), were regular speakers on a lecture circuit offering advice and giving demonstrations regarding physical culture and correct dress to various women's organizations throughout the United States.[17]

The reasons that first led Annie Jenness-Miller to adopt improved garments for her own use were "a backache and threatened invalidism" caused by heavy clothing and a cramped waist, both of which impeded natural form and carriage. But Jenness-Miller did not choose for everyday dress the radical short dress and trousers known as the Bloomer costume to improve her health. Rather, she chose a subtler and more enduring method, one that was evolutionary rather than revolutionary and that in her mind was both aesthetic and healthful. Her reform combined physical culture, artistic dress, and rational (common-sense) undergarments. Indeed, she noted that "the pioneers of dress reform did not sufficiently consider the elements of grace and beauty." Most significant, she took the cause to improve beauty and health beyond her own needs. For through publications and lectures, Annie Jenness-Miller and Mabel Jenness spread the message that women could enhance their beauty through exercise and by applying the principles of art to their clothing. As noted in chapter 3, the *Arena* applauded them for their efforts, particularly in reform of women's undergarments.[18]

Both women were influenced by the physical-culture movement that became increasingly popular in America in the 1880s and reached its peak in the 1890s. The most famous "physical culturist" was François Delsarte, and perhaps the most influential system used in America was one derived from his theory, which was based on the idea that there is a correspondence between the inner and outer nature of humans. The Delsartean method, which aimed at coordinating voice with gesture in order to express the emotions implied in music and drama, was incorporated into the program of study in the Monroe Conservatory of Oratory, where Mabel Jenness was a student from 1883 to 1884. Charles Wesley

Emerson, founder of the Monroe Conservatory, had been a student of Professor Lewis B. Monroe at Boston University. In 1878, when Monroe was dean of the School of Oratory, Steele Mackaye, who had introduced Delsartean theory to Boston, gave lectures on the philosophy of expression. It was these lectures that Charles Wesley Emerson attended and incorporated into the program at Monroe Conservatory, which now, incidentally, is Emerson College. Delsarte's techniques for natural expression were applicable to the new school of thought in oratory that emphasized natural expression. Natural expression was in opposition to the exhibitionism and artificial gesturing employed by such nineteenth-century orators as Edward Everett and Charles Sumner.[19]

While there is no evidence that Annie Jenness-Miller attended any classes at the conservatory, the records show that Mabel Jenness was enrolled. When she was a student the "Course of Instruction" included the following subjects: Dramatic Reading, which "embraces the philosophy of expression discovered by the great Delsarte of Paris," Prose Reading, Voice Culture, Declamation, Dramatic Action, and, of course, Aesthetic Culture, which included "the science of the beautiful in nature and art and the philosophy of taste and their application to habitual manners and the arts of expression."[20]

Charles Wesley Emerson, however, was equally drawn to the ancient Greek philosophy and the importance of the "coequal development of mind and body." In an article published in the first issue of Dress, and directly following Jenness Miller's introductory essay, Emerson stated that the Greeks knew "that God joins beauty and health in an indissoluble union, and no man can put them asunder." A close study of Grecian sculpture, Emerson observed, "discloses a still deeper principle than beauty," that is, unity, "a oneness of expression" of all the parts of the body "that gives such perfection to the whole figure." Thus unity was for Emerson the highest form of beauty. And it is through his system of vital exercises that one could cultivate a unity of the body. This form of bodily training, which goes beyond mere mechanical exercises, could produce unity and thus assure "both beauty and health to the person who can gain it." In addition to learning the correct exercises in order to achieve unity, Emerson stressed the need for a philosophy of taste and its application to habitual manners and the arts of expression. In his discussion of physical culture, Emerson also emphasized the need for clothing that would not hinder the free exercise of all muscles.[21] Both Annie Jenness-Miller and Mabel Jenness concurred with Emerson regarding the benefits of this sort of Delsartean-classical system of exercise, for they believed that "physical development involves health, unity, self-command, grace and beauty in logical and progressive order."[22] The publication of Mabel Jenness's Comprehensive Physical Culture (1891) no doubt was the culmination of thoughts previously presented to readers of Dress, beginning in 1887. In this work and in Annie Jenness-Miller's Physical Beauty, as well as through their articles in the journal and their public lectures, the ideas that the Jenness sisters presented to the public may well have been based on the knowledge gained through subjects studied by Mabel Jenness at the Monroe Conservatory of Oratory.[23] Indeed, another author and lecturer on improving women's health in dress, Frances S. Parker, also had been a pupil of Professor Lewis B. Monroe at the Boston University School of Oratory, where she, too, learned about Delsartean philosophy and took her own first steps toward dress reform. And perhaps the best-known follower of Delsarte, Henrietta Russell, also had studied with Monroe in Boston. Russell presented her system of physical culture and dress reform in a great number of lectures and demonstrations throughout the United States and Europe in the 1880s and 1890s.[24]

The relationship between the Jenness sisters and the Monroe Conservatory is evident in other ways as well. Indeed, the students at the Monroe Conservatory were aware of Annie Jenness-Miller's efforts to educate the public regarding the aesthetics of correct dress. The December 1896 issue of the *Emerson College Magazine* offered a series of articles on the subject of hygiene and aesthetic dress. Not surprisingly, these articles noted the importance of attaining unity through physical culture and quoted both Annie Jenness-Miller and Charles Wesley Emerson on the question of dress. In "A Plea for Rational Dress," Annie Blalock, teacher of "Physical Culture and Oratory" at Emerson College, drew again on the example of the Greeks. "The life and habits of the Greeks enabled them to reveal to the world almost ideal physical perfection. So it is to their statues [the Venus de Medici, and Venus de Milo], the despair and delight of all ages, that we turn for proper education in regards to women's forms.[25]

In addition to promoting the Delsartean ideas of physical culture and the Greek ideal, *Dress* included articles on "the effect of materials, colors, draperies, and general combinations, instructing our readers how to go at the work of emancipating themselves from the discomforts, dangers, and crudities of fashions which have no other reason for challenging popular favor than daring and novelty." Its editors invited correspondence on the subject of "How, What, When, and Where" regarding dress, and they offered the following advice concerning the aesthetics of clothing: "The question of what to wear can be answered by the analysis of what constitutes art and utility in dress," noting that the "human picture" is one grade higher than the painter's creation because the human must "unite utility with beauty."[26]

The influence of Jenness-Miller and Mabel Jenness was great in part also because they were popular lecturers. It was announced in the *Jenness Miller Magazine* in November of 1890 that they would give a series of lectures "in New York, Boston and other large cities during the winter season." Subjects included: "Healthful and Artistic Dress," "The Cultivation of Individuality," "Artistic Care of the Body," and "Congruities and Art in Dress." The first lecture, "Healthful and Artistic Dress," was illustrated with certain physical movements showing the difference between the grace and elegance gained by physical culture and the unartistic effects produced by fake dressing and the compression of the essential organs. They also showed eight costumes designed for different occasions.[27]

The lectures were so popular that imitators apparently sprang up all over the country. This phenomenon was cause for editorial comment in the magazine, in which Jenness-Miller explained that "correct, artistic and healthful dress rests on the firm basis of good, sound physical development" and that "before adopting artistic dress or giving a single public lecture upon the subject, both Miss Jenness and myself spent years in the study of physical development." She noted that other lecturers, Miss Case of St. Louis, Miss Bishop of New York, Miss Giddings of Massachusetts, and Miss Clara Holbrook Smith of Illinois, had all had training by the Jenness sisters.[28]

AMERICAN ARTISTIC DRESS: THE ARTIFACT

The literature that offers insight into the American adoption of the classical ideal for reforming women's dress also contains revealing descriptions and illustrations and patterns for the styles of dress considered to be artistic. Sources of knowledge include contemporary diaries, journals, magazines, advice publications, and extant garments. Descriptions and illustrations of artistic dress also appear in short stories and serialized fiction. The aesthetic lifestyle was a popular subject for fictional literature in women's magazines between 1881 and 1884, especially *Peterson's Magazine*. Reading this literature would allow women to imagine being an aesthete and offer them ways in which they could display artistic symbols as well. Or it might turn them against the style, for there was considerable ambivalence toward the aesthetic lifestyle in American society and thus in American fiction at the time.

One notable author of aesthetic fiction was Frances Hodgson Burnett, best known as the creator of the novel *Little Lord Fauntleroy*. Stories by her with an artistic theme appeared in *Peterson's Magazine*. Publishers illustrated aesthetic fiction with engravings that provided would-be aesthetes with ideas for making their own artistic gowns. Judith Ann Fuller describes the clothing and scenes in which artistic women are placed in a positive light, and she has observed that in many stories the artistic heroine wins her man over the less fortunate fashionable girl. The aesthete, however, was not always so pleasantly characterized, for in *The Coast of Bohemia*, William Dean Howells sees a threat in aesthetic dress and in women who wear it; the loose dress reflecting irrational forces in society and the breaking down of cultural boundaries. In the "Utterly Utter Boston Browns," Lydia Hoyt Farmer has a country character, Daisy Brown, reject the aestheticism and artificiality of her Boston cousins.[29]

While these fictional aesthetes of the period can enlighten us on some aspects of the aesthetic lifestyle and the perceived threat to the status quo, other sources, especially extant garments and advice literature, provide perhaps a more realistic perception of the style.

Styles of Artistic Dress Worn in America

Artistic, or aesthetic, dress can best be defined in nineteenth-century terms as any somewhat loose-fitting garment often worn without a corset that affords the wearer both comfort and grace. It was a category of dress that included varieties of house gowns (wrappers), which had been worn for years, but especially the tea gown. Yet it also included any garment, whether for daytime wear or for dinner or dance, that was designed using artistic principles and that had been selected for an individual based on these principles.

One of the chief improvements made by artistic dress was the possibility of freeing women from wearing a corset. Ideally, the artistic reform styles were designed with no band or constriction at the waistline. As noted by Steele and Adams in *Beauty of Form and Grace of Vesture* (1892), "There is positively no waistline in the natural body, no horizontal division whatsoever. . . . Not until the clothing of the figure is treated as one and indivisible . . . is the element of elegance, 'simplicity' in all classic costumes achieved."[30]

There were three basic styles of house gowns, also termed wrappers, which met this requirement: the Mother Hubbard, various configurations of the princess line, and the Empire style, mainly informed by historical garments—from the classical world through the eighteenth and early nineteenth centuries. The princess style was sometimes referred to as a tea gown, but in actuality tea gowns could also be constructed in the high-waisted Empire style or any other historic style, such as those designed by Liberty's. The support for all of these gowns was on the shoulders or, more ideally, according to Annie Jenness-Miller, evenly distributed over the whole body. In commenting on these styles, Steele and Adams observed that the "old pattern of a morning gown that for fifty years has been worn . . . is still pleasing . . . because of its unbroken front, unbroken, except by cord and tassels."[31]

Contemporary literature commented on the irony of adopting house-gown styles. A writer in *Dress* observed that "still the work goes on toward reform in dress and correct taste. To be sure the garments were first euphonized into tea-gowns; then all were astonished that their attractiveness had not been sooner discovered."[32] When making existing fashions meet artistic requirements, a designer might incorporate some of the elements of these gowns, particularly the princess style. However, it was not unusual for a dress to have the appearance of a small waist when in fact the gown had been draped over a princess-cut "gown form" that served as a lining. The "gown form" allowed the weight of the garment to be evenly distributed over the body rather than at the constricted waistline. Designers of gown forms recommended that women wear their "systems of underwear" that required no corset but offered a substitute "waist" or under bodice that had no or little stiffening.

The Mother Hubbard. The Mother Hubbard (see Fig. 5), as Steele and Adams noted, appears more like "a curtain hung from a ruffle at the bottom of the yoke and . . . it is still too long for free movement, especially when stooping." Without a girdle, the Mother Hubbard suggests "barrel-like bulk." Its good qualities, they pointed out, are overburdened with associations with "untidy surroundings and general discomfort." Rose E. Cleveland suggested that the Mother Hubbard when belted could be worn out of doors, but when left loose was strictly a negligé garment in shape, like a princess wrapper, and suitable only for the house. The Mother Hubbard craze of the 1880s had pioneering women adopting them for very practical reasons. As noted in chapter 1, debates raged over its attractiveness, or lack of it, as well as its appropriateness.[33]

The Princess Style. Historically inspired dress depicted in the paintings of the Pre-Raphaelites served as a model or source of the body-skimming princess style (figure 63), which is distinguished by vertical seams from shoulder to hem. The painters often drew on illustrations of women's medieval dress that called for

Fig. 63 A Jenness-Miller gown designed in the princess style, a design meant to evenly distribute the weight of the clothing on the body as well as create an illusion of slimness.

layering a sleeveless, sideless gown over a long-sleeved gown. Steele and Adams observed that such a charming arrangement had "its foundation in truth, for the garments of the Middle Ages were worn one over another, and of the same general form." Other than incorporating vertical seams and no defined waist, the artistic princess-style gown bears no resemblance to the fashionable cuirass bodice and dress style worn during the 1870s and early 1880s and also called the princess style; the shape of the fashionable princess gown was defined largely by undergarments and the stiffness of the dress itself, not by the body underneath it.[34]

The princess cut was highly recommended by *Demorest's Monthly Magazine* in 1878 because it lent itself to an unbroken line from neck to hem and was, therefore, more natural and graceful. The princess style often had a high collar or was cut low like a medieval dress. The aesthetic sleeves, with extra, gathered-in fullness rising above the arm's eye, varied in size. Fuller suggests that the English version had fuller sleeves. The fullness allowed ample room for movement of the arms. Fabrics suggested for artistic dress included cashmere, fine wools, "oriental" silks, fine camel hair, and satin. These fabrics would be soft and drape easily. Liberty fabrics were most appropriate. Colors in the aesthetic palette were cream, a dull faded red, sage Venetian green, reddish-brown, blue-green, and dove gray. Ornament was kept to a minimum. However, embroidery with crewel or silk yarns in floral or leaf motifs was quite acceptable, as was smocking, a technique largely associated with Liberty designs and popular on children's clothing because of the elasticity it provided.[35]

The princess style was a favorite for the tea gown. Designers often added a graceful Watteau pleated train to the back that hung from the top of the shoulders. This effect was considered quaint, like eighteenth-century gowns, and lent a gracefulness to the line of the body. The style also suggests the open robe of the eighteenth century. The obvious advantage of the princess style was a more even distribution of the weight of the garment on the body. According to Annie Jenness-Miller, the princess-style tea gown was the most popular style because it adapted more easily to the abused corseted figure than the coquettish Empire style, which best enhances the charms of the perfect figure.[36]

The Directoire and Empire Mode, Classical Derivations. The Directoire and Empire style was a high-waisted straight cut tubular gown (Fig. 64). It saw its greatest development as a fashionable style in revolutionary France and takes its name from being the fashion worn during the Directory and Empire periods. It continued as the dominant fashionable style into the 1810s and 1820s. The inspiration for the style came from the clothing worn in ancient Greece, the female chiton. An example can be seen in the sculpture of Diana by Praxiteles. The high-waisted style allowed women perfect freedom of their waists and thus an opportunity to move more gracefully than tight-fitting clothes would allow.[37]

Regarding the Empire high waist, Steele and Adams observed that if a horizontal line was unavoidable, "then it should be placed high, because the upper ribs are firm." The high waist also "makes the lower limbs seem longer, adding distinction to most figures." The high-waisted style also offered "fulness [in]

Fig. 64 Annie Jenness-Miller commented that this antique high-waisted style, often called the Empire, was in harmony with the women who were musically inclined, and they would have learned the art of dressing "in harmony" with their "bodily and mental powers." The style, she observed, would not be appropriate for everyone. (*Jenness Miller Monthly* [January 1894]: 9.)

the skirt . . . [which] conceal[s] the soft part of the body, which needs the utmost freedom for grace of carriage."[38]

The January–February 1888 issue of *Dress, a Monthly Magazine* observed that leaders of fashion were introducing the costumes of the Empire and Directoire periods for evening and house wear. Of course, the magazine warned, "These styles are confined to the indoor toilettes, as very few women could wear such gowns with ease and grace upon the promenade." It attributed women's lack of grace to years of abusive corset wearing that made their bodies lose the natural grace they once had.[39]

Sources of Artistic Gowns: Dressmakers, Patterns, Fabrics

Since aesthetics based on the Greek principles of art were central to Jenness-Miller's new concept of dressing, it is not surprising that examples of artistic dress frequently appeared in her magazine, *Dress*. Patterns for artistic gowns could be purchased from the Jenness-Miller Publishing Company (Fig. 65). These

THE great demand for the JENNESS-MILLER SYSTEM of artistic and hygienic patterns requires that they shall be placed on sale in every town and city, and we are now ready to establish agencies on the most liberal terms.

A handsome pattern case, in fancy wood, given free of cost to each agent purchasing a $10.00 (ten dollar) outfit. All communications from reliable business houses will receive our prompt attention. Our prices, at wholesale and retail, are as low as those of any pattern house in the world, with the advantage that each and every design is absolutely original with us, designed for the magazine DRESS, and for sale in pattern form.

Patterns of Costumes of every Description.

The JENNESS-MILLER BATHING SUIT, superior to all others, combining perfect support for the bosom, with freedom and beauty in general style.

Bust measures, 34 to 44 inches. Price of pattern, 30 cents each.

Pattern of Turkish Leglette for summer wear, with thin dresses. Waist measures, 24 to 32 inches. Price of pattern, 20 cents.

The Josephine Robe, the daintiest of toilets for piazza and parlor wear at summer resorts. Bust, 30 to 42 inches. Price of pattern, 30 cents.

Outing Costume for active sports. Bust, 30 to 42 inches. Price of pattern, 30 cents.

FOR SALE AT WHOLESALE BY

THE JENNESS-MILLER SYSTEM CO.,

EAST ORANGE, N. J.

All these patterns, as well as patterns of any and all costumes illustrated in DRESS, may be had at retail from our agents:

Mrs. A. Fletcher, 6 East 14th Street, New York City.

Miss C. Bates, 47 Winter Street, Boston, Mass.

Mrs. L. J. Lanphere, 316 7th Street, Des Moines, Iowa.

Mrs. S. W. Pike, 126 State Street, Chicago, Ill.

Mrs. R. H. Tonge, 8 Clayton Block, Denver, Colorado.

Mrs. H. S. Holmes, Cor. Coit & Joy Streets, New London, Conn.

W. V. Snyder & Co., 725-729 Broad Street, Newark, N. J.

Mrs. M. H. Ober, 332 Sutter Street, San Francisco, Cal.

Wilcox & Gibbs, 310 Fulton Street, Brooklyn, N. Y.

Edward R. Stover, 58-60 Fourth Street, Brooklyn, E. D.

Chas. S. Furst, 52 Newark Avenue, Jersey City, N. J.

ORDERS BY MAIL PROMPTLY ATTENDED TO.

artistic dresses, often described as "tea gowns," were fashioned after historic dress, particularly medieval and the classical Greek dress chiton. As noted previously, this type of dress had been available from Mssrs. Liberty and Company, London, since they opened their Dress Department in 1884. They offered the style into the late 1920s. Interestingly, an article by Bastien Le Farge in the *Jenness Miller Magazine* in 1891, titled simply "Artistic Clothing," did not give credit to the Liberty Company, but rather noted only that the increasing popularity of the Jenness-Miller System was not confined to the United States, "for it is well shown in the beautiful new gowns which had recently been presented to

Fig. 65 (opposite) Advertisement for ordering Jenness-Miller patterns listing agents that carry the patterns.

Fig. 66 Annie Jenness-Miller frequently advertised the pattern for the "Josephine gown" shown in the center. A photograph of her wearing the dress also appeared in *Dress*. The style is very similar to those advertised by the Liberty Co. (*Jenness Miller Monthly* 7 [November 1894]: 28).

the English public by Liberty & Co., of London." Le Farge observed that the gowns were created on a purely "hygienic" plan, which embraced all the principles of the Jenness-Miller System, and were as artistic as they were healthful.[40]

Yet not all the artistic gowns shown in *Miller's Magazine* were "tea gowns." With such names as "Daphne," "Calypso," "Josephine," and "Mona," these artistic dresses were described as being "house gowns" and for "visiting," "walking," or "dinner." These specific references suggest that artistic gowns were not meant strictly for entertaining at home (Fig. 66).[41] Annie Jenness-Miller favored a smocked version that she wore herself.

In their book, *Beauty of Form and Grace of Vesture* (1892), Steele and Adams discussed the artistic aspects of clothing that not only prevented distortion of the human body but created graceful illusions through the application of aesthetic principles of line, color, and form to dress. They provided eighty illustrations so that the reader would have ample visual sources to understand what artistic dress looked like. The illustrations and text gave women examples of how to wear artistic dress on any body type so that the gown appeared harmonious, graceful, and flattering to any woman, regardless of body size and shape. Steele and Adams shared Annie Jenness-Miller's belief that the current fashion for wearing corsets and tight-fitting clothing with unnecessary appendages was both unhealthful and debilitating.[42]

Regarding fabrics, Steele and Adams suggested that "it is desirable to get fabrics fascinating for their draping qualities, and to experiment with them; many artistic truths are to be learned in the practice." They recommended silks and velvets, velveteens, and wash silks for summer; silk crape and linen velours with a nap on both sides were suggested for evening cloaks. They suggested using the goods of the Associated Artists, which "are soft, heavy, of exquisite design and lasting quality, and very choice," and they even suggested appropriating upholstery goods if "they will serve to give an artistic result."[43]

Color was important for each individual. Steele and Adams, for instance, did not recommend "aesthetic" colors as suggested by Haweis in the 1870s. They held a different view: "It is the harmony of colour, grace of form, and fitness to the personality of the wearer that makes a gown beautiful; not richness of material, not cost of ornament. The most beautiful quality of a dress is its colour." Most important, they decried, "It is nothing if it is not becoming to the wearer." In a chapter titled "Beauty of Colour," they discuss color harmony, offering examples of the effect of various colors on the skin and hair color, as well as color associations, stating, for example, that "red expresses the glow of physical health."[44]

Where to have artistic gowns made was a problem. Steele and Adams noted that the dressmaker could not be relied on because "they betray an ignorance of anatomy or of art. One must think for one's self to design beautiful garments, at least at present." The problem was not easily resolved. In *Dress, and How to Improve It*, Frances Parker included a condensed version of the "Rules by Which to Determine the Artistic Value of Gowns," adopted by the Society for the Promotion of Physical Culture and Correct Dress of Chicago.

1. The lines of the gown should follow those of the natural body, as represented in classic sculpture; the arm-hold describing the top of the shoulder joint; the sleeve following the shoulder line, or at least not curve; the whole presenting the contour of the Venus de Milo, and not inward V-like lines.
2. Every part of the gown should be suspended from the shoulders, and should appear to be so suspended.
3. The dress should be loose enough to permit free and graceful movement.
4. The form of construction should be suited to the fabric—simple forms for heavy goods, and gathers for thin materials.
5. The costume should be genuine throughout. If made of two materials, its prototype would be the gowns of the early Middle Ages, one worn over another. If there is a pardonable simulation, that simulation should be consistent; i.e., where one material seems to be that of an undergarment (such as the guimpe), it should appear to be an undergarment every time that particular material appears.
6. The decoration of the gown should be subordinated to the gown itself; the ornament should serve, or seem to serve, the purposes of strengthening the edges, uniting the parts, or holding together.
7. The gown should be suited to the personality of the wearer, in color and texture and form.[45]

Frances Parker published her book "in answer to the many letters received from all over the country in regard to dress." In her pamphlet, as she called it, she provided many illustrations of gowns that had worked for her between 1888 and 1896. According to Parker, there were two problems with the dress-reform movement: the first was a lack of conviction; the second, an "absolute helplessness in the face of difficulties which present themselves when a departure from conventional dress is essayed." She sought to resolve the problem by offering suggestions for "modifying and adapting the conventional dress" so it would "approximate the comfort and beauty that the wearer desires." This was a sure way, Parker believed, to "change their ways."[46]

Patterns for all of the gowns illustrated could be purchased from Mrs. C. D. Newell, who had offered many practical suggestions for Parker's book. The patterns were available in eight sizes, 30–44, bust measurement. The cost for a cambric fabric pattern for both dress and petticoat was $3.00; paper patterns for dress and petticoat were $.50 each.[47]

Parker offered other places in Chicago where gowns could be made. These included dressmakers "who can suit the individual, who has an eye for color, who will finish a dress well; one who can make a dress that is comfortable and at the same time will not depart so far from the conventional that the wearer will be the 'observed of all observers,' if not the derided of all observers." She recommended Miss Annie M. Gibson, who "has designed some of the most

Fig. 67 A gown form such as those promoted by Jenness Miller and Kellogg served as a gown liner that would provide some support. This typical tea gown style, ca. 1891, is made with a separate gathered front. Courtesy The Kent State University Museum.

desirable dresses that I have," and Mrs. Robert Diefendorf, "a lady of excellent taste in design and finish," who "will make dresses at home or on order."[48]

Apparently there were several other places in Chicago where women could acquire reform garments in the 1880s. In 1887 *Dress* advertised that the Sanitary Publishing Co., on La Salle Street in Chicago sold the Bates waist, which was recommended and worn by Frances Willard. In November of that year the journal noted that Mrs. Pike's on Madison Street was a recognized dress-reform headquarters. Miss L. M. Aldrich also was mentioned as a Chicago source, in addition to the previously mentioned artists suggested by Parker. Steele and Adams recognized Mrs. Cressman and their Dress Reform Rooms. Kate Manville was another dressmaker in Chicago who provided reform dress. The label of a princess-style gown, with a typical "open robe" front, now housed in the National Museum of American History Smithsonian Institution, reads, "Kate Manville, Dress Reform Artist, Chicago."[49]

The problem of acquiring artistic dress was not easily resolved. Yet Annie Jenness-Miller was more positive about the possibilities than were Steele and

Adams, for she observed, "This art of making loose and beautiful gowns seems to have obtained among the best modistes in our cities, even among those who treated the idea with general dislike when it was first introduced."[50]

All of the promoters of artistic dress recommended that women wear reform undergarments underneath their artistic gowns. As previously noted in chapter 3, Jenness-Miller provided patterns for her system of undergarments. Parker and Steele and Adams illustrated the types they recommended and suggested a few places where these garments could be purchased. They all recommended replacing the corset with the bust supporter and removing whalebone from readily available "reform corsets," such as the Flynt Equipoise Waist.

For many women house gowns would be the extent of their venture into the realm of "artistic" dress. Patterns for various styles of house gowns were readily available to the home sewer from *The Delineator* and similar magazines (see Figs. 5 and 6). The August 1893 issue of *The Delineator* noted that artistic house-gowns are now considered necessary items of a complete wardrobe, and the dressy woman to obtain that individuality which is so desirable, selects her styles from those of the past generations and develops them in the most *fin de siècle* materials." When these gowns united the "semi-*négligé* adjustment of an ordinary wrapper" with trimness, they would be appropriate "for breakfast *en famille*, informal luncheons and afternoon tea." *The Delineator* observed that it was the optional close-fitting body liner that allowed the gown to have an appropriate close, trim fit. (See Fig. 67.) The body liner was similar to a gown form.[51]

WHO WORE AESTHETIC DRESS?

At first aesthetic dress was worn in public by only a few brave American women who espoused the artistic style as a way to express their connection with British aesthetic sensibilities and the artistic, sometimes Bohemian, subculture that supported it. The public display of artistic dress in the 1870s and 1880s would have been considered daring. Women who wore artistic dress at public gatherings may have been snubbing their noses at current hegemony—fashion and the status quo. Many (though not all) women who wore artistic dress at the time lived in areas where they could belong to an artistic set or group that enjoyed gallery openings or functions planned around an aesthetic theme. They were like any group that tries to be hip today. American aesthetes would have been keen followers of Oscar Wilde's lectures in America and might even have given receptions in his honor.[52]

Fortunately, Bohemians could enjoy the company of individuals who shared their interests and would not have cared about what others thought of them or if they were breaking social rules. They may have relished the thought of doing so. As innovators and early adopters of aesthetic style, these Americans nudged the boundaries of acceptability. However, artistic dress also became quite acceptable and fashionable in the manifestation of the tea gown and was worn for entertaining other women in private functions in the home. So while aesthetes and women living a bohemian, artistic lifestyle adopted artistic dress, including tea gowns, for specific public occasions—studio gatherings, gallery openings, or fêtes of some kind—other women wore the tea gown as an acceptable fashion for quiet entertaining in the privacy of the home with family or female friends. And even the fashionable tea gown was viewed as a reform garment. The phenomenon is curious because it follows the course that negligé clothing (underwear) has taken in recent times—that of becoming outer wear. What was once private and hidden becomes visible and more public. And the tea gown confirms, in fact, that this fashion process has historical precedence.[53]

Two highly visible women who wore no corsets and advocated reform were Charlotte Perkins Gilman and Frances E. Willard. Perkins attended the Rhode Island School of Design and made a living by teaching art and gymnastics. She is perhaps best known, however, as the author of "The Yellow Wallpaper" and *Women and Economics* (1898).

Frances Willard, renowned as the founder of the National Women's Christian Temperance Union and also a prominent educator (onetime president and dean of the Evanston College for Ladies, which was taken over by Northwestern University), was the first president of the National Council of Women. Miss Willard, as noted in the *Arena*, was "brave and outspoken in her advocacy of physical freedom for women, recommending often and heartily Elizabeth Stuart Phelps' dress reform book titled *What to Wear*."[54] Willard's advocacy included writing on the subject in a pamphlet titled *Dress and Vice*, published by the Women's Temperance Association. In an article titled "On Bondage," which appeared in *Dress* (1887), Willard shared her agony over the loss of freedom in dress as a young girl:

> I wonder how many women go back in thought, as I do at this weary hour, to the time when they first lost their liberty? During sixteen blessed years I had feet uncramped, limbs unfettered, trunk unbandaged, hair untwisted, and, largely as a consequence, spirit blithe as a singing skylark. But there came a day—alas! The dark day of my youth—on which I was literally caught out of the fields and pastures as was ever a young colt; confronted by a long dress that had been made for me, corsets and high-heeled shoes had been bought, hair-pins and ribbons for my straying locks, and I was told that it simply "wouldn't answer" to "run wild" another day. Company from the city was expected; I must be made presentable; I "had got to look like other folks."

Willard clearly shared the beliefs of Jenness-Miller, for, as Willard wrote, "Near me on the walls of my study hang Annie Jenness-Miller's picture and engravings of her new costumes. I look up at them with a prayerful heart, saying, 'How long, O Lord, how long?'"[55]

The subject of dress reform was never far from her thoughts, for in her opening address to the National Council of Women in 1891, she expressed her views on the subject: "Woman is a creature born to the beauty and freedom of Diana,

Fig. 68 The Willard gown was designed for women who worked in the National Women's Christian Temperance Union offices. It was expected that the Jenness-Miller system of undergarments would be worn with it (*Dress, a Monthly Magazine* 2 [Nov.–Dec. 1888]: 126).

but she is swathed by her skirts, splintered by her stays, bandaged by her tight waist, and pinioned by her sleeves until—alas, that I should live to say it!—a trussed turkey or a spitted goose are her most appropriate emblems."[56]

Willard's advocacy also extended to action. She persuaded Annie Jenness-Miller to design a graceful dress for the workers of the National Women's Christian Temperance Union (Fig. 68). The dress was created using the Jenness-Miller plain princess "gown form" and would, no doubt, have been worn with other elements of the Jenness-Miller Dress System. In a photograph taken in her home in England in 1895, Willard wears what appears to be comfortable dress, artistic in design, of the sort advertised by the Liberty Company and promoted by Willard's friend, Annie Jenness-Miller (Fig. 69).

Fig. 69 Frances Willard in the cottage Reigate, England, 1895, wearing a Liberty-style dress. From Anna Adams Gordon, *The Beautiful Life of Frances E. Willard* (1898), 225.

There are many examples of various types of house gowns, wrappers, tea gowns, and artistic dress in costume collections in Europe and the United States. Not many, however, have a known provenance. We may know the designer or store through the garment label but rarely more than that. The documentation of the rare garments often tells us something about the women who wore the garments. Sometimes they leave notes telling us about their gowns, with others there are family histories to peruse for information. It appears that many of these women, as was the case with both Gilman and Willard, were educated and involved in sports or the arts. One strong individual and educator who wore aesthetic dress was Elizabeth Crocker Lawrence, who chose an aesthetic dress for her portrait, which now hangs over the fireplace in a dormitory living room at Smith College. Lawrence was sports-minded, having won the first Smith College tennis tournament in 1882. After graduating from Smith, Lawrence studied at Radcliffe College and the Boston Society of Natural History. She later received a master's degree from Smith (1889) and, in 1891, a Ph.D., from the Boston University School of Gymnastics. She taught at Williams College and was secretary-treasurer of the Association of Collegiate Alumnae (later the American Association of University Women) and for twenty-one years served as treasurer of the Association to Aid Scientific Research by Women (1900–21). The aesthetic gown worn for the portrait is in the collection of the Northampton Historical Society, Northampton, Massachusetts. The design of this gown is similar to a high-waisted Empire gown.[57]

The Cincinnati crafts community was home to another young woman who wore aesthetic dress. Eliza Jane Randle (Becker) was the youngest daughter of an English sign painter who became a successful painting contractor in Cincinnati. Eliza studied wood carving with the artist Benn Pitman and at the Art Academy. She won many prizes for her work until arthritis forced her to lay down her tools. Eliza Randle was another free-spirited determined woman, for she did not marry until after she could no longer work as an artist. Her aesthetic gown, dated 1880–1885, is a typical princess style with open robe (Fig. 70). The gown is in the collection of the Cincinnati Art Museum.[58]

Fig. 70 Eliza Jane Randle's aesthetic dress, 1880–1885 (1988.138). Courtesy Cincinnati Art Museum. Gift of Mrs. Horace Reid Jr.

Fig. 71 Gown worn by Idelle Emma Rising Peters, Lancaster, Ohio, ca. 1880s. Courtesy Caroline Rockwood.

Gowns similar to Eliza Jane Randle's were worn by women in Lancaster and Medina, Ohio. The two dresses, now in the Historic Costume and Textiles Collection at Ohio State University, are made in the open-robe princess style. But they contrast greatly in fabric and intended use. Both were worn by young women. Idelle Emma Rising Peters of Lancaster wore her very artistic gown to a formal occasion in the 1880s. The photograph of her wearing the gown suggests an artistic setting, perhaps the photographer's studio (Fig. 71). The gown is made from heavy plain silk in gold and blue and has a substantial train. While the gown that belonged to Marie Louise Bliss of Medina is similar in style, the fabric is blue chambray trimmed with white braid (Fig. 72). It came with a small bustle pad. According to Bliss, she wore her gown to high school. The simplicity of the gown seems appropriate for a young girl. The cotton fabric meant the dress could be laundered easily for daily wear.

In her examination of the Wisconsin Historical Society collection, Judith Ann

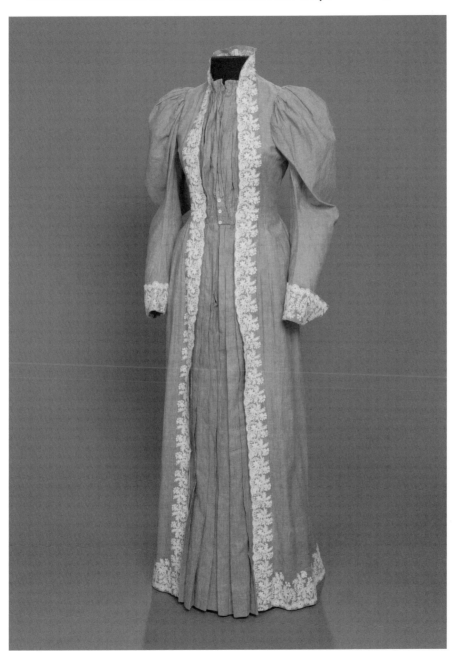

Fig. 72 Gown worn by Marie Louise Bliss, ca. 1886. Courtesy, Historic Costume and Textiles Collection, The Ohio State University.

Fuller found two tea gowns with known provenance. She identified the wearers as Annie Richards Crank of Oregon, Wisconsin, and Helen Hohlfeld of Madison, who had the opportunity to travel in Europe on several occasions with her husband, a noted Goethe scholar. Both dresses are dated from the early 1880s, 1882, and 1883 respectively. Both are cut with princess seams and have shirred front panels with an attached under bodice. In terms of art and health, it must be acknowledged that the under bodice of Hohlfeld's gown contains stays, nine in all, and a waist cincher; Crank's under bodice, however, has no stays. Hohlfeld's gown is "aesthetic" red cashmere and silk brocade, has a "Medici" sleeve fitted at the arm's eye but full at the wrist as well as a Watteau pleat in back. Crank's gown is made from a combination of brownish-red and brown wool, velvet, and glazed cotton and has a low-set belt in the medieval style. Since these gowns were made at the behest of each individual, the decision about stays would have been made by the client, with, perhaps, the dressmaker's recommendations.[59]

In 1896 the *Woman's World and Jenness Miller Monthly* included photographs of actresses and opera stars wearing artistic dress. The August issue illustrated Madame Emma Eames-Story, an American prima donna, who "wears no corsets." The photograph of another uncorseted prima donna, Mme. Antoinette Sterling, appeared in the September issue. In October, the magazine included a portrait of an actress, Jane Harding, wearing an artistic gown. By offering their readers these examples of famous women, clearly the editors were continuing to argue for "correct dress" along artistic lines.[60]

 ## WHERE ARTISTIC DRESS WAS WORN IN AMERICA: FICTION AND FACT

Judith Ann Fuller discusses the space given to artistic dress in popular American women's magazines, noting that *Peterson's Magazine*, although it rarely promoted artistic dress, frequently printed short stories and serialized fiction with "aesthetic" characters. The stories not only describe aesthetic styles and symbols but also suggest places where they were worn. Some of these stories take place at resorts, such as Saratoga, New York, and Mount Desert, Maine, where artistic dress would have been acceptable and appropriate dress. Other stories occur in Boston, as in "The Utterly Utter Boston Browns," where not only is the dress artistic but the houses are as well, being Gothic or Queen Anne in style. These stories support the notion that artistic dress was worn at resorts and for special occasions, such as to parties with artistic themes. Tea gowns, of course, were always appropriate in the home. In these stories it is a rare occasion for an aesthete to wear her artistic dress when traveling or for a public occasion that is not deemed "artistic."[61]

The references to aesthetic dress in stories appearing in *Peterson's Magazine* begin in the 1870s. An 1877 story places the heroine as an aesthetic "model" with auburn hair and in graceful robes. In 1881, in "Paste and Diamonds," Agnes James clothes her aesthetic heroine in a large-brimmed hat and "artistic" cottons. In "A Mount Desert Episode," by Katherine Keene, the setting is the resort community Bar Harbor, Maine, where artistic Bostonians are part of the scene. Artistic clothing worn by the character Daphne in "Two Wise Guardians," by Fanny Driscoll, consists of "a princess dress made from Indian design fabric" and headdress of ivy leaves. In a story set in the resort town Saratoga, New York, Emma Garrison Jones has the young artistic Dot in "Dot's Farewell" catch the young millionaire sought by her two older conventional sisters who are at the resort to find wealthy husbands. "An Esthete's Heart," by Mary Hayes, mentions many characteristics of aesthetic dress. The story is a parody. The main character, a country girl named Tilly, desperately wants to be "artistic" but only grasps superficial details rather than understanding the principles. She is contrasted with her two "aesthetic," urban cousins, who dress in quiet, simple artistic gowns and appreciate the beauty of nature and art.[62]

Two stories by Frances Hodgson Burnett that appeared in 1884 have aesthetically minded heroines. In "Lindsay's Luck," Lindsay lives in an artistic Gothic house and wears flowing artistic gowns. In "Miss Crespigny," the heroine holds "aesthetic soirees," and it is noted that she is striking because she is artistic. Fuller notes that young aesthetic heroines usually are accomplished in art—sketching, music, or painting—and often "catch their man," although not always.[63]

Whether in fiction or in fact, aesthetic dress became associated with the artistic lifestyle and the women who associated themselves with an artistic set or bohemian circle and who wore the style to galleries and studio open houses. For some, the dress was a costume suitable for specific occasions; others chose to wear it more frequently to express their artistic lifestyle. Yet it must be assumed that many women who adopted the artistic style were doing more than affecting a lifestyle. Their clothes presumably reflected a belief that they were improving their bodies by wearing reform clothing and that by making this change they would be augmenting both their health and their beauty.

Articles that appeared in *Dress* and statements in etiquette books also provide hints about where artistic dress was worn. Because artistic dress bordered on the negligé, etiquette required that it remain a house gown. However, after women became accustomed to seeing aesthetes wearing artistic dress in public, the rules began to break down. Women who wore tea gowns at home for private entertaining with close friends began to wear them for "at homes" and for dinner. Rose Cleveland observed that "loose 'aesthetic' dress, which is only a modification of our grandmother's gowns, is often worn in quiet, retired places, and certainly possesses the virtue of being cool and aesthetic in effect." Cleveland commented that summer resorts allowed latitude in the matter of toilette, with the exception, perhaps, of the more fashionable resorts, which would offer little freedom from ceremony in the matter of clothing.[64]

Annie Jenness-Miller's magazine *Dress* remarks on the pervasiveness and versatility of the tea gown, observing that "everyone wears it; tea gowns are worn for all sorts of home entertainments." In 1887, in an article titled "Dress Reform and Dress Gossip," the writer (S. L. S.) mentioned that in London "tea gowns are worn as much at dinner as at tea." Dinner was a noontime meal while tea was taken in the late afternoon. Although Helen Gilbert Ecob stated that the tea gown was meant only for the drawing room, gowns styled with a high waist and in the princess style were recommended by Steele and Adams in the 1890s for evening wear.[65]

By the 1890s the tea gown had been popular for many years. It was regularly offered in the Sears and Roebuck Catalog as a ready-made dress. The tea gown, a negligé garment meant for use in the home, was designed along aesthetic lines and gave the designers and dressmakers a model or prototype for artistic dress. Annie Jenness-Miller often used the princess style for a variety of garments that fit her demands for "correct dress," which were designed according to art principles and would be worn with no corset.

ℰ PROMOTION OF ARTISTIC DRESS: THE WOMEN'S CLUBS

One of the goals of Annie Jenness-Miller's lecture series apparently was to establish dress clubs in major cities. The purpose of the dress clubs would have been to serve as a mutual support group for women desiring to improve their health by adopting artistic dress. One of the most prominent was the Society for the Promotion of Physical Culture and Correct Dress established in Chicago under the auspices of the women's club. Indeed, Annie Jenness Miller had noted in *Dress* (1888) that the Chicago dress club, "formed during my recent visit to that city, where I gave two lecturers on Healthful Dress . . . has the honor of being the largest Dress Club now in existence with 150 members."[66] She further noted: "Before I left Chicago the practical step of organization, with constitution and by-laws, had been carried forward, and I had the honor of making the christening speech. The most important step was that of inducing the Women's Club to accept the Dress Club as an auxiliary, and it showed the liberal and progressive nature of these Western women that the proposition was so readily accepted."[67]

This Chicago dress club, which met in rooms of the Women's Club, on the first Tuesday of the month at 3 p.m. beginning June 5, 1888, was not only the largest in the United States but perhaps the most liberal. For, as noted in the *Arena*: "So far as freedom of the waist region goes, the Physical Culture and Correct Dress society has taken the most advanced ground. The corset and even the 'health waist' are condemned, and one of the 'rules for determining the artistic value of gowns' is this: 'Is the dress loose enough to permit free and graceful movement, allowing a possible suggestion of the play of muscle? Does it appear to be easy by the absence of seams stiffened by whalebones?'"[68]

Frances Mary Steele, one of the founders of the club, said much about the importance of studying "classic sculpture." She remarked upon what a change it was when women no longer cared to have their gowns fitted over corsets but even desired beauty like the form of the Venus de Milo. She believed that it was utter hypocrisy—unconscious, perhaps—for anyone to profess admiration for classic sculpture who admired a fashionably dressed woman. Another prominent club member, Frances S. Parker, observed in *Dress, and How to Improve It* that "the Venus de Milo has stood the test of ages as a model of grace and beauty" and that "grace" could be acquired.[69]

Frances E. Russell, noted dress reformer and chair of the Dress Committee of the National Council of Women, believed that others should follow the Chicago example, averring that "the object of the Physical Culture and Correct Dress Society is 'mutual help in learning the highest standards of physical development, and mutual counsel toward realizing those standards in practical life.'" She liked the name (though rather long) and the object of the society. Russell believed that there was a call for, and a need for, local organizations like the one in Chicago to carry forward the work of women's emancipation in dress.[70]

Fig. 73 Artistic gown featured by the Society for the Promotion of Physical Culture and Correct Dress of Chicago at the Columbian Exposition in 1893.

In 1892 the *Arena* carried a symposium of papers on women's dress. In her essay for this forum, Frances M. Steele commented on the difficulty women had in achieving a more beautiful natural form of dress. The courage to try to do the right thing came, she stated, through the mutual support of clubs. She noted, in particular, the "two hundred and fifty thoughtful women in Chicago who have, for four years, encouraged each other in study upon artistic lines." That is one hundred more than the membership in 1888.[71] In 1893 the club contributed to the dress-reform action at the Columbian Exposition.

Mrs. Henrietta Russell, director of physical culture for the Exposition and a leader in the Delsartean movement, appeared on the program as an illustration of the modern idea of Greek drapery.[72] Artistic dress as studied by the Physical Culture and Correct Dress Society of Chicago was represented by Frances Steele, "a quiet symphony in gray."[73] Of particular interest was the dress exhibit of this Chicago club. For on mannequins having "the proportions of Venus de Medici were shown a working dress and apron, a street suit, and reception gown and several evening dresses" (Fig. 73). All were intended to reveal the beauty of a woman's form when unbounded by a corset. Of course, the organization condemned the use of the corset and the "health waist." Clearly, they promoted the classical ideal for, as the club calendar revealed, "the study committee earnestly recommends that each member supply herself with a photograph of the Venus de Milo . . . and visit many times the statuary in the Galleries of the Art Institute," for "to appreciate a beautiful form is the very first lesson we have to learn concerning perfect physical development."[74]

ADOPTION OF ARTISTIC DRESS

The question often arises regarding the number of women who actually adopted reform clothing. Numerous letters written to Jenness-Miller were concerned with this question. As one correspondent observed, "Why should time be given to getting up a healthful style of dress for the women who least need it, when hard-working women are still left in the bondage of clothes?" To these questions Jenness-Miller replied that the benefits of sensible dress were not confined to any class of women, and reform efforts were not directed to either the rich or poor, but to all women regardless of class or conditions. "Yet, a dozen letters have come to us from women of leisure and social prestige for every one received from hard-working—housewives, sewing and shop girls—in other words, ladies with leisure to think, and the social security to warrant the courage of their convictions, have very generally been the ones to . . . advance the cause of healthful dress." Jenness-Miller observed that the rule admits exceptions, but out of twenty women with whom they talked, in various public offices and stores, only one was found to listen with ears of favor to the pleadings of sensible dress; the rest frankly admitted that they would rather suffer in the most uncomfortable of fashionable dresses than be odd—in other words, they would wear any absurd and extreme device in clothes bearing the stamp of Paris rather than be out of the "latest style."[75]

The Jenness sisters believed that by applying the classical principles of art to their clothing and by wearing the reform underclothing and artistic gowns women could truly dress individually and avoid the caprices of fashion that were preventing them from enjoying good health and from dressing in an aesthetically pleasing manner. And they believed that basic to this was a healthy body, which could be attained through physical culture.

There is no doubt that the ideas of physical culture and artistic, healthful dress were widespread during the 1880s and 1890s. The Jenness sisters clearly reached many women through their magazine, their books, and, of course, their lectures to various women's organizations. No doubt through their efforts as well as those of others the connection between health and beauty reached a large audience. The standard for physical culture and correct dress was naturalness and individuality as defined by the Greek ideal of beauty. It did not matter that the representation of the Venus de Milo was not really "natural"; the statue was after all the most natural-looking female form that could be publicly displayed.

It is apparent, then, that the adoption of artistic and correct dress was advanced and adopted by upper- and middle-class women, women who were involved with women's clubs and organizations. These educated women who surely must have admired Frances Willard and been greatly interested in the happenings of the Women's Building at the Columbian Exposition in Chicago were different from the artistic set and Bohemians who first wore aesthetic dress. The clubwomen represented the new woman of the 1890s. These same women embraced the new fads for sports as well. By their acceptance of activities that could improve their physical bearing, whether sports or physical culture, the activities became more than fads; they became fashionable. They became to a limited degree an accepted part of the American lifestyle. Indeed, as activities and sports for women became more acceptable, then clothing that was worn for these activities became more acceptable as well. This new acceptance led to later developments in reform of women's dress.

Although toward the end of its publication the *Jenness Miller Monthly* continued to carry photographs of notable women who wore artistic dress, the magazine focused less and less on physical culture and correct dress. Concomitantly, although the ideas of Delsarte were for a while incorporated into programs of physical education in schools, they soon lost favor with educators. The ideas of physical culture and rational dress, however, were not forsaken, for they appeared in other arenas, especially the new field of dance. As Ted Shawn mentioned in a history of modern dance, advocates of the modern dance movement were greatly influenced by Delsarte. Shawn, in fact, believed that it was Delsarte's wife, the dancer Ruth St. Denis, and Isadora Duncan who led women to freedom in dress by adopting flowing classical Greek gowns for dance.[76]

The reform in dress being advocated by the Jenness sisters was both intimate and subtle and therefore not obvious. The rational undergarments were not visible, and the artistic garments worn over them were meant to be close in design to acceptable fashions of the day. Yet the widespread promotion of artistic dress designs based on art principles certainly aided dress reform in America, especially the lectures and publications by both the British and American proponents of the cause, and particularly those of the Jenness sisters. On the continent of Europe artists and designers involved with the Modern Design Movements were similarly engaged in the reform of women's dress.

CHAPTER SIX

Artistic Dress and the Modern Design Movement on the Continent

On the European continent much of the impetus for reforming women's dress along artistic lines came from individuals aligned with the modern design movement at the turn of the century. Highly decorative fashionable clothes made of stiff fabrics and worn with corsets obviously were not in accord with new concepts of design promoted by artists, architects, and designers associated with Art Nouveau, Jugenstil, or Secessionstil in Germany, Austria, and other parts of Europe.[1] These modernists shared the American and English moral aesthetic argument for reform that equated good health and the natural body with beauty unique to each individual. An especially prominent idea was the aesthetic concept that beauty lies in the fitness of an object to its purpose. Other aesthetic arguments also provided strong motives for reform. These architects and designers saw the need to create forms and objects for living. For them all objects—the house, its furnishings, and the people in it—should be in aesthetic accord. That is, the clothes should correspond to the interior of the house, as well as to the personality of the individual who lived there. All objects should work together to create a personalized beauty reflective of the individual.

INFLUENCES FROM ABROAD

Artistic dress did not suddenly emerge unannounced on the continent of Europe. Artists, designers, and architects were very aware of the earlier artistic developments in improving women's clothing that had occurred in Britain and

America. The Liberty Company based in London had been supplying fabrics in Europe since the 1880s. Their shop opened in Paris in 1889 and they had several branches in other cities as well. Most artists sensitive to the issues of modernity in the late nineteenth century were aware of the philosophies of John Ruskin and William Morris, on which the modern design movement was founded. While the British and Americans tended to adopt a historical approach, the Germans and Austrians were more futurist and accepting of new technology.

The Japanese influence was widespread in the modern movement, and elements of an Asian aesthetic are apparent in a substantial amount of the new art and design. Leonie von Wilckens observed that Asian influence occurred in technique, symbolism, choice of motif, and color. Japanese motifs—the wave, fish, flowers, and birds—became apparent in almost all expressive arts: the fine and decorative arts, as well as theater and ballet.[2]

British influence had occurred early with the establishment in 1864 of the Austrian Museum for Art and Industry (Österreichisches Museum für Kunst und Industrie) on the model of London's South Kensington Museum (renamed the Victoria and Albert Museum). In many respects the Vienna institution and its adjoining school provided the setting for the revival of arts and crafts in Austria. However, the British influence on the Continent, especially in Austria, had its first real impact on modern art when the Glasgow School of Art, represented by Charles Rennie Macintosh and his wife, Margaret Macdonald, exhibited their assemblage of furniture and textiles in 1900 at the Eighth International Exhibition in Vienna. The Glasgow School also exhibited at Turin in 1900; therefore, it is clear that the Continent was well acquainted with modern British style.

The Glasgow artists drew on design elements that were applied geometric forms, which in later developments became integrated into the form of the object. This was especially true with the Macintoshes and became apparent in Vienna with Koloman Moser's and Josef Hoffmann's work for the Wiener Werkstätte (see below). The black and white color scheme used for the Glasgow exhibit also, no doubt, had an impact on Gustav Klimt, on the early work of Moser, and on the designs of other artists working in the Wiener Werkstätte. While it is clear that the artistic communities on the Continent were influenced by artists and designers from abroad, their interpretations of the new concepts were strictly their own.[3]

 ## The Modern Design Movement in Germany and Dress Reform

Artistic reform of women's dress in Germany, as elsewhere, gained impetus from architects, designers, and artists who were in the forefront of the modern design movement that brought profound changes to architecture and the decorative arts and crafts. *Jugenstil* is the term usually used to describe this movement in Germany. The name *Jugenstil* is from the Munich journal *Der Jugend,*

established in 1895 to publish works of avant-garde artists and writers. Indeed, Munich was the first center for the German version of Art Nouveau.[4]

The artistic-dress reform movement in Germany, although influenced by the earlier aesthetic reform in Britain and America, had its own character, both in the manner it was introduced to the public and in the creation of specific styles of dress. The movement had several components. Starting with Krefeld, Germany, in 1900, there were exhibitions of artistic dress in a number of cities. These were reviewed in newspapers and art journals. Several books by artists and physicians provided theoretical bases for the movement. Schools and programs of study in the applied arts embraced the idea that artistic clothing was an art form. Eventually, department stores and fashion magazines promoted the new concept of artistic reform dress.[5]

In 1907 Minna Cauer, a prominent women's-dress reformer, summarized the theoretical basis of the movement. Cauer observed that the question of dress reform would never be settled until women took it upon themselves to assert their independence and strike out for themselves on commercial and professional lines, at the same time asserting their right to dress as they pleased and refusing to conform to the dictates of tailors and manufacturers. In reflecting on artistic reform, she, too, declared that individuality must be carried out in a woman's gown, so that it and its wearer would be one harmonious whole. Furthermore, she wrote, true reform in dress must combine utility and beauty and health; that is, beauty of fitness and the beauty of form. Embracing the precepts of artistic reformers throughout the West, Mrs. Cauer argued that women must think for themselves in regard to their homes and personal adornment and bring these both into harmony with their new individuality.[6]

The German modern design movement had its roots in Munich. Indeed, an early illustration of reform dress can be found in Bruno Paul's 1897 drawing *The Fountain of Youth*, which appeared in the Munich paper *Simplicissimus*, as well as in a tapestry designed by Otto Eckmann, titled *The Arrival of Spring*, circa 1897 (Fig. 74). Yet it was a Belgian, Henry van de Velde, who was the most ardent promoter of artistic dress reform in Germany. Indeed, van de Velde was one of the earliest and best-known activists in the modern design movement on the Continent. He lived and taught in Germany from 1900 until the outbreak of the First World War. Although most prominent as an architect and designer, he created women's reform dress, planned reform-dress exhibitions, lectured frequently on the subject, and presented his theories in a number of publications devoted to modern design.[7]

In *Deustche Kunst und Dekoration* (1902), van de Velde put forth his "New Art Principles in Modern Women's Clothing." He believed that the earlier hygienic (anti-corset) movement for dress reform failed because beauty was not a consideration with these reformers. However, Van de Velde also felt that women were indeed the victims of the fashion profession, which had a primary interest in profits and little real interest in beauty.[8]

In support of a new artistic dress, van de Velde also noted that they (architects) had finally found out that women's dress must be as sensible and homogeneous as a piece of furniture or carpet. This was a new decorative idea and one that made dress immediately a piece of art. Like other artistic reformers, van de Velde further suggested that clothing should express a woman's individuality but that this individuality should be suppressed in street wear because the clothing should be defined by place and circumstances; that is, clothing should adapt to private, general, or ceremonial spheres. Regarding the specifics of dress, he supported the aesthetic concept that everything should be fit to purpose and that each material has its own beauty, "an expression of its life." He felt that the artists' task was to awaken this life—to give life to the cloth. Van de Velde denounced the revival of historical styles and called for a new modern style using new forms, new materials, and new techniques. Functionalism for van de Velde was essential to the beauty in all objects, not only clothing. Any ornament had to be abstract and organic.[9]

Fig. 74 (opposite) Otto Eckmann, *The Arrival of Spring*, ca. 1897. Tapestry made by the Kunstgewerbeschule, Scherrebek (established 1896). Courtesy Schleswig-Holsteinisches Landesmuseum, Schleswig, Germany.

Exhibitions of Reformkleid

Van de Velde was perhaps repeating the text of a talk he gave at the first German exhibition of artist-designed reform dress, which was held at the town hall in Krefeld in April 1900. Dr. Deneken, director of the Kaiser Wilhelm Museum in Krefeld, had asked several well-known architects, artists, and designers to create "Reformkleid" for this event, which was held in conjunction with a tailors' exhibition. The artists who exhibited were indeed well known and included van de Velde himself. The other artists in the exhibition also aspired to bring modernity to the world of art and raise the level of respect for the applied arts. They included Alfred Mohrbutter and Curt Hermann of Berlin; Richard Riemerschmid, Bernard Pankok, Otto Krüger, and Margarethe von Brauchitsch from Munich; and Paul Schultze-Naumburg.[10]

The exhibition had an impact on those who visited and on those who were informed of it by newspapers and through the publication of an *Album* with a forward by Mrs. Maria van de Velde. In critiquing the Krefeld exhibition, Maria van de Velde mentioned two mistakes. First, she noted, the quality of construction was imperfect, but second, and even more neglectful, the artistic garments did not approach the idea of reform decisively enough in the cut and composition of the dresses. The central idea, she argued, was to invent more logical, healthier, and beautiful clothing than fashion can manage.[11]

Maria van de Velde commented further on the decisive gap between real innovators and those content with "artistic interference only in the ornaments." Designs that fell into the latter category were those of Schultze-Naumburg, Curt Hermann, and Alfred Mohrbutter, although van de Velde thought Mohrbutter showed tendencies toward liberation. She placed her husband, Henry van de Velde; Richard Riemerschmid; and Margarethe von Brauchitsch among the innovators.[12]

The types of gowns presented by the artists varied in style, amount of ornamentation, and in intended use. Where the gown would be worn, that is, its
intended use, determined the style and decoration. There were ball gowns, house
gowns, and tea gowns, as well as dresses for concerts, walking, visiting, parties,
and gardening. The cut of the Krefeld dresses reveal that the corseted small
waist was not considered beautiful by any of the designers. In terms of style,

Fig. 75 The fullness of this
gown by Alfred Mohrbut-
ter suggests the Mother
Hubbard style; it also
mimics the "blouse dress"
or jumper style. From
Mohrbutter, *Das Kleid der
Frau.*

Fig. 76 An Alfred Mohrbutter design, this artistic gown is cut in the princess style yet suggests a high waist of the Empire and Directoire styles. Many illustrations and photographs of reform style gowns show similar combinations of the basic elements of the princess, Mother Hubbard, and Empire styles.

most were a variation of a princess cut with variety in fullness, sleeve type, and jacket length. The gowns could be quite loose or barely skimming the body. Some gowns were a modified princess style with a waistline defined just below the breasts. Another popular style was similar to the Mother Hubbard, with a set-in yoke placed just above the breasts and a gathered skirt falling from the breast line or just above it (Fig. 75). Sleeves frequently had fullness from arm's eye to the elbow, or wrist to elbow in imitation of the medieval styles that appeared frequently in British and American aesthetic dress (Fig. 76).[13]

Gown descriptions include a wide range of fabric types, with light silks used most often for society dresses and heavier silk or wool for street dresses. Velvets often were used for tea gowns. Street dresses, of course, were plainer and simpler than society dresses. Pleating to contain fullness and add an organic decorative effect was placed on upper sleeves, bodices, and vertically on the skirt (Brauchitsch). Other dresses had applied ornamentation. Gowns designed by van de Velde and

Fig. 77 Henry van de Velde's velvet gown with applied Art Nouveau embroidery designs. Many of the gowns created for the Krefeld exhibition of artistic dress were embellished with embroidery created in the curvilinear Art Nouveau style. From Mohrbutter, *Das Kleid der Frau*.

Mohrbutter often incorporated embroidery and appliqué of curvilinear motifs usually associated with the Art Nouveau style (Fig. 77).[14] Henry van de Velde apparently preferred Liberty silks for his Krefeld dresses. However, since he was involved in the design of silks manufactured in Krefeld, he also incorporated these in having dresses made up for his wife and her younger friends.[15]

The success of the Krefeld exhibit generated exhibits of artist-designed reform dress in other cities as well—Leipzig, Dresden, Wiesbaden, Darmstadt, and Berlin. The Leipzig exhibition took place in autumn 1901 under the guidance of Adolf Thiele. That year a special division for artistic clothing also was

set up in Dresden in conjunction with the Exhibition of Art and Industry. Clothing was also shown at the exhibition center in Darmstadt in 1901. Although artists and architects took credit for designing artistic dresses, most dresses were made by someone other than the artists. Peter Behrens's designs, for instance, were made up by Klar Blay of Darmstadt.[16]

Peter Behrens, architect, designer, and founding member of the Munich Secession in 1892, along with his wife, Lilli, designed artistic clothing for women. While there are few records of Lilli's designs, those of Peter Behrens are well documented. His designs for the Leipzig exhibition of artistic reform dress are very severe and have little ornamentation (Fig. 78). Behrens's style contrasted sharply with the styles of van de Velde and Mohrbutter, which had soft flowing lines and decorative applications. Leonie von Wilckens noted that contemporary critics thought Behrens's designs were too cold and masculine. His well-published society dress, however, was better received, in part, no doubt, because it did have flowing ornamentation at the hemline. Behrens's designs for a two-piece walking dress reflect the later commentary by Schultze-Naumburg that one alternative for a street dress is a skirt and jacket. In their simplicity, Behrens's designs were more like those of fellow architect Richard Riemerschmid, who had exhibited in Krefeld in 1900. However, while Riemerschmid's style is simple and stark with no ornamentation, most of his designs do have a defined waist, an element that would not be appreciated by many dress reformers unless worn without a corset (Fig. 79).[17]

The Berlin exhibit focused on two of the best-known supporters of women's reform dress in Germany, the artists Paul Schultze-Naumburg and Else

Fig. 78a&b On the *left* is a sketch for a reform dress by decorative-arts designer Peter Behrens, 1902; on the *right* is a photograph of his wife, Lilli (with their daughter), in a similar *Strassenkleid*. From *Deutsche Kunst und Dekoration* 1, no. 4 (1909).

Oppler-Legbaud. In 1902 Schultze-Naumburg published a book-length study
titled *Die Kultur des Weiblichen Körpers als Grundlage der Frauenkleidung,* which
dealt with the need to free women's body through dress reform. In his lecture
for the Berlin exhibition titled, in translation, "The Movement toward the Formation of a New Women's Costume," Schultze-Naumburg noted that the goal
of the exhibition was to encourage fainthearted women and to transform theoretical propaganda into practical action. He did not believe that the dresses in
the exhibit were the final solution to the problem. The dresses in the Berlin
exhibit met most reformers' expectations for reform dress. They had to hang
from the shoulders, free the body from the need to wear trousers, and conform
practically and aesthetically to their respective purposes: house dress, society
dress, walking dress, visiting dress, etcetera.[18]

Schultze-Naumburg's designs in this exhibition included several dresses with
an Empire-styled high waist; all of these were society gowns (Fig. 80). In writing

about a suitable style for artistic reform dress, Schultze-Naumburg thought that three designs were appropriate: a loose dress falling freely from shoulder to heel or held in by a belt fastened just under the breasts or at the hips; a two-piece close-fitting costume made of a skirt and jacket; and the "blouse dress," which was a blouse with a sleeveless gown worn over it with waistline under the breasts or at hips. This garment is much like the late-twentieth-century American jumper. An example of a blouse dress designed by Else Oppler-Legbaud (Fig. 81) is a walking dress, a practical, functional garment that would contrast greatly with

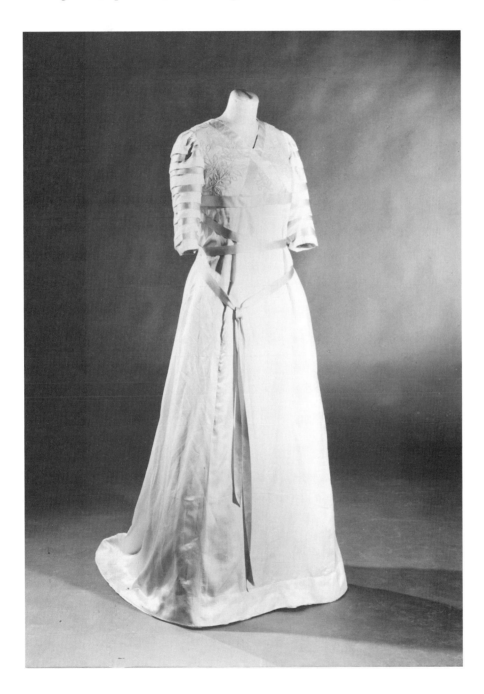

Fig. 80 An artistic reform dress (society dress) designed in the style of Paul Schultze-Naumburg. Courtesy Historisches Museum, der Stadt Wien

Fig. 81 *Strassenkleid,* by Else Oppler-Legbaud. From Mohrbutter, *Das Kleid der Frau.* The style of the garment was a blouse dress, or what we today call a jumper and blouse. The dress was included in the exhibition of artistic women's dress held in Wertheim's Department Store in 1904.

the more highly embellished society dresses that were made by various professional firms such as Herrmann Gersen in Berlin.[19]

Of the professional dressmakers who exhibited reform clothing in Berlin, the most influential was Else Oppler-Legbaud, who had studied under van de Velde in Berlin. In 1903 she took charge of the reform-dress department in Wertheim's, a large department store in Berlin. She was a versatile artist, for her designs for interiors earned her silver and gold medals at art exhibitions held in Leipzig and Turin.[20]

At about the same time as the Berlin exhibition, the Wiesbaden Society for Fine Art arranged an exhibition for women's clothing in which Peter Behrens, Alfred Mohrbutter, and Schultze-Naumburg took part. In writing about the Wiesbaden exhibit in *Dekorative Kunst,* Oscar Ollendorf offered his theoretical opinions, saying that dresses should conform to artistic laws and that artists were particularly equipped to design women's dresses not only because of their knowledge of drawing a woman's body and the functions of ornament but also for their sensitivity to color and, above all, their sense of fantasy and awareness of the effect of the homogeneous whole.[21]

As noted by Leonie von Wilckens, Else Oppler-Legbaud organized an exhibition of artistic clothing in 1904. For this exhibition, Anna Muthesius spoke on the progress made in artistic reform dress, noting improvement in construction, color, materials, and in the individual fit and suitability to the wearer.[22] Anna Muthesius was one of several Germans who, after 1901, gave extra support to the artistic-dress reform movement by publishing theoretical work on the subject. Muthesius used the term *Eigenkleid* (proper or personal clothing) to define the new artistic

Fig. 82 Anna Muthesius in a gown of her own design. From Mohrbutter, *Das Kleid der Frau*.

dress. For her the concept of dressing to express individuality was imperative; the dress should conform to the needs of the individual and express the unique creativity of the artist. She also designed many of her own dresses (Fig. 82).[23]

Reform Publications

Henry van de Velde, Anna Muthesius, and Paul Schultze-Naumburg were joined in their efforts by others writing on the need for artistic dress reform. These authors also provided ethical and aesthetic arguments for reforming women's clothing. They included Alfred Mohrbutter, Heinrich Pudor, and Adolf Thiele.[24]

In his text on women's dress, *Das Kleid der Frau* (1904), Alfred Mohrbutter repeated observations made by Henry van de Velde and Anna Muthesius, stating that women think they dress individually when, in fact, they continue to be the slaves of fashion. Like van de Velde, Mohrbutter believed that cloth alone could make a good dress, through the beauty of its pleats, which allow for movement, which in turn enhances the fabric. He, too, believed that the choice of fabric and color depends on the destination of the dress. In *Das Kleid der Frau* Mohrbutter included illustrations of several gowns and sketches for gowns of his own design, as well as designs by several women who had reform-dress salons in various German cities. Dress-reform artists represented in Mohrbutter's text included Anna Muthesius, a house dress (Hauskleid); Marie Hartmann, a society dress; P. A. Winker, a street dress, summer dresses, house dress, and society dress; E. Friling, a visiting dress; Else Oppler-Legbaud, a visiting dress, theater dress, street dress (blouse dress), and festival dress; Dr. Elly B., a visiting dress; Fia Wille, a summer afternoon dress; and Clara Müller, a society dress.[25]

In 1903 two publications from Leipzig appeared to further the cause of artistic reform. The art critic Heinrich Pudor published *Women's Reform Clothing*, in which he championed the notion that women's clothing should follow beautiful forms. Adolf Thiele, author of *Toward a Philosophy of New Women's Dress*, put his words to action by directing the exhibition for artistic clothing in Leipzig.[26] In *Women's Clothing*, in a chapter titled "Improvements in Women's Clothing," C. H. Stratz observed that improvements had been made in women's clothing for recreation, but he stressed the point that, until women improved their bodies and quit depending on corsets (even reform corsets), there would be no true reform of women's clothing. He suggested that women adopt the Japanese kimono for use in the home, noting that Dutch and Indian women had substituted it for the house dress.[27]

The media supported efforts of artistic-dress reformers, which, of course, was crucial to the communication of the new style. Franz Lipperheide's *Illustrated Women's Newspaper* regularly reported on the exhibitions and included illustrations of many so-called reform dresses that were not designed by artists but rather came from leading ateliers who wanted to follow the times. The journals of the Jugenstil promoted the new style. Both *Dekorative Kunst*, published in Munich, and *Deutsche Kunst und Dekoration*, published in Darmstadt, reported on artistic-dress exhibitions held between 1900 and 1904. Publications of the women's associations featured artistic dress as well. These included *The New Female Clothing* and *Healthy Women*.[28]

Women's Clubs

The various women's organizations that early on were most concerned about the hygienic and practical needs of women's dress held several exhibitions where artistic dress was featured. Von Wilckens stated that the Club for the Improvement of Clothing and the Club for People's Hygiene united to organize a Reform-Clothing Festival in Berlin in December 1902. All of the participants at the festival wore clothing of the new style. Brigitte Stamm noted that in 1906 the Free Association for Improvement of Female Dress worked with the Third German Art and Craft Exhibition in Dresden. This exhibition featured fourteen reform dresses, Liberty fabrics, underwear, and accessories.[29]

Writing on the German dress-reform movement in the *Independent* in 1905, Else Oppler-Legbaud noted that we "enter the fray with ethical, hygienic and esthetic arguments." In writing, she summarized the artistic theory regarding dress, stressing the idea that the beauty of the natural human form should be appreciated and that the new artistic reform dress actually offered individuality, not a uniformity of dress. And, again, she declared that the form of the dress should depend on its intended use. She applauded Mohrbutter for designing a reasonable, practical street dress along artistic lines—a dress that, in her mind, was most difficult to make artistic. Her own designs, for which she also used soft drapable Liberty silks, reveal a fitness to purpose as well. That is, a street dress was simple compared to a more diaphanous and decorated society dress, ball gown, and festival dress.[30]

Regarding the form of artistic dress, Oppler-Legbaud noted that the reform dress was "never allowed to fit so closely to the body . . . as French fashion requires." When a belt was worn, the dress was fastened either directly under the breasts or rested on the hips, in order to avoid the wide, loose dress, which was neither practical nor aesthetic. The form of dress, she concluded, reiterating van de Velde's thoughts, depended on its use, whether to be worn "at home as a working dress, a street dress, or in society only."[31]

Effectiveness of the Reformers' Crusade

In commenting on progress, Oppler-Legbaud observed that the practical street dress had caused the most difficulty. No bloomers were being worn; but skirts now were to the ankles, and the weight of garments was distributed from the shoulders, especially the dress (jumper) worn with shirtwaists, what Schultze-Naumburg termed a "blouse dress." Sometimes the garment was designed so the weight was distributed onto the hips.[32] Oppler-Legbaud noted that at the time (1905) the reform dress was seen everywhere in society, at theaters, concerts, and in the streets, and it only depended on artists and tailoresses to impart variations and quality technique to dispel the last trace of prejudice in conservative quarters. The prejudice of tailoresses and dressmakers had been overcome. Those who lacked skill to make reform dress had at first refused to promote it in belief that it was in opposition to their interests, but after a few dared to make them, others quickly followed so that by 1905 every German town had a few artists producing reform clothing.[33]

AUSTRIA

In Austria the Arts and Crafts Movement had its earliest impetus with the founding of the Wiener Secession in 1897 by a group of progressive artists, architects, and designers who defected from the more conservative association, the Künstlerhaus, which had been the only exhibition space for contemporary works. The group included Gustav Klimt, Josef Hoffmann, Joseph Maria Olbrich, Koloman Moser, and Carl Moll. Greatly influenced by the British Arts and Crafts Movement, they demanded new aesthetic forms of expression in keeping with modern life. The motto on their exhibition building, the Secessionhaus, completed in 1898, reads "Der Zeit ihre Kunst, der Kunst ihre Freiheit," or "To the Age its Art, to Art its Freedom." The title of the Secession magazine, *Ver Sacrum*, marked their direction toward a rebirth for art in Austria.[34]

Although it is doubtful that women's dress was a consideration when they placed the motto on the building, it could be applied to dress: "to every age its dress, to dress its freedom." Several members of the Secession very clearly held this point of view. Koloman Moser designed many gowns for the women in his family. In 1902 a number of artists and authors associated with the new art movement—Josef Hoffmann, Alfred Roller, and Hermann Bahr—published their theories and opinions on why women's dresses needed to change in *Dokumente der Frauen*. Certainly the Wiener Werkstätte (Vienna Workshop), organized in 1903 by Moser, Hoffmann, and Fritz Wärndorfer, was receptive to reform in dress. The Wiener Werkstätte added a textiles department in 1909 and a fashion department in 1911 under the direction of designer Edward Joseph Wimmer-Wisgrill.[35]

Gustav Klimt and Emilie Flöge

Gustav Klimt, a famous Viennese artist, no doubt believed in dress reform for women. In his portraits women are often clad in long, loose flowing garments that may have been of his own design. It has been said that Klimt collaborated with his close friend Emilie Flöge in designing reform dresses for her fashion salon in Vienna (Fig. 83). Indeed, the modern reform dresses would have been appropriate to the interior of the salon itself, which was a Wiener Werkstätte commission designed by Moser and Hoffmann in 1904. Investigation into the source of Flöge's designs for an exhibition on Klimt and Flöge at the Vienna

Fig. 83 Design of a summer reform dress made in Emilie Flöge's fashion salon and photographed by Gustav Klimt. A series of these photographs appeared in *Deutsche Kunst und Dekoration* 1, no. 9 (1907): 64–73.

History Museum, in the late 1980s, was inconclusive about whether Klimt collaborated with Flöge. Some scholars believe that Flöge may have told her customers that her clothes were designed by Klimt because of his status as an artist. It is highly likely that the designs were Flöge's own. On the other hand, it is also possible that Klimt sketched out ideas for dresses that were then worked up by seamstresses in Flöge's workshop in Vienna. The Flöge gowns that appear in the art journal *Hohe Warte* (1905–1906) are similar to the very stark styles of the German reform artists, especially those of Peter Behrens. Emilie Flöge often wore reform-style gowns herself. She posed for the photographer D'ora wearing a loose, ruffled artistic gown (Fig. 84), and on many occasions for Klimt.[36]

Fig. 84 Emilie Flöge wearing an artistic reform dress. Photograph taken by D'ora, ca. 1907.

Architectural historian Udo Kultermann believes that Flöge's gowns carry Klimt's imprint. He argues that the dress worn by Flöge in Klimt's 1902 portrait could only have been designed by Klimt. He observed that the geometric motifs (circles and squares) and flowing, shapeless style show exactly the reform ideas that were later to be seen in Wiener Werkstätte designs. In support of his argument for Klimt's impact on the design, Kultermann refers to a photograph of Flöge wearing a dress that also carries Klimt's characteristic style, exhibiting a mixture of geometric and floral motifs. The dress is similar to designs found in a collection of Klimt's drawings owned by Zamuel's Gallery in New York. The drawings, which date to 1903–1904, were studies for portraits. Regardless of who actually designed the dresses, one thing is certain: they were meant to be reform dresses.[37]

Klimt remained true to his appreciation of the avant-garde reform style, for in 1916 one of his patrons and supporter of the Wiener Werkstätte, Fredericke Maria Beer, wore a Wiener Werkstätte harem outfit for her portrait by Klimt. Her niece commented in a letter that her aunt had all of her dresses made by the Wiener Werkstätte at that time. Beer later had the harem outfit made into a dress.[38]

Photographs of Klimt lead us to believe that he thought that men, too, should have the option to be comfortable. He often wore a loose gown, even on occasions when other men wore suits. Of course, a loose, flowing smock was a privileged garment for an artist. Hermann Bahr, a poet, critic, and Klimt's supporter and friend, apparently also wore a similar gown, which may have been designed by Klimt to emulate a Japanese kimono. Such an exotic garment would be quite acceptable for these young artists who were infatuated with all Asian objects, a passion shared by many artists of the modern design movements.[39]

Koloman Moser

Klimt was not alone in his dislike of fashionable dress. Many artists who became associated with the Secession, the School for Arts and Crafts (Kunstgewerbeschule) connected to the Austrian Museum of Art and Industry (Österreichisches Museum für Kunst und Industrie), and the Wiener Werkstätte also held a similar aversion for the dictates of Paris. Koloman Moser, painter, graphic artist, and designer, was one of the most active reformers in Vienna and a key figure in the Austrian modern design movement. Along with several other young artists, Moser was a founding member of the Vienna Secession. He provided the relief decorations for the building that housed the Secession artists, the Secessionhaus, designed by Joseph Maria Olbrich. Moser frequently exhibited with Josef Hoffmann at the Secessionhaus and contributed to their journal, *Ver Sacrum*. In 1898, Moser began teaching at the Kunstgewerbeschule. In 1903, he and Josef Hoffmann became artistic directors of the Wiener Werkstätte, with Fritz Wärndorfer as administrator and financial director. They started small but soon became international leaders in the Arts and Crafts Movement. Their honest approach to design was applauded at exhibitions in Berlin, London, and Dresden. The taste for black and white executed in geometric precision suited the taste of the avant-garde in art. In 1907, Moser left the Wiener Werkstätte to pursue a career as a set designer, interior designer, and graphic artist.[40]

Moser produced several dresses for his wife and sisters. These are now housed in the costume collection (*Mode Sammlung*) of the Vienna History Museum. All of the gowns would have hung from the shoulders and free the waist. The gown designed for Moser's wife, Data, is a society dress, *Gesellschaftkleid* (Fig. 85), made of printed linen. The style is loose-fitting with no defined waistline. A matching long coat accompanies the dress, a copy of which is on display in Vienna at the museum. The gown of Moser's mother is made of black silk. It has no defined waist, trim along the seamlines, and pleats on the sleeves for added interest (Fig. 86). Leopoldine had a dress dated 1900–1905 (Fig. 87) made in a similar style from

a dark red silk fabric. These designs are similar to other reform gowns in the collection of the Vienna History Museum, one of which was designed in the style of
Paul Schultze-Naumburg (see Fig. 80).[41]

As noted by Daniele Baroni and Antonio D'Auria, Moser had already designed an entire collection of reform clothes in 1900. By the end of 1906, Moser
turned out to be the most incisive in following the theoretical directions set
forth by Schultze-Naumburg. The novelty of Moser's designs, they point out,
consisted of a simplicity of line, sometimes resembling a kimono, and an absence of excessive trimmings such as lace, fringes, or a crinoline. Moser greatly
influenced his students, especially Wimmer-Wisgrill, who later became head
of the Wiener Werkstätte fashion department.[42]

In 1895 Moser traveled to Munich and immersed himself in the local artistic circle, which included the avant-garde artists who were just beginning to publish their magazine *Der Jugend*. At this time Moser would have been aware of the artistic rumblings for dress reform that were coming from abroad. The idea of *Gesamtkunstwerk*, the integration of all visual design elements to create a total artwork, was by now well accepted. The need to have clothing be in harmony with the environment as well as with the uniqueness of each individual conformed with the concept of *Gesamtkunstwerk*.[43]

From very early on, both Moser and Hoffmann adopted geometric forms, which became the hallmark of Wiener Werkstätte products. Clearly, such designs were a favorite of Klimt's. Delight in geometric forms created a split in the early years of the Secession. In the 1890s, according to Baroni and D'Auria, there

Fig. 86 An artistic reform gown designed by Koloman Moser for his mother. Courtesy Historisches Museums, der Stadt Wien.

Fig. 87 An artistic reform dress designed by Koloman Moser for his sister Leopoldine. Courtesy, Historisches Museums, der Stadt Wien.

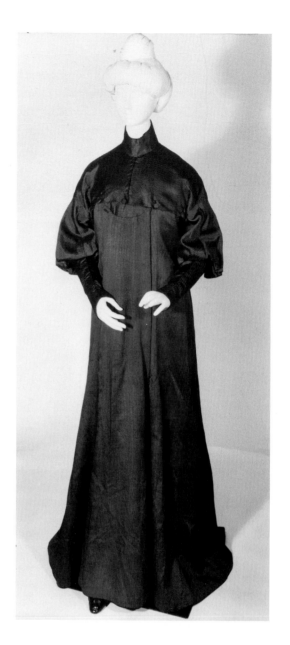

was a shift toward an understanding of form based on an internal search, either for organic or for more geometric elements of an abstract nature. The line became the principal element—a potent means of expression and abstraction. The works by British designers such as Walter Crane provided guidelines for this new approach to the decorative arts. Moser came into contact with Charles Rennie Macintosh, Crane, and others, and he studied Japanese art, particularly Katagami stencil techniques. Moser's studies of line and form led quickly to an emphasis on geometry. Moser, as Baroni and D'Auria attest, had such a mastery of expression—geometric and chromatic interpretation, "use of typographic characters, references to Oriental emblems and kaleidoscopic fantasies"—that he may rightly be considered one of the founders of modern graphic art.[44]

Josef Hoffmann

While Moser concentrated on expressing his modern concepts of design and
the need for clothing reform through the execution of various art projects, others focused more on writing about them. Josef Hoffmann, Moser's friend and
colleague, accomplished both. Hoffmann frequently worked with Moser on
projects, especially after the establishment of the Wiener Werkstätte in 1903.
More important for this study, however, is that Hoffmann also designed reform
gowns for women (Fig. 88). Unfortunately, there are no extant Hoffmann-de-
signed garments; only illustrations remain. Hoffmann's writings in *Die Wage*
reveal his attitude and beliefs about the need to improve women's clothing. In
an essay entitled "The Individual Dress" ("Das Individuelle Kleid"), he expressed

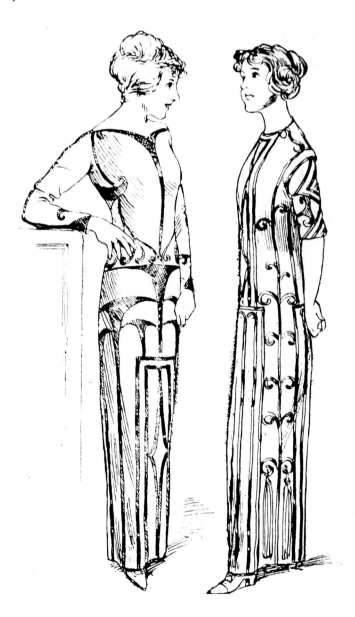

Fig. 88 An artistic gown
designed by the Viennese
architect Josef Hoffmann,
ca. 1910.

Fig. 89 Meliva Roller wearing a reform dress with elements of traditional regional dress and embroidery. The setting is an exhibition of modern interior furnishings. Courtesy Picture Archive, Austrian National Library.

his astonishment that in a time when everyone wants to be original and special, so few people appear really original. In their outer appearance they (women) subjugated themselves ostentatiously to fashion. He felt that individuals should express their uniqueness in their dress, "that we should be able to recognize them through their dress and how they wear it." For instance, Hoffmann continued, "the dandy should appear to be a dandy, the dignified, dignified, a modest girl should dress simply, a serious one in dark clothes, the energetic in clothes that do not hamper, an unpretentious person should wear plain clothing," and so on. He believed that people should stand above the tailor so that the tyranny of fashion would be broken and the individual sense could achieve its rights. Hoffmann suggested specifically that clothes should be light and allow movement and that they should be made so they could be put on fast and easily without the help of a second person.[45] Hoffmann's arguments clearly fall within the realm of the aesthetic principle of "fitness." His philosophy is expressed in his clothing designs.

Dokumente der Frauen: *Roller, Bahr, and Loos*

During the early years of the twentieth century, the condition of women's fashion became a topic of interest in the arts community in Vienna. In March 1902, *Dokumente der Frauen* offered the opinions of several Viennese artists, designers, architects, and doctors regarding women's clothing. Professor Alfred Roller, director of the Angewantekunstschule (the Vienna School of Arts and Crafts) and of the Vienna Opera, included his opinions in the form of a letter. Roller believed that women should not go to male artists for clothing designs of the future, but rather that more women and girls who had an understanding of their own particular clothing needs should be trained in the arts to solve the problem of dress. He believed that it was important for women who worked to have clothing that would facilitate the act of work and, like the new sports clothing, the function should create the form. For him, clothing should be seen as a facilitating tool, whether it was for work, climbing, mining, or deep-sea diving, or for a circus artist.[46]

Roller noted that women in public had worn mainly ornate clothing unsuitable for work. He believed that the "fake" items of dress could be removed without being conspicuously absent—"buttons that don't button, ribbons that don't tie, laces that don't lace," and so on. He also felt that other hurdles needed to be removed. First, the tight waist (corset) had to go. Second, the decoration should be incorporated into the design. There was no need to mask stitches or pockets; they should become part of the ornament. Women must break with the lies of these fake items applied to dress—fabrics, skirts, sleeves, hems, pockets, and collars (Fig. 89).[47]

Of the other writers in *Dokumente der Frauen,* Hermann Bahr is perhaps in most agreement with Hoffmann and Roller, for he declares that a dress is beautiful if it is a perfect skin of a person and it has no deception (no fake ribbons or sleeves). Furthermore, he believed that reform dress should be distinctive for each individual person and that it could change with age, body changes, and set of mind. For him, to be elegant was to be natural.[48]

The well-known architect Adolf Loos, a prolific essayist who feared no subject, was not a member of the Secession or involved with the Wiener Werkstätte. It is not surprising that his comments on women's fashion are far from bland: "Lady's Fashion, you horrible chapter of cultural history. You tell hidden lusts to mankind. If one turns your pages, the soul is shaky in view of the terrible aberrations and incredible vices." Writing initially in 1898, the sensible, if frequently contentious, Loos believed that women's clothing forced them to achieve equality with men through the power of the clothing to appeal to man's licentious nature, to his pathological sensuousness (forced on him by the culture of his time, of course). In the future, he believed, equality would no longer be achieved by sensuousness but rather by the economic and spiritual independence of woman gained through her work. This, perhaps, is one of the most accurate futurist appraisals of the period.[49]

Wiener Werkstätte

Both Koloman Moser and Josef Hoffmann could publicize and propagate their ideas for modern design in Vienna through exhibitions at the Secession and teaching in the Kunstgewerbeschule. What they needed, however, was a place for the production and sale of objects based on their principles. In 1903, with financial backing from Fritz Wärndorfer, the Wiener Werkstätte came into being to fill this need.

From the beginning, the designers and the craftspeople, the ones who actually built the objects, had equal billing. The operation allowed patrons to deal directly with artists, which was the usual Austrian method for selling art. Few dealers in art were very successful. Indeed, many Austrian artists, Oskar Kokoschka in particular, lived in Germany to be closer to dealers who offered a friendly reception for their works. However, as Jane Kallir has observed, in many respects the rise and fall of the Wiener Werkstätte reflects an inherent difficulty in the marriage between creators of art and dealers or sellers of art. The Wiener Werkstätte was a business enterprise handicapped by artistic principles, just as the Secession was an artists' organization with commercial problems.[50]

There were several foreign models for the Wiener Werkstätte enterprise. The first was Ashbee's British Guild of Handicrafts, which Hoffmann visited in 1902. Others were two German organizations: The United Workshops for Art and Crafts, founded in 1897, to which Peter Behrens and Hermann Obrist belonged, and the Dresden Crafts Workshop, founded in 1898. The philosophy of the Wiener Werkstätte echoed that of Ruskin and Morris, the earlier Secessionists, and the English and German modernists. In their work program for the Wiener Werkstätte, Moser and Hoffmann declared, "The work of the art craftsman is to be measured by the same yardstick as that of the painter and the sculptor!" If our cities, houses, rooms, furniture, clothes, jewelry, language, and feelings fail to reflect the spirit of our times, "in a simple and beautiful way, we shall be infinitely behind our ancestors!" They clearly evoked the spirit of the German *Gesamtkunstwerk.*[51]

Like the earlier Secessionist artists, the Wiener Werkstätte received good publicity from the start, particularly from the Munich journal *Deutsche Kunst und Dekoration* as well as from Hermann Bahr and the art critic Bertha Zuckerkandl. One of the first major commissions was for the Stocket mansion in Brussels, designed by Hoffmann, which to this day remains one of the best known and admired Werkstätte creations. The Werkstätte contributed to a number of European art exhibitions as well as to international trade exhibitions. Its members established sales branches in Vienna, most notably on the Graben, the most fashionable street in the center of the city.[52]

The Wiener Werkstätte produced a variety of decorative objects, furniture, jewelry, and textiles. In 1905 it established a textile workshop to produce hand-printed and hand-painted silk designs. Werkstätte members designed and manufactured large amounts of fabrics designed by the leading artists: Moser, Hoffmann, and others. The textile department thus had some control of the fabrics used in the interior of buildings and houses as well as those for garments then possibly worn by people who lived in them. The textile workshop was another step on the way toward integration of the arts.[53]

Beginning in 1907, artists in the Wiener Werkstätte began designing costumes for the Cabaret Fledermaus, a café with lighthearted music, dance performances, and other theatrical productions. However, it was not until 1910, under the able direction of Wimmer-Wisgrill, that fashion was first introduced, and then it occurred at the Karlsbad branch, not in Vienna. Vienna did not see a fashion sales room until the following year, when a fashion shop was opened next to the salesroom on the Graben. Finally, in 1914 the Werkstätte established a separate "factory" for fashion production and then opened more showrooms in 1916 and 1917. Branches were opened in other cities, including Marienbad, Zurich, New York, and Berlin. By 1928, in its twenty-fifth year, the Wiener Werkstätte was producing objects such as silver work; gold work; metal work; sheet-metal work; leatherwork; bookbindings; knitwear; beadwork; embroidery; woven, printed, and painted fabrics; ceramics; carpets; wallpaper; and lacework.[54]

Kallir interprets the Wiener Werkstätte line as incorporating two basic trends: that of the loose fitting reform dress created by Flöge, Klimt, and Moser, and its reinterpretation as an Empire mode by the French designer Paul Poiret. Bertha Zuckerkandl referred to the reform dress as a "flour sack," so she must have been thinking of the gowns designed by Klimt and Moser, which were very full and loose-fitting with no defined waist at all. Attributing the first reform style to Flöge, Klimt, and Moser, however, neglects the very real possibility of its having origins closer to home, that is, in the creations of the German reformers previously discussed in this chapter. It also neglects to give credit to the classical and medieval models promulgated by the Liberty Co. These designs had been available since 1884 in Liberty catalogs and through many depots and shops in Europe, including Paris.[55]

In the early years of the Wiener Werkstätte, until about 1914, the textile and fashion department experimented with many ideas. In fact, there was an attempt to assimilate many design sources—the Empire waist, reform ideas, and Asian touches. Harem pants, which may have come from Poiret, appear to have had some success, for they survived into the twenties. Harem pants and other such styles were viewed as exotic or "artistic" dress, not really fashion (and indeed, only really wealthy, artistically inclined women purchased these clothes in the early years). During the First World War, patriotism placed fashions from France in a bad light. Many designers began to express an Austrian aesthetic with an emphasis on historical styles such as Biedermeier, which echoed French Empire forms.[56] The Wiener Werkstätte began to design low-key clothing that reflected the somber tone of the war. After the war the fashion department emerged as a respected institution, showing fashions abroad on a regular basis in the late teens and twenties. It gained extra prestige by being the "shop" for many actresses. It is ironic that the textile and fashion department grew during the twenties, while the Werkstätte itself began a steady decline, finally closing its doors in 1932.[57]

Since fashion photography was used so little in Austria, the Wiener Werkstätte "line" was presented to potential mail-order customers through small watercolor sketches with fabric swatches attached to mail orders. The drawings, however, except for the first line executed by Mela Köhler, an artist in the fashion department, were little more than vague representations of the actual garments. Kallir notes that they evoke a Werkstätte feeling rather than the exact style. Two sets of fashion prints, *Wiener Mode* (*Viennese Fashions*) and *Das Leben eine Dame* (*The Life of a Lady*) were executed and published in 1914–1915 and 1916, respectively. Although created outside the Werkstätte, they do depict

Fig. 90 Two reform dresses, one for evening events and the other for visiting. From *Wiener Mode* 18 (1905): 11.

Fig. 91 A summer dress in the reform style. From *Wiener Mode* 20 (1907): 881.

accurate designs, since the drawings were made by Hoffmann's former students or former employees of the Werkstätte. The published portfolios reveal all the prevailing fashion trends of these periods—the Empire style, the harem pants, and the Biedermeier historical revival.[58]

Fashion in the Reform Style

During the years 1902–1903, *Wiener Mode,* the leading conservative "Viennese Fashion" magazine, also available in Germany and other European cities, included variations of the new modern style of artistic dress and reported on exhibitions of artistic reform dress held in cities throughout Europe in the early years of the century. Terms used in *Wiener Mode* to define artistic dress were "reform dress," "new style," "Liberty style," "princess style," and even several references to "bride's reform dress" (Figs. 90 and 91). The reform models were interspersed with illustrations of high fashion. *Wiener Mode* also included advertisements for reform underwear.

Through promotional efforts at arts and crafts exhibitions, fashion shows, portfolios, and feminist advocacy, knowledge of artistic reform dress made its way to other parts of Europe. In Sweden, Norway, and the Netherlands there was increasing interest in reform in women's clothing. Although this interest included reform of undergarments, the solution often fell into the artistic range of reform garments. The Wiener Werkstätte style was undoubtedly much appreciated.

The Netherlands

The dress-reform movement in the Netherlands began in earnest with the establishment in 1899 of the new Dutch Society for the Improvement of Women's Dress (de Vereeniging voor Verbetering van Vrouwenkleeding, or V.v.V.v.V.). Impetus for the organization came from knowledge of a similar German society established in 1896 and of an exhibition of women's work in The Hague in 1898, where a competition was held for the design of a reform costume for women who worked. The society published a monthly magazine with articles about improving health through improved underwear and hygiene. However, as noted by Carin Schnitger, "after 1903 the interest in artistic design grew." Membership in the organization increased to two thousand, and there were branches in several cities. The organization also held lectures, produced brochures, and held exhibitions of reform clothing with the cooperation of shopkeepers who regularly sold reform dress.[59]

The new artistic dress and its relation to modern art drew the attention of women who were artistically inclined. The writers Marie Metz-Konig and Anna van Gogh-Kaulbach wore artistic dress, as did musicians and singers Catharina van Rennes, Auke Schierbeek, Jeanette Molsbergen, and Alida Noorderweir-Reddingius. These women would have had no difficulty in finding examples of artistic dresses illustrated in the *Maandblad der Vereeniging voor Verbetering van Vrouwenkleeding (Monthly [Paper] of the Dutch Society for the Improvement of Women's Dress)*. These artistic gowns were all loose-fitting, cut full with a yoke or in the princess style.[60]

For the most part, promoters and designers of artistic dress in the Netherlands relied on the publications and designs of Henry van de Velde, Alfred Mohrbutter, and Paul Schultze-Naumburg. Most of the styles made by Dutch artists were simple princess styles, more like the designs of Peter Behrens or an adaptation of the Directoire or Empire styles promoted by the Liberty Company (Fig. 92). The Liberty Company had a dress department in the fashion firm of Metz and Company in Amsterdam. Examples from Liberty's 1905 catalog, *Dress and Decoration*, appeared in the Dutch artistic magazine *The Woman and Her Home* (*De Vrouw en haar Huis*).[61]

Perhaps one of the best-known artistic-dress reformers was Madame de Vroye, who moved from Paris in 1901 to live in The Hague. She offered expensive, elegant reform dress in the princess style to the moderate women of the

Fig. 92 Dutch reform dress. From *Maandblad der Vereeniging voor Verbetering van Vrouwenkleeding* (April 1, 1901): 43.

V.v.V.v.V. In 1903, she edited her own magazine, *Refome,* which catered to an audience that embraced the new art. At the Berlin exhibition of women's artistic reform dress, Die Neue Frauentracht, held in 1903, Madame de Vroye presented a group of gowns that were very favorably received for their elegance.[62]

It is curious that few male artists in the Netherlands are credited with designing artistic dress. Carin Schnitger suggests that ideally women would have designed their own clothes since their garments in theory had to be an expression of the individual. Certainly this was a major thesis of many of the artistic-dress reformers.[63]

Yet, there is one well-known man who designed women's dress, the painter Jan Toorop. Toorop depicted reform styles of artistic dress in several lithographs, including *Arbeid voor de Vrouw* (*Work for Women*), 1899 (Fig. 93), and *Delftsche*

Fig. 93 An 1898 Jan Toorop lithograph depicting women in reform dresses. The anvil reads "Work for Women." From *Deutsche Kunst und Dekoration* (1899).

Slaolie (*Delft Salad Oil*), 1894. The latter work depicts batik cloth, which would have been familiar to Toorop, who grew up in Java, where batik-designed fabric was the traditional decorative technique. Batik designs in cloth were familiar to the Dutch, who had been importing them as trade items for years. After an exhibition of batik fabrics in 1883, batik became a technique widely used in the Dutch new art movement in the 1890s, and the exotic nature of the fabric made it popular with modern designers everywhere.[64]

Students at the newly established Trade School for the Improvement of Women's and Children's Dress in Amsterdam (established in 1909) were exposed to works by artists and architects of the Dutch new art movement, which had a preference for new geometrical forms usually associated with early Wiener Werkstätte design.[65] In March 1917, the Wiener Werkstätte took part in a fashion show held in Amsterdam under the artistic direction of Otto Lendecke. Lendecke's fashion journal, *Die Damenwelt,* reported enthusiastically about positive comments by the Dutch press: "Among the exhibiting firms, the Wiener Werkstätte, so well known here by the individual character of its textiles, and the totally different style of its cutting and makeup. Its contribution struck me as a style of fashion in its own right!"[66]

Scandinavia

Interest in reform dress in Sweden and Norway was spearheaded by Christine Dahl, who had studied reform dress in America. Dahl spoke regularly on the subject of the need for reforming women's dress; most of her suggestions were

Fig. 94 *Anna Muthesius,* by Fra Newbery. From the cover of *Der Jugend,* no. 93 (1904). Mrs. Muthesius, the author of a book on women's clothing reform, *Das Eigenkleid der Frau* (1903), is shown wearing a blue and green batik dress in the reform style.

based on hygienic principles. In order to avoid wearing a corset and to have the support of clothing fall on shoulders, Dahl devised a princess-style dress. She patented her design, which was sold by the Steen & Strom Company in Christiana. Scandinavian efforts at reforming women's clothing became better known when a doctor from Copenhagen wore Dahl's princess dress during the 1896 International Congress for Women's Work and Women's Endeavors. This predated most of the German efforts toward artistic dress reform. Scandinavians had an opportunity to see Austrian crafts in Stockholm in April 1916, when the store Nordiska Kompaniet organized an arts and crafts exhibition in which the Wiener Werkstätte showed its latest clothing models, as well as leather, glass, jewelry, and tableware.[67]

The relationship between reform dress worn in Britain and that adopted by women on the Continent may best be summed up by Margaret Swain's reflections on the personal relationships of individuals involved in these efforts. In an essay on Jessie Newbery, Swain refers to the close friendship between the Newburys from Scotland and the Muthesius family from Germany that lasted until the First World War. When Anna Muthesius published her book on dress reform, *Das Eigenkleid der Frau* (*The Proper Dress of Women*), photographs of the Newburys' two daughters and Anna's friends the Macdonald sisters are used as illustrations. Fra Newbery painted a portrait of Anna Muthesius in which she wears a dress made out of batik of either Dutch or Dutch Indies origin (figure 94). The connections among the German, Dutch, and British artistic endeavors for reform were clearly cemented when the art magazine *Der Jugend* reproduced the portrait of Anna Muthesius for its cover in 1904.[68]

CHAPTER SEVEN

Fashion, Dress Reform, and the New Woman

No great movement springs suddenly into existence.
—Helen Gilbert Ecob, 1900

There is little evidence to reveal just how many women in Europe and America actually wore reform dress. Nonetheless, from the mid-nineteenth century to the early years of the twentieth century there were plainly many advocates of reform dress striving to move toward what they perceived to be more comfortable, healthful, and beautiful clothing. Between the turn of the century and the end of the First World War—less than twenty years—many changes took place in women's dress. Some of them reflect the efforts of the reformers. The move toward rationality continued in the twentieth century, with the strongest voices coming from the arts communities, especially from the reformers who advocated applying the principles of art to dress.[1]

This final chapter considers the impact of the reformers in "making fashion rational" in the twentieth century. It considers the impact of each reform style—trousers, underwear, and artistic dress—on future fashion and the reasons for the eventual acceptance of these styles. It also addresses the connection of high-fashion designers to reform efforts, particularly the efforts of avant-garde designers Paul Poiret and Mariano Fortuny, who are often credited, wrongly perhaps, with freeing women from constricting clothing. This chapter also incorporates the voices of early-twentieth-century women in the form of reports on the progress reformers thought they had made toward improving women's dress. Finally, this chapter addresses the legacy these reformers left for women and their impact on styles of clothing worn during the remainder of the twentieth century.

ℰ What Became of the Reform Styles?

In many respects, fashion capitulated to the efforts of the reformers well before the First World War. Indeed, after each reform style was introduced, it took on a life of its own. Bloomers, or some form of bifurcated garment, were worn for classes in physical education and all sorts of outdoor activities. Indeed, for sports women needed comfortable clothing, which they often devised themselves. Women denounced heavy and restrictive undergarments, and many of them refined and reduced the number of undergarments they wore, adopting the reform style universally until central heating relieved many women of the need for extra warmth. The very stiff steel and whalebone corset became passé, although many women did wear lighter corsets, some in a reform style; yet others wore no corset at all. Ultimately, the philosophy of the aesthetes took hold. The lighter-weight medieval and classically inspired gowns of the artistic reformers gained support with the makers of fashion. This support allowed artistic reform dress to become an acceptable fashion.

Trousers

The problem with women's dress, as argued by reformers in the mid-nineteenth century, was that it was harmful to women's health—women's outer clothes were too voluminous, heavy, and bulky; skirts and trains were too long and dragged on the ground; and the weight was distributed unevenly on the body. The underclothes were too heavy, women wore too many petticoats and other layers, and the corset was worn much too tight. In addition, underwear provided no warmth in winter and was too hot in summer. In short, many women felt encumbered by fashion. Feminists added the complaint that their cumbersome clothes were politically at fault because the burden of fashion prevented women from partaking in the public world of politics, business, and commerce. In order to eliminate these problems, both health reformers and feminists adopted loose trousers worn under short skirts, a style that came to be called the Bloomer costume.

Although reformers promoted trousers as street wear for women throughout the second half of the nineteenth century, their efforts to make trousers an alternative to fashion were successful only in the area of active sports and then largely for events that occurred away from public view—mountaineering, hiking, and bicycling. However, women did have a choice of skirt, trousers, or a skirt worn over trousers for these activities. As more leisure time gave women the opportunity to engage in these and other sports, they could experience wearing trousers. Of course, in colleges many young women were required to wear a bifurcated gymnasium suit. Indeed, the gymnasium outfit, which served as inspiration for the Bloomer, continued to be worn for calisthenics and physical-education classes in schools well into the twentieth century, sometimes with a skirt attached. Apparently women's wearing trousers in public places went against strong gender roles and ideas of propriety or etiquette in dress. Pants were not considered feminine and hence were deemed unattractive on women. Cultural expectations of women definitely placed restrictions on their wearing trousers. Acceptance occurred only when trousers seemed a truly practical and logical choice for a specific activity.

Reform Underwear

In the early 1870s, when health reformers decided to solve women's clothing problems by devising lighter-weight and less restrictive underwear and promoting the abolition of the corset, they were more successful than they had been with trousers. Underwear reform had a broader base of activists and greater acceptance in part because it was more subtly subversive; the changes could not be seen. The idea of returning women's bodies from the distortions caused by heavy, stiff, and rigid underwear to a more natural human shape was a desire of the artistic reformers as well as of the feminists, physicians, and hygienists. Reformers with an artistic perspective were some of the most ardent supporters, and many developed underwear systems of their own. The new underwear systems offered many improvements—even distribution of the weight of the clothing, fewer undergarments, and the demise of the corset.

Reform underwear promoted by these reformers became popular, although it was difficult to convince women to leave off their corsets. Some women adopted simple bust supporters that looked very much like tightly fitting, yet boneless and cordless under bodices, or a reform-style corset that was softer and had less stiffening than fashionable corsets, something similar to Annie Jenness-Miller's "model bodice." (See Fig. 45.) Others chose to replace the corset with an early form of the brassiere, or what they also called a bust supporter, a garment that fitted over the breasts and not over the upper torso as a "bodice" would fit. Of course, as the outer dress became simplified, less rigid and cumbersome, underwear styles conformed to it. The introduction of central heating in homes also eliminated the need for excess underwear. These new systems of underwear clearly solved some of the problems of unhygienic clothing. Nonetheless, problems remained—the tightness, weight, and length of the outer garment.

Artistic Dress

In Europe and America artistic reformers argued that beauty was apparent only in a body that had not been misshapen by the fashionable corset. In many instances they recommended a return to earlier forms of dress, designs based on classical Greek or medieval dress. The aesthetic concept of fitness to purpose was a dominant theme, one that supported the idea that dress should correspond to the individual woman. Yet these reformers believed that the body as it appears in nature could be improved through exercise and enhanced by making choices of clothing styles and colors based on the principles of art.

The princess- and Empire-style garments that Liberty advocated in London and that Annie Jenness-Miller promoted in America in the 1880s and 1890s were advertised as acceptable "fashionable dress" in "the reform style" in Europe after 1905. Most of all, major fashion designers discovered that the simplicity of antique classical dress would enhance the natural beauty of the female form. When fashion designers began to copy the simple, artistic reform styles and recreated a new Empire or Directoire look in 1907, referring to it as the new reform style, the New Woman of the twentieth century quickly adopted it. How many women actually went without a corset under these garments is not known. Images in magazines are misleading, for fashion illustrators of the period often made women fit a corseted fashionable ideal that was even more unnatural than the effect of the corset in normal circumstances; photographs would provide more accurate examples.

Offering "A New Philosophy of Fashion" in 1900, Helen G. Ecob stated the case clearly for the artistic reformers, observing that the problem with "contemporary dress" was that it "attempts to conform the human figure to the prevailing fashion." Her solution was to draw on science and art to force fashion to conform to the human figure. "Intelligence," she declared, "must be applied to dress." Her thoughts were clearly in accord with the artists of Europe and America when she stated that "the science of dress" was based on two basic laws. The first was the law of necessity wherein the means were adapted to the ends. In her view, "Every ornament must have a purpose." The second law was "the demand of the aesthetic nature of beauty." The first aim of scientific dress was to set up a standard of beauty for the feminine form based on the study of nature. "Dress," she believed, "must adapt itself to the laws of . . . the human body."[2]

Ecob argued that the tyranny of the trade was a serious obstacle and "their despotism will cease only when women combine to demand stability and intelligence in design." Furthermore, she suggested, "We must learn to distinguish between good and bad fashions through the application of art criticism, just as we learn the worth of literature, or feel the laws of literary art." In order to accomplish this, Ecob proposed a school of design that would assume that dress is "a philosophical study that raises the profession to a dignity becoming so serious a subject." Dress, she stated, is related to economics, medicine, art, social questions, and ethics. The school would provide systematic and comprehensive training in "this difficult branch of decorative art" and be a sort of bureau of intelligence open to the average woman. The curriculum would include: anatomy and physiology, art anatomy and drawing, physical training, color theory, historic art and the history of dress, principles of ornamentation and textile design, sewing and drafting, cutting and fitting, designing, and the economics and ethics of dress.[3]

Most of all, Ecob argued, "Woman's new relations to the industrial world call for the evolution of clothing suited to her new activities. As men and women cooperate in comradeship in the work place, comfort and good taste must replace attraction as the emphasis of dress."[4]

THE IMPACT OF REFORM: THE SUM IS GREATER THAN ITS PARTS

Efforts toward improving women's dress were, of course, related. The artistic reformers would have worn a trousered outfit for mountaineering, hiking, and similar outdoor activities, and they quite enthusiastically adopted union suits and favored shaped under bodices and bust supporters in place of a corset. Annie Jenness-Miller's nonradical "improvements" for women confirm this. For not only were her dress designs largely artistic, in that she acted on the belief that clothing designs should be based on art principles, she was also an advocate for women's wearing reform undergarments and she promoted comfortable trousered garments for outings and other outdoor activities. To dress correctly, women would have to wear her artistically designed dresses with her system of reform ("correct") underwear, which replaced the corset with her model bodice if needed. These dresses were meant for all occasions, for use both at home and in public. Her most radical suggestion was the "business suit" for women that consisted of a short skirt worn with gaiters. Her success centered on her ability to work within and around existing ideas of propriety and appropriateness and, of course, in concealing her methods.[5]

The Fashion Business and Reform Garments

The extent to which women adopted trousers, improved their undergarments, and wore artistic dress reveals the distaste that advocates of clothing reform had for fashionable dress. Yet little has been said about how the fashion industry felt about these promoters of anti-fashion. The producers of fashion—dressmakers and department stores, and indeed the *haute couture*—were not immune to the efforts of the reformers. Some supported their efforts. Since they needed to maintain their client base in order to survive, the professionals had to produce clothing that fit the requirements of their customers. They could not ignore the needs of the public, and clearly women's needs changed from the mid-nineteenth century to the early decades of the twentieth century. Not only was there a growth in population and more wealth but women's roles were changing. Many more women were employed outside of the home and attending universities and colleges.

As observed by Helen Ecob, the new women needed clothing appropriate to their new public activities. They wanted clothing that emphasized practicality rather than femininity. Women also had more time to pursue leisure activities that required activity-specific, comfortable, and appropriate clothing.

Reform Efforts of the Haute Couture

Dress-reform efforts within the world of the *haute couture* actually occurred as early as the mid-nineteenth century. Although many may not view the creation of the cage crinoline as "reform," in many respects it was an improvement. It lightened the overall weight of the clothing worn by women by reducing the number of petticoats they needed. When Charles Frederick Worth altered the shape of the crinoline after it had reached enormous proportions in the mid-1860s, this, too, could be viewed as an improvement. Furthermore, while they were not ready to give up the corset, or suggest trousers for everyday, many high-fashion designers agreed with the reformers when it came to the creation of artistic dresses (tea gowns) and clothing for sporting activities. Although couturiers such as Charles Frederick Worth and his sons made their reputations on elaborate court gowns and ball gowns, their elite customers also needed clothing for other occasions. In fact, their clients were often the first women to take up preoccupations that required special clothing—for example, elaborate entertaining at home, bicycling, yachting, and shooting. Dresses worn for other daytime activities or for evening pursuits would not do, nor would a gymnasium costume or a bathing suit. Clients of the *haute couture* included not only women of the aristocracy but also the wealthy bourgeoisie, actresses, dancers, and opera singers. Among them were newsworthy women such as the dancers Eleanora Duse and Isadora Duncan, socialite Peggy Guggenheim, and member of the aristocracy Queen Marie of Romania.[6]

Designers often made up special gowns for these women to wear when posing for their portraits. Apparently the tea gown was a favorite for informal portraits. Diana DeMarly believes that the timeless quality of tea gowns, based as they were on historical style, made them appropriate selections for portraits. Sitters for the artist M. Dagnan-Boureret, for instance, often wore "timeless" gowns designed by Jean Phillipe Worth.[7]

There are a number of examples of couture involvement in reform efforts. As noted in chapter 2, Worth et Cie., appeared to be more than willing to accommodate the reformers. The London branch set up a booth at the 1883 Rational Dress Association Exhibition held in Prince's Hall, London, with designs suggested by the Rational Dress Association. Worth et Cie., entered the competition with garments for a variety of occasions and competed for first prize in the evening-dress category. Worth even went so far as to produce a "Dress of the Future" for Mrs. E. M. King, the sponsor of the exhibition. Her futurist garment had no skirt and included short knickerbocker trousers in a vaguely seventeenth-century man's style (see Fig. 38). Worth et Cie., received a silver award for the artistic design of their evening dress (Fig. 95).[8]

Fig. 95 Worth evening gown with trousers, shown at the Rational Dress Association Exhibition in Prince's Hall, 1883.

Impact of Aesthetic Reform on Couturiers

Of all the dress-reform efforts, it is clear that the artistic-dress reformers had the most influence on fashion. The clothing created by artistic reform-minded artists and designers became accessible to the fashion world not through advertising as we know it today but rather by a more informal means. Communication about artistic dress occurred at an individual level through the women who wore it. Wider publicity would have come, however, through favorable commentary by art critics and journalists who gave vivid accounts of clothing worn by aesthete women to art exhibitions and from their reports on reform gowns shown at arts and crafts and fashion exhibitions. Such favorable coverage was in stark contrast to the reaction of the press toward women's wearing trousers in public in the mid-nineteenth century.

The public was made aware of artistic dress promoted by the Liberty Company through magazines such the *Queen,* Liberty's own sales catalogs, and the expansion of its shops and depots throughout Europe and America between the mid-1880s and the early twentieth century. As noted in chapters 5 and 6, artistic ideas for dress spread quickly throughout Europe. In Italy the reform dress took the name of "style liberty." Efforts were aided by art magazines such as *Dekorative Kunst* and *Deutsche Kunst und Dekoration,* whose writers commented very favorably on artistic styles. Frequent exhibitions of artistic dress also communicated the reformers' efforts in promoting the new aesthetic ideal for women's dress.

Artists and designers involved in the modern movement were receptive to exotic new ideas from abroad. Aesthetic ideas and design forms from Japan, Turkey, and the Near East all became sources for new ideas and expressions of taste. These new aesthetic ideas were often incorporated into the clothing designs of artistic reformers, along with the romantic, historical expressions influenced by classical Greece, the Middle Ages, and the Renaissance. It would have been practically impossible for designers of couture clothing to have no contact with these artistic efforts, especially when, as was frequently the case, the designers themselves were interested in the modern movement in the arts and looking for ideas to express this new-found modernity through fashion design.

In 1913 the *Independent* commented on the influence of the artistic reformers on fashion, noting that "the women of Germany and France, in their recent dress reform movements, developed designs that satisfied the artistic sense as well as the desire for comfort, and their influence has had a great deal to do with shaping new styles."[9]

Although a number of designers were clearly sympathetic to the reformers' efforts, the two most often linked with artistic reform of dress are the early-twentieth-century avant-garde designers, Paul Poiret and Mariano Fortuny. Both were in tune with the efforts of the artistic-dress reformers in Germany and Austria, yet there were obvious differences in their approach. Poiret worked from inside the couture business; Fortuny created his designs as an extension of his art enterprises, which included theatrical design.

Paul Poiret. Artistic dress promoted in the 1880s generally did not include constricting undergarments. The gowns were meant to free the body and allow it to retain its natural shape. Women were advised to wear reform undergarments with them, which meant, of course, that no corsets, bustles, or constrictions of any kind would be worn. Yet in the early twentieth century, Paul Poiret claimed that it was he who freed women from the corset. From the previous discussion of artistic-reform dress in Britain and Europe, it should be clear that women had many opportunities to free themselves of the corset long before Paul Poiret came on the fashion scene.[10]

Although previous scholars have pointed out that Poiret was not solely responsible for freeing women from corsets, there has been little recognition of the reciprocal influence between Poiret and the designers of artistic dress in Germany and Austria or of the possible influence on him of the classical styles

promoted by the Liberty Company. Poiret also claimed to have invented the brassiere, but we know, of course, that the reformers of underwear had long been promoting a similar garment, a bust supporter, as a reform undergarment. Wearing it allowed women to discard the corset (see chapter 3).[11]

Garments that Poiret designed in 1908 (and later) that were very much in keeping with the artistic reformers' philosophy included his "pantaloon skirts," a two-piece garment with a tunic-like dress worn over long trousers (Fig. 96) and his Directoire gowns (Fig. 97).

After his marriage in 1904, Poiret traveled continuously in Europe, discovering new movements in the decorative arts and meeting artists and architects. He met Emilie Flöge, Gustav Klimt, and Josef Hoffmann in Vienna. Poiret was aware, therefore, of the reform dress being promoted within the artistic community, and certainly he would have been aware of the artistic gowns offered by the Liberty Company, which, in fact, opened a shop in Paris beginning in 1890. Paul Poiret clearly was not the first designer to adopt the Directoire high-waisted style. His own high-waisted "Directoire" dresses are not that much different from

Fig. 96 (left) Pantaloon skirts by Paul Poiret, 1911. Shown as "Female dress of tomorrow" in *Le Choses de Paul Poiret vues par Georges Lepape.*

Fig. 97 (right) High-waisted gowns inspired by nineteenth-century neoclassicism. From *Les Robes de Paul Poiret racontées par Paul Iribe,* 1908.

the Liberty offerings of a much earlier date. It is ironic, perhaps, that by the 1920s, Poiret was creating dress designs for Liberty's.[12]

There was considerable interaction between Paul Poiret and the Wiener Werkstätte. Poiret was especially impressed with their hand-painted silks. He later used examples created by Wiener Werkstätte designer Dogobert Peche. In fact, the head of the Wiener Werkstätte fashion department, Edward Joseph Wimmer-Wisgrill, emphasized that Paul Poiret had picked up the general reform elements of artistic dress and adopted them "for the whole civilized world."[13]

The influence, however, was no doubt reciprocal, for Otto Lendecke, who began to work for the Wiener Werkstätte in 1911, had worked for Poiret in Paris prior to his arrival in Vienna. Lendecke produced many fashion designs, dresses, textiles, stage designs, and ballet costumes. In 1917 Lendecke established the magazine *Die Damenwelt,* a short-lived but beautiful fashion paper formulated in an artistic manner rather than as a fashion periodical.[14]

Paul Poiret saw the Wiener Werkstätte exhibit in Rome in 1911 and became so fascinated with Hoffmann's pavilion and Klimt's paintings that he immediately set off for Vienna. It was not until 1912, however, that Poiret was able to visit Hoffmann's famous pavilion, the Palais Stoclet in Brussels. As noted by Werner J. Schweiger, Poiret purchased many Wiener Werkstätte products in Vienna: "He bought so much that the products of the WW, the Austrian interior decorating industry and the Kunstgewerbeschule came to exert a very strong influence on Paris fashion in 1912."[15]

In writing about the fashions of the Wiener Werkstätte, Jane Kallir described the line as incorporating two basic trends: the "Reformkleid" (reform dress) and its re-interpretation by "the French designer Poiret." When Kallir states that Poiret's contribution was the revival of the classical style, she was apparently unaware of the efforts of the artistic reformers in producing classical styles, as well as other historically inspired designs, especially the medieval and Renaissance silhouettes. Certainly, the styles promoted by the German and some Austrian artistic designers in the first decade of the twentieth century reveal a propensity for a high "Empire" or classical Greek waistline.[16]

Another element that appears in both Wiener Werkstätte designs and those of Poiret is the influence of what has been called Orientalism. Both the Werkstätte and Poiret produced pleated, Middle Eastern–inspired harem pants. Poiret's harem pants predate the brightly colored costume designs of León Bakst for the Ballet Russes, which were appearing on stage all over Europe. The exotic colors and styles were new and exciting, and they were greatly admired not only by the artistic community but by their general audiences as well. The popularity of the ballet in turn helped sales of harem pants. Interestingly enough, Mariano Fortuny also produced pleated trousers. All of these designers created the harem trousers as lounging pajamas, not as street wear.[17]

Mariano Fortuny. Mariano Fortuny y Madrazo was a painter who created clothes. His ideas were largely divorced from fashion, yet his clothes were worn

by many fashionable women. Although born in Granada, Spain, Mariano Fortuny spent his formative years in Paris and then settled in Venice, where he became an accomplished artist, theatrical designer, photographer, and architect. Yet today he is perhaps best known for his textiles and the design of the finely pleated "Delphos Robe" (dress), which he patented (Fig. 98).

Fortuny used pleated silk for the Delphos dress, which was cut narrow and straight to hang loosely from the shoulders. Sometimes it was gathered in at the waist or just under the breast "as in the manner of Directoire or Empire gowns." The style of Fortuny dresses relates to the artistic reform dress of the period in that they both freed women from constraints of the corset and other restrictive undergarments. As Guillermo De Osma has argued, the real reformers were the artists and aesthetes who, like Fortuny, wanted to create a new style of dress, one that would "liberate the body, allow for complete freedom of movement, provide comfort and warmth, and, above all, be beautiful."[18]

As in the case of Poiret, Fortuny traveled widely, especially in England and France. He had contact with the artistic community and the artists and designers in the modern movement. One objective of the European modern design movement was to break down the barriers of traditional art. Fortuny shared this view, believing that sculpture, paintings, etchings, photographs, and dresses were of equal artistic value.

Fortuny was familiar with the work of Arthur Lasenby Liberty, Walter Crane, Henry van de Velde, Peter Behrens, Gustav Klimt, Josef Hoffmann, and Koloman Moser, all of whom in one way or another aided the development of artistic dress in Europe. Fortuny also would have been knowledgeable about the Greek classicism found in the paintings of Albert Moore, Frederick Leighton, Sir Lawrence Alma-Tadema, and William Godward, who had exhibited their works in the Beinnale in Venice. Another source of influence on Fortuny's designs was his personal experience with Asian and Arabic art, which he gained from his father, who had been an accomplished painter. As noted by De Osma, painting, particularly Venetian painting, was also a main source of inspiration. Fortuny was able to incorporate ancient Greek, Venetian, and exotic elements into his work.[19]

Fortuny, as De Osma argued, was greatly influenced by all elements of the artistic world, by art and artistic dress, critics, patrons, and the *literati*. He was well prepared to create garments that glorified the human body in the way that the clothing worn in ancient Greece had done. From De Osma's point of view, Fortuny in a very personal and quiet manner forced reform dress to become acceptable fashion.[20]

There was a degree of escapism or theatricality found in many types of reform dress, including the tea gowns of the British aesthetes, the Empire and princess styles of the artistic reformers, and the Greek styles of Liberty, Poiret, and Fortuny. Many styles had historical elements that were for the most part unrelated to fashion. The extent to which reform styles differed from fashion placed them in a sphere that went beyond fashion, and thus by wearing these new reform styles women could feel that they were indeed escaping from the constraints of fashion. In its ability to transport the wearer beyond reality, to a new level of personal awareness, artistic reform dress actually aided in the eventual modification of that reality. De Osma has observed that this quality to transcend is usually the function of great art; but then the designers thought of their dresses as art.[21]

Promotion of Artistic Dress: The Poiret and Fortuny Methods. Fortuny's success in promoting his designs owes in part to his clientele. Unlike Poiret, who made larger-than-life public gestures to gain attention for his creations, Fortuny gathered around him devoted friends and clients who appreciated the quality and timelessness of his dresses and textiles. Fortuny's supporters included the writers Gabriele D'Annunzio and Marcel Proust, entertainers Eleanora Duse and Isadora Duncan, Queen Marie of Romania, and many socialites and aristocrats in Europe as well as wealthy Americans. Peggy Guggenheim maintained a palace in Venice and was a great admirer of Fortuny. By wearing the Delphos dress, or through making references to Fortuny's works of art, his friends provided a link between Fortuny's Venice and the world at large.[22]

While Fortuny's gowns were at first usually worn only in the home, women in the visual and performing-arts fields often wore them on stage and even in public. Ruth St. Denis wore Fortuny's Knossis scarves for performances of Indian dances in Berlin in 1907. Isadora Duncan, who revived Greek dance, and who performed frequently throughout Europe, also was an admirer of Fortuny. Duncan frequently wore classically inspired Greek dress, both on and off the stage. She considered herself to be a dress reformer. Her clothing allowed her to dance in a style far removed from the stiffness of the traditional ballet. In many respects Duncan reformed the dance and paved the way for the later innovations of Shawn, Duse, and Martha Graham. Duncan's performances revealed dance full of movement and expression. The director of the Ballet Russes, Sergei Diaghilev, and the designer Bakst had seen Duncan perform in Russia during her tour in 1906. Bakst, in particular, reinterpreted her dress for such ballets as *Narcisse* (1911), *Daphnis et Chloe* (1912), and *Après-Midi d'un Faune* (1912).[23]

Fortuny's influence on women's clothing reform cannot be denied. Yet it can be said that the popularity of the Ballet Russes largely created the demand for Fortuny's dresses and cloaks with their exotic names. Clearly, there was a mutual impact. Even Poiret admired and copied Fortuny's work, creating his own version of the Delphos dress in the 1910s and selling Fortuny's tunics as early as 1908. Fortuny's influence on reformers in the United States became a reality after his gowns were exhibited in New York in 1914. Two years later, Belle Armstrong Whitney used Fortuny gowns to illustrate "ideal dress" in *What to Wear, a Book for Women.* Whitney believed that Fortuny's gowns fulfilled all her conditions for the ideal dress, which should be above fashion and change: "efficiency, simplicity, personality, quality materials and a high standard of workmanship and artistry."[24]

Other artists who followed Fortuny's lead include several Italian dressmakers. One was Maria Monaci Gallenga (Fig. 99), who also had been a painter. Madame Babani opened a shop in Paris in 1919 selling her own Fortuny-like designs, as well as Liberty fabrics and Fortuny's garments and materials. A third dressmaker who relied heavily on the Ballet Russes and Fortuny designs was Madame Bertillon. While these women created dresses in the genre of Fortuny, none of their work is considered to be as refined as Fortuny's.[25] Nonetheless, they were expanding the possibilities for women to wear a "reform style."

Poiret's method of promoting both his Paris fashion house and his interior-design workshops was different from what couturiers like Worth had been doing. Indeed, his flamboyant approach was such a departure from the rather subdued tactics of most couture houses that Worth admonished him for it. Poiret

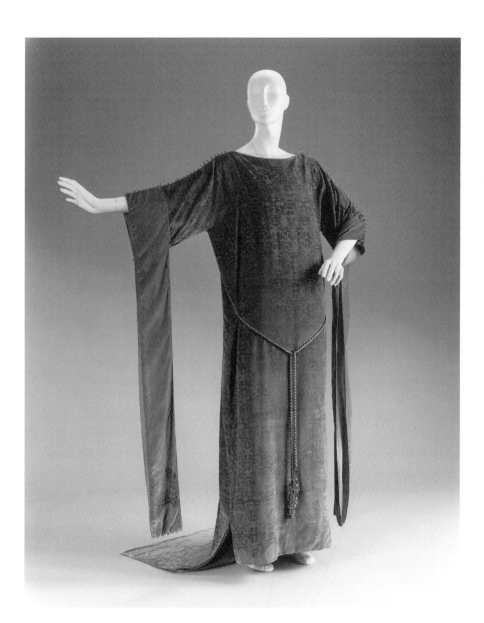

was not like other couturiers—he thrived on promotion and flaunted his successes. Illustrations of Poiret's gowns appeared in many fashion publications.
The first of these were the albums devoted exclusively to Poiret designs. The
initial album, *Les Robes de Paul Poiret racontées par Paul Iribe,* appeared in 1908;
the second, *Les Choses de Paul Poiret vues par Georges Lepape,* came out in 1911.

Two new fashion magazines devoted to Art Deco, *Gazette du Bon Ton* (1912–
14, 1920–25) and *Journal des Dames et des Modes,* featured Poiret fashions on a
regular basis and greatly improved spreading fashion news to the public. Illustration was likewise important in *Les Modes, Vogue,* and other publications. The
exposure raised fashion illustration to an art form and communicated fashion
ideas to the public. Another aspect of the theater that aided the dissemination
of fashion ideas was the publication *Comoedia Illustre,* which devoted many pag-

es to *haute couture* between 1908 and 1912. The illustrators for these magazines—Paul Iribe, Georges Lepape, Georges Barbier, and Roman de Tirtoff, better known as Erté—helped to place new couture designs well within the context of Art Deco, thus establishing for the art of illustration a distinction unknown to previous artists of the genre.[26]

Poiret was the first couturier to make a fashion tour of major European cities. He would show his latest fashions, using fashion models, and give lectures, appearing in Berlin, Vienna, Brussels, Moscow, St. Petersburg, and Munich. He also took his entourage to the United States, where he was lauded by the women of fashion and denounced by moralists and ministers. Poiret had his models attend the races at Longchamps, where they could parade around in his new styles with ease.[27]

Both Poiret and Fortuny designed costumes for the ballet and theater, where members of the audience could easily spot a new creation and later order a similar gown or cloak. It is quite clear, then, that all the performing arts—dance, opera, theater, ballet—shared the designing talents of the couturiers for the creation of sets and costumes and that notable dancers, actresses, and opera singers were capable of communicating the latest styles both on and off the stage.[28]

Through early-twentieth-century promotion of artistic reform styles in fashion magazines such as the *Wiener Mode* and the *Queen,* and through the efforts of artists and avant-garde designers such as Fortuny and Poiret, reform dress became a more viable choice. Indeed, this promotion of reform styles as a fashion choice made these styles more accessible and hence gave the idea of wearing reform dress greater agency for women who, perhaps, had previously thought they could not be comfortable wearing styles that might be considered *outré.* Promotion was a key to their success. The Wiener Werkstätte also made the new styles acceptable to the public through distribution of postcards. The styles would seem fresh and appropriate to a new generation seeking change.

CONTEMPORARY REPORTS ON THE PROGRESS OF REFORM DRESS: AN AMERICAN PERSPECTIVE

It is safe to say that the movement to improve women's dress that emphasized artistic and healthy principles certainly benefited from the successful promotional efforts of Poiret and Fortuny, whose gowns nearly replicated the efforts of the artistic reformers. But these successes were largely at the high end of fashion. What were middle-class reformers saying about the progress they had made in improving their dress? What were designers of women's artistic dress saying about progress? Early-twentieth-century magazines published women's reactions to changes in dress styles. These commentaries report on the progress made in dress reform and reveal individual, personal feelings about the success of the movement in general.

Writing in 1903, Elizabeth Dryden observed that "the dress reformer, or physical culturist attired in her eccentric garbs, has lived to see her dreams real-ized: strangely enough the tabooed theories have been gradually adopted, but vanity, and not common sense won the day." She continued: "The tight waist was given up grudgingly . . . and proof of its decline is seen in the pathetic appearance among us of a provincial creature gorgeously arrayed and sticking to her eighteen-inch waist." Indeed, Dryden argued, "It took a smart bicycle, golf or walking suit on a healthy, good looking woman, to show how comfort, neatness, and style might be combined; and to make the least natural of us feel ridiculous." Of course, she declared, reformers had an obligation to the athletic woman, for one could not golf or fence in a corset. She goes on to note that women who engaged in athletics learned to "stand tall," which gave them the physique they needed to discard the laced waist, the corset.[29]

Although women were very aware of the changes and improvements that had been made in their clothing, they were not satisfied. Many of them did not believe that reform ideas had been totally successful. For instance, Anna G. Noyes wrote in the *Independent* that while progress had been made in the elimination of the hoop skirt, the reduction in weight and number of petticoats, and the acceptance of the one-piece undergarment worn next to the skin, for the most part she wanted to see improvement, not simply change. "Clothes don't get better," she said. "They are just different."[30]

In an article titled, "Hygiene, Dress and Dress Reform," Dr. Dudley A. Sar-gent, writing in the *Journal of Home Economics* in 1910, observed that "some evils have gone, some are on the wane or disguised, while some are still boldly dis-played. . . . Those who urge reform now do so on authority [of] . . . scientific research . . . and physiological laws." Obviously, progress had been made: the economic conditions of women's lives had changed, making the return to me-dieval, classical, or Asian styles unlikely. Yet, Sargent noted, women had to work out their dress reform in relation to the demands of living. He argued that women had a "moral obligation" to adopt "the light weight walking skirt and shirtwaist and the lightweight one piece dress, provided the undergarments, especially corsets, if worn, are properly made." He lamented that the high-waisted dress (worn in the previous year), which could have freed women from constraints of corsets, suffered in the hands of the caricaturists. Instead of accepting the soft lines down from the raised waist, women were wearing tightly fitting under-garments to maintain "the figure" and more often than not, the outer skirt had the same tightness, necessitating the long corset. Sargent argued that women should train their muscles so that they did not need corrective corsets.[31]

Writing in 1914, Marguerite Wilkinson observed that "in our present period of development women's clothing does not express the personality of the indi-vidual woman." Women, she wrote, were still prey to absurdities in fashion. They still lived their lives in obedience to conventions. True individuality and appropriateness in clothing would come naturally, she believed, after women had their own life, work, interests, burdens, responsibilities, and "she will gradually find her own proper clothing to go with them—that which is essentially suitable." Echoing the words of many artistic reformers who drew on aesthetic arguments, Wilkinson continued, declaring that the beauty of garments lies in their possessing "wholesome appropriateness . . . [and] suitability to the uses for which they are made—their essential simplicity and sincerity."[32]

In 1913 an article in the *Independent* noted that progress had been made in a variety of ways. After recognizing the influence of the Germans and French regarding artistic dress, the article observed that there were now more choices of clothing styles that allowed greater scope for individual expression and taste. The new colors and color harmonies and soft, rich fabrics (the journal was referring no doubt to Liberty's) meant that clothing could fall into the "graceful lines of a Tanagra figurine." In addition, the article continued, there was no wasp waist of a corset: "The weight of women's clothing as a whole is only half or a third of what it used to be." Four dresses, the author observed, could be packed in the space that was formerly filled by one. One-piece dresses allowed the weight of the clothing to be supported from the shoulders, hips had fewer and lighter skirts to hold up, and the skirt no longer trailed behind. A thirty-two-inch waist was now permissible where formerly a twenty-inch waist was thought proper. And, although some women still wore the corset, it was worn lower and was softened through the use of rubber webbing in place of steel and whalebone.[33]

Yet for all these positive comments regarding the demise of the corset, in 1915 the corset makers were still successful in turning fashion toward their products. Writing on corsets in the *Ladies Home Journal,* Edith M. Burtis argued, "The day of the corsetless figure is gone, and if you would be in fashion you must be corseted." The corsets, she believed, met the reformers' needs: comfort, hygiene, but also grace and charm never before obtained in corsetry. The article claimed that much harm had been done by the "no-corset" fad. The new corsets, it maintained, "support the abdomen and the bust and allow freedom over the diaphragm," and, harking back to arguments from centuries past, Burtis continued by saying that the corsets "brace the spine and force the body to stand in an erect, natural position."[34]

By 1922, Jane Barr took notice of the progress made in improving women's dress: corsets had been discarded, heels and collars lowered, and one-piece dresses were the rule. However, reformers were still looking for improvement; now they wanted to have the freedom to wear knickerbockers (Bloomers) instead of skirts for sports.[35]

In commenting on the influence of painting on the art of dress in 1927, Sonia DeLaunay observed that it was some time before the First World War that fashion began to free itself from the stranglehold of fashion; "It got rid of the corset, the high collar, all those elements of women's dress demanded by the aesthetics of fashion but which were contrary to hygiene and freedom of movement." DeLaunay attributed the improvement to "the change in women's lives [which] has provided the revolution. Women are increasingly active."[36]

In the early twentieth century, as each new generation came along, fewer and fewer young women were exposed to the corset and other restrictive garments; so it was not surprising that they would naturally accept trousers for specific activities; lighter, less restrictive underwear; and the new softer, less restrictive outer garments promoted by the fashion industry as the "reform style." As noted by several of the American commentators on the progress of reform, a number of events and cultural shifts aided the change in attitude about reform dress. Yet clearly women's clothing reform came about through evolution rather than revolution, a process that makes it difficult to assess the success of the various efforts.

Our judgment of what constitutes reform in women's dress from the 1850s to the 1920s is, unfortunately, clouded by our own experiences with clothing. We have difficulty comprehending that shortening a skirt to two inches above the floor would be viewed by women in the nineteenth century as a significant improvement. Mary E. Tillotson's reaction upon seeing the Bloomer after altering her clothing to improve her health is enlightening—she went home and immediately started cutting away more of her own costume. Her piecemeal reaction to change suggests the hesitancy of women to make any alterations that were too blatant, even when they felt that their clothing was endangering their lives. (See chapter 2.)

Many women worked at making fashion rational by altering their garments in ways that appear to us as subtle, but for them were not—shortening skirts, reducing layers of underwear, supporting garments from the shoulders rather than from the waist. For us these changes may seem trivial because we have no understanding of what their clothes felt like. Nineteenth-century women wore heavy and restrictive clothing compared to ours; for them these alterations were significant efforts toward reform. Annie Jenness-Miller's efforts were most profound in this regard and obviously reflect the attitudes of many women, who wanted change but in an unobtrusive way.

Each type of garment introduced as a reform dress remained as a "style" possibility for a considerable amount of time. Some garments introduced as "reform" were already classic styles; some became classics. Trousers were perhaps the most problematic garment—even the bifurcated "leglettes," an undergarment sold by Annie Jenness-Miller, came under scrutiny for being somewhat *outré* for the times—though loose full trousers and leggings were acceptable for sports activities. It is curious that in the development of women's clothing for sports, although the Bloomers or knickerbockers were worn for certain activities (especially mountaineering and bicycling), the skirted gymnasium suit was the normal costume for school physical education classes, and shortened skirts became the standard costume for sports played by women—tennis, bowling, ice skating, croquet, and golf. Skirts for sports activities are vestiges left over from when women were expected to wear skirts in public. Indeed, women often had a skirt to match their sporting attire, so they could be appropriately dressed after climbing a mountain. Some of these traditions remain today: women still wear tennis dresses and skirts, golfing skirts, and skating dresses; for field hockey, tradition demands a kilted skirt. It is curious that the shortened skirt became shorter, rather than being replaced by shorts, for there are no rules prohibiting shorts or trousers for these activities, except perhaps in some educational institutions.[37]

While trousers for leisure activities gained in popularity over the years, especially with the advent and popularity of slacks and jeans, and later Bermuda shorts and short shorts, these were very feminized garments. They did not have the cut of men's trousers. It may surprise us to realize that it took until the women's movement of the 1970s for women to be "allowed" to wear trousers for white-collar jobs and for teaching, and then it was a struggle. Until then, trousers were deemed inappropriate for women to wear for these jobs. The patriarchy refused to give up trousers as a symbol of male supremacy in the workplace, except for menial positions, of course, where some type of "work clothes" uniform was, and is to this day, usually worn. Even at the turn of the twenty-first century, young women are advised to forego the trousered suit for job interviews.

Perhaps the most effective way in which women made fashion rational was through the adoption of reform undergarments. Some of these reform styles, like the drop-seat knit union suit, remain as practical, warm, undergarments for winter wear. The soft knit undershirts are similar to the warm wool knit under vests promoted by Jaeger. Even undergarments similar to Jenness Miller's leglettes have been offered in place of a half-slip. And we are thankful to the designer of nineteenth-century equestrian tights for our standard winter wear of footed nylon tights. The nineteenth-century reform garment called the bust supporter, now given its French name of "brassiere," gained eminence as the garment of choice for the support of the breasts. The corset eventually gave way to a girdle—only to be revived for a period as a "Merry Widow" undergarment, which, although introduced in the 1940s, became popular in the 1950s as an appropriate undergarment to wear with strapless evening gowns. Then in the 1980s, the corset was revived again by Gaultier as "the bustier," a garment popularized by Madonna and then worn as either a "showy" undergarment or, sometimes, an outer garment worn discreetly, or not, under a jacket. (Indeed, in the late twentieth century, beginning in the 1960s, many earlier underwear items besides the corset—corset covers, chemises, and petticoats—that could be found in vintage clothing markets, became acceptable as outer wear.)

Simplicity in dress evolved in the 1910s, in part owing to the artistic reformers but also, perhaps, because the increasing number of women in the workforce needed simple, serious clothing for the business environment and for ease of travel to and from work. Historicism in fashion has seen the revival of many earlier styles that were promoted as reform dress. Artistic styles have been popular. The neoclassical style—the Empire and Directoire derived from the classical Greek chiton—has remained as a standard, often being revived by designers who want the look of simplicity and associations with the classical world. There was almost no decade in the twentieth century when the style was not present.

The high-waisted Greek chiton became a reform style in the first decade of the century, and it continued as inspiration for fashionable garments designed by the couture into the teens—by Poiret, Lucile, the notable English designer who became Lady Duff Gordon, and many others. The tubular, slim styles in the 1920s were as simple as any Greek chiton, and the 1930s saw the bias-cut body-hugging creations of Madame Grès and Madeline Vionnet. Designers continued to draw on the classical silhouette in the 1940s and 1950s. The style clearly became a classic for lingerie, formal wear, and bridal gowns. It was not surprising to see it reappear in earnest in the 1996 collections of Givenchy.

The princess line has also remained as a classic style, occasionally revived as a dominant look, as in the 1960s when Jackie Kennedy helped to make it popular. With historicism in fashion so prevalent in the later years of the twentieth century, it was not surprising to see a princess-style revival in the 1980s and 1990s. The obviously comfortable Mother Hubbard style is another classic used for intimate apparel, and it still appears in nightgowns, bathrobes, maternity clothing, and housecoats. Even the more elaborate styles of tea gowns based on vaguely medieval and Renaissance styles are apparent in wedding dresses, which often draw on historical styles for inspiration.

The legacy of reform is also seen in education. Indeed, the philosophical principles and arguments remain intact. It may be no surprise that the principles of art are still applied to dress and taught in college and university courses in fashion design, with consideration given to individuality. When the ideas moved into the realm of popular culture, we saw publications such as *Color Me Beautiful* and, interestingly at virtually the same time, the literature on how to dress for success. The progression toward modernity that provided women new options for dressing—trousers, reform underwear, and comfortable artistic dresses—in many ways paralleled the evolution in women's roles. As observed above, these new forms of dress eventually were transformed into the comfortable styles that we wear today.

Notes

1. Introduction: Fashion, Health, and Beauty

1. On the history of nineteenth-century fashion, see Caroline R. Milbank, *Couture, The Great Designers* (New York: Stewart, Tabori, & Chang, 1985); Valerie Steele, *Paris Fashion: A Cultural History* (New York: Oxford University Press, 1988), and *Fashion and Eroticism* (New York: Oxford University Press, 1985); and Philippe Perrot, *Fashioning the Bourgeoisie,* trans. Richard Bienvenu, (Princeton: Princeton University Press, 1994).

2. See Thorstein Veblen, *Theory of Leisure Class* (New York: Macmillan, 1899). See also Perrot, *Fashioning,* 87–112. Regarding the pervasiveness of fashion ideals, see Joan Severa, *Dressed for the Photographer* (Kent, Ohio: Kent State University Press, 1995).

3. See Susan Kaiser, *The Social Psychology of Clothing* (New York: Macmillan, 1992); and William Leach, *True Love and Perfect Union* (New York: Basic Books, 1980).

4. See *Dress, a Monthly Magazine.*

5. Primary literature on the need to reform women's clothing includes a wide variety of contemporary nineteenth- and early-twentieth-century magazines in Europe and America, such as the *Lily, Sibyl, Arena, Aglaia,* the *Rational Dress Society Gazette, Deutsch Kunst und Dekoration,* and *Dress, the Jenness Miller Magazine.*

6. Many reformers embraced the need for all three—trousers for sports, underwear changes for comfort and health, and artistic dress for beauty.

7. Not every question is relevant to each chapter; however, the impetus and effect of the promotion of reform garments will be discussed from a European and an American (United States) perspective. Since the publication of Stella Mary Newton's *Health, Art, and Reason: Dress Reformers of the Nineteenth Century* (London: John Murray, 1974), additional information on dress reform has become available, especially on the efforts toward reform on the continent of Europe.

8. See William Hogarth, *An Analysis of Beauty* (London: T. Reeves, 1753); and Sir Joshua Reynolds, *Discourses on Art,* ed. Robert R. Work (New Haven: Yale University Press, 1975). See also Jean-Jacques Rousseau, *Émile; or, Treatise on Education* (New York: Appleton, 1904); Dr. William Buchan, *Advice to Mothers* (Boston, 1809); and William Alcott, *The Young Mother* (Boston: Light & Stearns, 1836), 50.

9. See Perrot, *Fashioning,* 87–112; and Steele, *Paris Fashion,* 136–38. For a discussion of Victorian fashion, see Otto Charles Thieme, "With Grace & Favour, Victorian and Edwardian Fashion in America," in *With Grace & Favour,* ed. Otto Charles Thieme (Cincinnati: Cincinnati Art Museum, 1993), 26–86.

10. *The Delineator* (Aug. 1893): 123. For contemporary commentary on the tea gown, see Steele, *Paris Fashion,* 84–89, and *Dress, a Monthly Magazine* 1 (Nov. 1887): 276–77; 1 (Jan.–Feb. 1888): 601; 1 (Feb. 1888): 456; and 1 (Apr. 1888): 652–53. See also Anne Bissonette "At Home at Tea Time: The Distinctive Tea Gown of the Victorian Era," *Lady's Gallery* 4, no. 5 (1997): 8–14, 58.

11. See Gerilyn G. Tandberg, "Towards Freedom in Dress for Nineteenth-Century Women," *Dress* 11 (1985): 11–30. See also Sally Helvenston, "Fashion on the Frontier," *Dress* 17 (1990) 4–45.

12. "Rational Dress," *Knowledge* (Oct. 16, 1885): 334.

13. Tandberg, "Towards Freedom," 25, 29.

14. Thorstein Veblen, "The Economic Theory of Women's Dress," *Popular Science Monthly* 46 (1894): 198–205. See also Veblen, *Theory of Leisure Class.*

15. G. Armytage, "Modern Dress," *Littell's Living Age*

153 (1883): 165; and Elizabeth Ann Coleman, "Acquiring a French Wardrobe," in *With Grace & Favour*, ed. Otto Charles Thieme, 1–3.

16. Armytage, "Modern Dress," 165–67. See also George Simmel, "Fashion," *International Quarterly* 10 (1904): 130–55.

17. Armytage, "Modern Dress," 166; Perrot, *Fashioning*, 168–74.

18. Margaret Walsh, "The Democratization of Fashion: The Emergence of the Women's Dress Pattern Industry," *Journal of American History* 66, no. 2 (Sept. 1979): 301–13; and Claudia Kidwell, "Paper Patterns," in *1876, A Centennial Exhibition*, ed. Robert C. Post (Washington, D.C.: Smithsonian Institution Press, 1976), 126–29. For further information on American magazines, see Frank L. Mott, *A History of American Magazines* (Cambridge: Harvard University Press, 1938–68).

19. See Annie E. Myers, *Home Dressmaking: A Complete Guide to Household Sewing* (Chicago: Chas. H. Sergel & Co., 1892). Chapter 20, "The Dressmaker at Home," describes how customers worked with their dressmaker. See also William Leach, *Land of Desire: Merchants, Power and the Rise of a New American Culture* (New York: Pantheon Books, 1983).

20. See Claudia Kidwell and Margaret C. Christman, *Suiting Everyone: The Democratization of Clothing in America* (Washington, D.C.: Smithsonian Institution Press, 1974); Susan Benson, *Counter Cultures: Saleswomen, Managers, and Customers in American Department Stores, 1890–1940* (Urbana: University of Illinois Press, 1986); and Michael B. Miller, *The Bon Marché: Bourgeois Culture and the Department Store, 1869–1920* (Princeton: Princeton University Press, 1981).

21. Brigitte Stamm, "Das Reformkleid in Deutschland" ("Reform Dress in Germany") (Ph.D. diss., Technical University, Berlin, 1976), 22–25. See also Werner Sombart, *Wirtschaft und Mode* (Berlin, 1902).

22. Lois Banner, *American Beauty* (New York: Alfred Knopf, 1983), 17–18. See also Arthur Schlesinger, *Learning How to Behave: An Historical Study of American Etiquette Books* (New York: Macmillan, 1946); Perrot, *Fashioning*, 87–112; and Severa, *Dressed for the Photographer*.

23. C. Willet and Phillis Cunnington, *The History of Underclothes* (London: Michael Joseph, 1951), 154–55.

24. See Steele, *Fashion*, 62–65.

25. Ibid., 65–66. The Gibson Girl look refers to the popular idealized drawings of women by Charles Dana Gibson that appeared in many magazines of the period.

26. Ibid., 66–71.

27. See Willet and Cunnington's *The History of Underclothes* for a full discussion of changes in nineteenth-century underclothing.

28. See Thieme, ed., *With Grace & Favour*. For a discussion of how corsets have been viewed by twentieth-century scholars, see Helene E. Roberts, "The Exquisite Slave: The Role of Clothes in the Making of the Victorian Woman," *Signs: Journal of Women in Culture and Society* 2, no. 3 (1977): 554–69; and David Kunzle's response to it, "Dress Reform as Antifeminism: A Response to Helene E. Roberts' 'The Exquisite Slave . . .'" *Signs: A Journal of Women in Culture and Society* 2, no. 3 (1977): 570–79.

29. Willet and Cunnington, *Underclothes*, 15.

30. P. and R. A. Mactaggart, "Some Aspects of the Use of Non-Fashionable Stays," in *Strata of Society* (London: Costume Society, 1974), 23–24.

31. Willet and Cunnington, *Underclothes*, 14–17.

32. P. and R. A. Mactaggart, "Stays," 20–21.

33. Steele, *Fashion*, 42.

34. Ibid., 42–43.

35. Banner, *American Beauty*, 24–25.

36. The idea that simplicity was an admirable quality linked to ideas of beauty appeared in most etiquette books and served as a warning to women who tended to overdress. Simplicity was a quality many women admired. See Lilah Reichley, "Lucy Webb Hayes: An Advocate of Republican Simplicity in Dress" (master's thesis, Bowling Green State University, 1994). The idea of simplicity also had connections to the classical world and concepts of democracy in America. See Patricia A. Cunningham, "Simplicity of Dress: A Symbol of American Ideals," in *Dress in American Culture*, ed. Patricia A. Cunningham and Susan V. Lab (Bowling Green, Ohio: Popular Press, 1993), 180–99.

37. Jane B. Donegan, *Hydropathic Highway to Health: Women and Water-Cure in Antebellum America* (New York: Greenwood Press, 1986), 136. See also Andrew Combe, *The Principles of Physiology Applied to the Preservation of Health and to the Improvement of Physical and Mental Education* (London, 1834). The linkages among health, exercise, and beauty are addressed in Elizabeth Stuart Phelps, *What to Wear* (Boston: J. R. Osgood, 1873); Frances M. Steele and Elizabeth Livingston Steele Adams, *Beauty of Form and Grace of Vesture* (New York: Dodd, Mead and Co., 1892); Frances Stuart Parker, *Dress, and How to Improve It* (Chicago: Chicago Legal News, 1897), 7, 13, 25; Annie Jenness Miller, *Physical Beauty, How to Obtain and How to Preserve It* (New York: Charles L Webster, 1892), 11, 49–62; and Lydia Hoyt Farmer, *What America Owes to Women* (Buffalo: Charles W. Moulton, 1893).

38. Susan E. Cayleff, *Wash and Be Healed. The Water-Cure Movement and Women's Health* (Philadelphia: Temple University Press, 1987), 11–12. See also Samuel Thomson,

New Guide to Health Prefixed by a Narrative of the Life and Medical Discoveries of the Author, 2d ed. (Boston: E. G. House, 1825).

39. Cayleff, *Wash and Be Healed*, 11–12. See also James C. Whorton, *Crusaders for Fitness. The History of American Health Reformers* (Princeton: Princeton University Press, 1982).

40. Cayleff, *Wash and Be Healed*, 13–15.

41. Ibid. See also Jayme A. Sokolow, *Eros and Modernization. Sylvester Graham, Health Reform, and the Origins of Victorian Sexuality in America* (London and Toronto: Associated University Presses, 1983), 155.

42. Cayleff, *Wash and Be Healed*, 14. See also William A. Alcott, *Health Journal and Independent Magazine* 1 (1843): 29.

43. Whorton, *Crusaders*, 113–14.

44. Cayleff, *Wash and Be Healed*, 14–15 ; Sokolow, *Eros*, 155–57.

45. Cayleff, *Wash and Be Healed*, 18, 68–73; Whorton, *Crusaders*, 106–7.

46. Whorton, *Crusaders*, 24–25; Cayleff, *Wash and Be Healed*, 20–24.

47. Harvey Green, *Fit for America* (New York: Pantheon Books, 1986), 85, 89–90, 91, 94.

48. Catharine Beecher, *Physiology and Calisthenics for Schools and Families* (New York: Harper Bros., 1856), 53, 80, 83, 160; Green, *Fit for America*, 92–93.

49. Beecher, *Physiology*, 87, 91.

50. Ibid., 100, 182.

51. Ibid., 185.

52. Some believers thought that exercise would dampen sexual passions and then stretched the argument by pronouncing that ill health was the result of immoral behavior, particularly sexual behavior. See Patricia Vertinsky, "Rhythmics—A Sort of Physical Jubilee: A New Look at the Contributions of Dio Lewis," *Canadian Journal of History of Sport and Physical Education* 96 (1978): 36–37, 40; Green, *Fit for America*, 184–185; and Dio Lewis, *New Gymnastics for Men, Women, and Children* (Philadelphia: Ticknor and Fields, 1862). See also "Caroline Maria Seymour Severance," in *American Reformers, an H. W. Wilson Biographical Dictionary*, ed. Allen Whitman (New York: H. W. Wilson, 1985), 733–34.

53. Green, *Fit for America*, 191; Lewis, *New Gymnastics*, 56, 256.

54. Green, *Fit for America*, 95; Beecher, *Physiology*, v, 9. See also Barbara Novak, *Nature and Culture* (New York: Oxford University Press, 1980).

55. Green, *Fit for America*, 100. See also Banner, *American Beauty*.

56. Beecher, *Physiology*, 9.

57. Dio Lewis, *Five-Minute Chats with Young Women and Certain Other Parties* (New York: Harper & Brothers,

1874), 49. See also Martha H. Verbrugge, *Able-Bodied Womanhood. Personal Health and Social Change in Nineteenth-Century Boston* (New York: Oxford University Press, 1987), 41.

2. Trousers: The Rational Alternative to Skirts

1. See Elizabeth Stuart Phelps, *What to Wear* (Boston: J. R. Osgood, 1873), 19–21. Phelps's comments originated in a paper given to the New England Women's Club (published also in four numbers of the *Independent*). Phelps's arguments were instrumental in convincing the club to undertake an active program for reforming women's underwear, as discussed in chapter 3. See also Gayle V. Fischer, "'Pantalets' and 'Turkish Trousers': Designing Freedom in the Mid-Nineteenth-Century United States," *Feminist Studies* 23, no. 1 (Sept. 1997): 111; and Anne L. Macdonald, *Feminine Ingenuity* (New York: Ballantine Books, 1992).

2. For further discussion of Dr. Walker's efforts toward dress reform, see Allison Lockwood, "Pantsuited Pioneer of Women's Lib, Dr. Mary Walker," *Smithsonian Magazine* 7, no. 12 (Mar. 1977): 113–19; and Charles M. Snyder, *Dr. Mary Walker, the Little Lady in Pants* (New York: Arno Press, 1974). See also Valerie Steele, *Paris Fashion: A Cultural History* (New York and Oxford: Oxford University Press, 1988), 164–65; and Shelly Foote, "Bloomers," *Dress* 6 (1980): 1–10. For a full discussion of the efforts to have women adopt trousers in the nineteenth century, see Gayle V. Fischer, *Pantaloons and Power: A Nineteenth-Century Dress Reform in the United States* (Kent, Ohio, and London: Kent State University Press, 2001).

3. Jane B. Donegan, *Hydropathic Highway to Health: Women and Water-Cure in Antebellum America* (New York: Greenwood Press, 1986), 136. See also note 12, p. 157, where Donegan discusses feminists' views on fashion and Gerrit Smith's comments on dress reform.

4. Patricia C. Warner, "The Gym Suit: Freedom at Last," in *Dress in American Culture*, ed. Patricia A. Cunningham and Susan V. Lab (Bowling Green, Ohio: Popular Press, 1993), 141–42; and Elizabeth Ewing, *History of Children's Costume* (New York: Charles Scribner's and Sons, 1977), 65–66. Pantalets worn under a cage crinoline would have offered a degree of modesty if the crinoline were to flip up in a gust of wind.

5. Kate Luck, "Trouble in Eden with Eve: Women, Trousers, and Utopian Socialism in Nineteenth-Century America," in *Chic Thrills: A Fashion Reader*, ed. Juliet Ash and Elizabeth Wilson (Berkeley: University of California Press, 1993), 202.

6. Anne Wood Murray, "The Bloomer Costume and Exercise Suits," *Waffen und Köstumekunde* 24 (1982): 111; Luck, "Trouble in Eden," 204, 296.

7. Murray, "Bloomer Costume," 111–12. See also "Mrs. Kemble and Her New Costume," *Lily* 2 (Feb. 1850): 24; and Amy Kesselman, "The Freedom Suit: Feminism and Dress Reform in the United States, 1848–1875," *Gender and Society* 5, no. 4 (Dec. 1991): 496–97.

8. Warner, "Gym Suit," 142–43.

9. Jennifer Scarce, *Women's Costume of the Near and Middle East* (London: Unwin Hyman, 1987), 73, 103, 156, 166–67.

10. Warner, "Gym Suit," 144–47.

11. Murray, "Bloomer Costume," 113–15; "How to Begin," *Godey's Lady's Book* (July 1841). See also Warner, "Gym Suit," 144–45.

12. Elizabeth Smith Miller comments on her adoption of the short dress and trousers in "Reflections on Woman's Dress, and the Record of a Personal Experience," in "Symposium on Women's Dress, Part I," *Arena* 6 (1892): 491–95. See also commentary by Amelia Bloomer in Frances E. Russell, "A Brief Survey of the American Dress Reform Movements of the Past, with Views of Representative Women," *Arena* 6 (1892): 326.

13. "Female Attire," *Lily* 3 (Feb. 1851): 2; Murray, "Bloomer Costume," 111; and Kesselman, "Freedom Suit," 498. See also Mary E. Tillotson, *History ov [sic] the First Thirty-Five Years ov [sic] the Science Costume Movement in the United States* (Vineland, N.J.: Weekly Independent and Job Office, 1885); and Donegan, *Hydropathic Highway*, 138.

14. "Letters," *Sibyl* 1 (Aug. 1856): 23.

15. "Bloomerism," *Lily* 4, no. 10 (Oct. 1852): 85. The letter had previously appeared in the *Water Cure Journal*.

16. Angeline Merritt, *Dress Reform, Practically and Physiologically Considered* (Buffalo, N.Y.: Jewett, Thomas and Co., 1852), 86–95, 126.

17. Jeanette C. and Robert H. Lauer, "The Battle of the Sexes, Fashion in 19th Century America," *Journal of Popular Culture* 13, no. 4 (Spring 1980): 248–58.

18. William Leach, *True Love and Perfect Union: The Feminist Reform of Sex and Society* (New York: Basic Books, 1980), 249.

19. Robert E. Riegel, "Women's Clothes and Women's Rights," *American Quarterly* 15 (1963): 395; and Kesselman, "Freedom Suit," 498–501, 503n, 504–506. See also Frances E. Russell, "A Brief Survey," 327.

20. D. C. Bloomer, *Life and Works of Amelia Bloomer* (New York: Schocken Books, 1975), 71–72.

21. "Geauga County Had a Bloomer Girl Too, in the 1870s," *Cleveland Plain Dealer Pictorial Magazine* (June 20, 1948): n.p.

22. Ibid. See also *Pioneer and General History of Geauga County* (Geauga County Historical and Memorial Society, 1953), 657–58; and Mona Hodges Benton, "History of South Newbury, Geauga County, Ohio" (1947 [typescript]), 1, 2, 5.

23. *Pioneer History*, 658.

24. Tillotson, *History*, 36–37, 40.

25. "Dress Reformers in Congress," *Northern Ohio Journal* 5 (Sept. 5, 1874): 3.

26. Ibid. See also, "American Free Dress League," *Geauga Republican*, Sept. 16, 1874.

27. "Dress Reformers," 3. For a photograph of Mary Tillotson, see Joan Severa, *Dressed for the Photographer* (Kent, Ohio: Kent State University Press, 1995), 274–75.

28. Bertha Monica Stearns, "Reform Periodicals and Female Reformers: 1830–1860," *American Historical Review* 37 (July 1932): 697; Leach, *True Love*, 244.

29. Donegan, *Hydropathic Highway*, 153–55. For a photograph of Lydia Sayer Hasbrouck, see Severa, *Dressed for the Photographer*, 238–39.

30. "List of Dress Reformers," *Sibyl* (Sept. 1, 1858) and (July 15, 1859). See also Judith Ann Fuller, "Artistic Reform Dress in Wisconsin Collections: 1880–1890" (unpublished master's thesis, University of Wisconsin, 1977), 119–20. For an example of a woman wearing trousers for work, ca. 1869, see Severa, *Dressed for the Photographer*, 278–79.

31. See Donegan, *Hydropathic Highway*, 137; and Harry B. Weiss and Howard R. Kemble, *The Great American Water Cure Craze* (Trenton, N.J.: Past Times Press, 1967), 41. For images of women wearing trousers in Dansville, see Severa, *Dressed for the Photographer*, 250–51.

32. Donegan, *Hydropathic Highway*, 137, 140; *New Graetenberg Reporter* 2 (January 1850): 29.

33. Kesselman, "Freedom Suit," 497–98. See also "Bloomerism," 85; and *Water Cure Journal* (Feb. 1850, June 1850, Feb. 1851, and Aug. 1851).

34. Donegan, *Hydropathic Highway*, 138 n26, 141.

35. Ibid., 138.

36. Ibid., 146 nn57–58, 147.

37. Ibid., 141–42 n43.

38. Ibid., 146 n56.

39. Ronald L. Numbers, ed., *Prophetess of Health: Ellen G. White and the Origins of Seventh-Day Adventist Health Reform* (Knoxville, Tenn.: University of Tennessee Press, 1992), 135.

40. Ibid., 141. See also Fischer, *Pantaloons*, 126.

41. Ibid., 144–46.

42. Ibid., 146–57.

43. Alison Lockwood, "Pantsuited Pioneer of Women's Lib., Dr. Mary Walker," *Smithsonian Magazine* 7, no. 12 (May 1977): 113–19.

44. Tillotson, *History*, 14–15; and Kesselman, "Freedom Suit," 506–7.

45. Tillotson, *History*, 34–37, 40–41.

46. Ibid., 146. In the 1890s the sanitarium in Battle Creek continued to advocate dress reform. See *The Battle Creek Sanitarium Dress System* (Battle Creek, Mich.: Sanitary and Electrical Supply Co., [1890]).

47. Kesselman, "Freedom Suit," 500, 505–6; and Donegan, *Hydropathic Highway*, 137 n12.

48. Kesselman, "Freedom Suit," 506; Donegan, *Hydropathic Highway*, 137 n12; and Tillotson, *History*.

49. Robert Fletcher, *History of Oberlin College* (Oberlin, Ohio: Oberlin College, 1943), 307–8, 317, 320–22; and Amy Louise Reed, "Female Delicacy in the Sixties," *Century Magazine* 90 (Oct. 1915): 904.

50. Warner, "Gym Suit," 147–54; Sally Sims, "The Bicycle, the Bloomer and Dress Reform," in *Dress and Popular Culture*, ed. Patricia A. Cunningham and Susan V. Lab (Bowling Green, Ohio: Popular Press, 1991), 125–45. See also Claudia Kidwell, *Women's Bathing and Swimming Costume in the United States* (Washington, D.C.: Smithsonian Institution Press, 1968).

51. Warner, "Gym Suit," 147–54; Sims, "Bicycle," 133–34.

52. Shirley Sargent, *Pioneers in Petticoats* (Los Angeles: Trans-Anglo Books, 1966), 395; Dolly Connelly, "Bloomers and Blouses Plus Waving Alpenstocks," *Smithsonian Magazine* 7, no. 7 (1976): 126–31; and "Women in Trousers," *American Agriculturist* 36, no. 9 (Sept. 1877): 344.

53. Foster R. Dulles, *America Learns to Play* (New York: Appleton-Century Co., 1940), 266–67.

54. Murray, "Bloomer Costume," 113–15; Marian Tinling, "Bloomerism Comes to California," *California History* 61 (Spring 1982): 22–24.

55. "Dress Reform at the World's Fair," *Review of Reviews* 7 (Apr. 1893): 313.

56. Frances E. Russell, "Freedom of Dress for Women," *Arena* 8 (1893): 76. See also Jeanne M. Weimann, *The Fair Women* (Chicago: Academy Chicago, 1981).

57. Russell, "A Brief Survey," 339, and "Freedom," 76; Weimann, *Fair Women*, 534.

58. Weimann, *Fair Women*, 531–34.

59. Ibid., 533.

60. See "Symposium on Women's Dress, Part I," in *Arena* 6 (1892): 488–507, and also in the "Symposium," the commentary on practical business by Annie Jenness Miller (495–98) and Frances E. Russell (499–503), and the commentary on artistic dress by Frances M. Steele (503–507); as well as Helen G. Ecob, *The Well Dressed Woman* (New York: Fowler and Wells, 1893), 7, 225, 129.

61. Russell, "A Brief Survey," 338–39.

62. Dora de Blaquière, "Modern Dress Reformers," *Leisure Hour* 33 (1884): 558.

63. Murray, "Bloomer Costume," 107–8. See also Sarah Levitt, "From Mrs. Bloomer to the Bloomer: The Social Significance of the Nineteenth-Century English Dress Reform Movement," *Textile History* 24, no. 1 (1993): 27–37.

64. "The Bloomer Costume," *Chamber's Edinburgh Journal* (Oct. 15, 1851): 280–81; "Bloomerism, or the Female Invasion," *Bartley's Miscellany* 30 (1851): 644.

65. "Fashionable Vagaries," *Chamber's Edinburgh Journal* (July 15, 1871): 418; *Rational Dress Society's Gazette* 1 (Apr. 1888): 1.

66. De Blaquière, "Modern Dress Reformers," 561.

67. G. Armytage, "Modern Dress," *Littell's Living Age* 153 (1883): 166–67.

68. "Rational Dress," *Knowledge* (Oct. 16, 1885): 334.

69. Ibid.

70. *Rational Dress Society's Gazette* 1 (Apr. 1888): 6; Ada S. Ballin, *The Science of Dress in Theory and Practice* (London: Sampson Low, Marston, Searle & Rivington, 1885), 184–85.

71. Mrs. E. M. King, "Preface," in *The Exhibition of the Rational Dress Association. . . . Catalogue of Exhibits and List of Exhibitors* (1883), reprint (New York and London: Garland Press, 1978), 4; and ibid., "Remarks, No. 2," 35.

72. Ibid., 12, 16, 33; and De Blaquière, "Modern Dress Reformers," 562.

73. Fletcher, *Woman First*, 3; Patricia Vertinsky, "Rhythmics—A Sort of Physical Jubilee: A New Look at the Contributions of Dio Lewis," *Canadian Journal of History of Sport and Physical Education* 96 (1978): 36–37 nn20 and 28. See also Elizabeth Blackwell, *The Laws of Life, with Special Reference to the Physical Education of Girls* (New York: G. P. Putnam, 1852).

74. Fletcher, *Woman First*, 4–5, 13.

75. Ibid., 45 n9, 164 nn39 and 64.

76. De Blaquière, "Modern Dress Reformers," 558–59.

77. Ballin, *Science of Dress*, 188, 269–71, 222–23, 225.

78. *Exhibition*, 7–11, 13, 15–17, 19–20, 27–34.

79. De Blaquière, "Modern Dress Reformers," 557–59, 562.

80. See *Queen* (Aug. 22, 1896): 367; (Nov. 28, 1896): 1045; and (Dec. 26, 1896): 1238. See also Frances E. Russell, "The Rational Dress Movement in the Columbian Year," *Arena* 9 (1893): 315.

81. Helene E. Roberts, "The Exquisite Slave: The Role of Clothes in the Making of the Victorian Woman." *Signs* 2, no. 3. (1977): 568–69. See also Hugh Nisbet, "Fin de Siècle Dress and Its Effects," *Englishwoman* 3 (1896): 265–68; and Mrs. E. R. Pennell, "Cycling," in *Ladies in the Field*, ed. Lady Greville (London: Ward & Downey, 1894), 264.

82. Brigitte Stamm, "Das Reformkleid in Deutschland" ("Reform Dress in Germany") (Ph.D. diss., Technical University, Berlin, 1976), 15–20; Heinrich Lahmann, *Die Reform der Kleidung* (*The Reform of Clothing*) (Stuttgart, 1903), 4.

83. Levitt, "From Mrs. Bloomer to the Bloomer," 35–36. For a discussion of the bicycle craze in France, see Steele, *Paris Fashion*, 173–76.

84. See Steele, *Paris Fashion*, 162–67; and Pierre Dufay, *Le Pantalon Feminin* (Paris: Charles Carrington, 1906).

3. The Invisibles: Hygienic Underwear, "Dress Systems," and Making Fashion Rational

1. John Leighton [Luke Limner], *Madre Natura versus the Moloch of Fashion* (London, 1874), 71–73. Regarding the corset controversy, see also Valerie Steele, *Fashion and Eroticism* (New York and Oxford: Oxford, 1985).

2. Mrs. M. M. Jones, *Woman's Dress: Its Moral and Physical Relations* (New York: Miller Wood Pub., 1865), 24–29.

3. Elizabeth Stuart Phelps, *What to Wear* (Boston: J. R. Osgood, 1873), 34–36.

4. Ibid., 32–36, 77–92.

5. Ibid., 88.

6. Ibid., 88–91.

7. Ibid., 33–34.

8. See Abba Goold Woolson, *Dress-Reform* (Boston: Roberts Bros., 1874).

9. "The First Union Suit," *Textile World,* July 29, 1905, 139; Allison Lockwood, "Pantsuited Pioneer of Women's Lib., Dr. Mary Walker," *Smithsonian Magazine* 7, no. 12 (Mar. 1977): 113–19.

10. Deborah Jean Warner, "Fashion, Emancipation, Reform and Rational Undergarments," *Dress* 4 (1978): 24–29.

11. See Deborah J. Warner, "Women's Pavilion," in *1876: A Centennial Exhibition,* ed. Robert C. Post (Washington, D.C.: National Museum of History and Technology, Smithsonian Institution, 1976), 165; and Warner, "Fashion," 29. See also Anne L. Macdonald, *Feminine Ingenuity, Women and Invention in America* (New York: Ballantine Books, 1992), 103–6, 199–206.

12. See Warner, "Women's Pavilion," 165.

13. Ibid. See also, Claudia Kidwell, "Paper Patterns," in *1876, A Centennial Exhibition,* ed. Robert C. Post (Washington D.C.: Smithsonian Institution, 1976).

14. Warner, "Fashion," 29. See also "A Healthful Corset," *Demorest's Monthly Magazine* (Mar. 1874): 109; "Suitable Corsets," *Demorest's Monthly Magazine* (May 1874): 188; and "Healthful Dressing," *Demorest's Monthly Magazine* (Feb. 1876): 96–97.

15. Warner, "Fashion," 29.

16. Ibid. See also, "Advertisement for the Ferris 'Good Sense" Corset," *Dress, a Monthly Magazine* 1 (Sept. 1887): 185.

17. Annie Jenness-Miller, "The Reason Why," *Dress* 1 (May 1887): 7.

18. Ibid.

19. Annie Jenness-Miller, *Physical Beauty, How to Obtain and How to Preserve It* (New York: Charles L. Webster, 1892), 50–51, 172–75, and "How, What, When, and Where," *Dress, a Monthly Magazine* 1 (June 1887): 57.

20. See *Dress, a Monthly Magazine*: "Our Own System" (June 1887): 65–67; "The Model Bodice" and "Ribbed Union Suit" (Feb. 1888): 474; and "Leglettes" (Mar. 1888): 527. For further discussion of underwear, see *Jenness Miller Monthly*, Irma, and "How to Do Everything Right," 7 (Feb. 1894): 15; and Annie Jenness-Miller, "The Jenness Miller System of Dress" 7 (Mar. 1894): 22.

21. "Advertisement," *Dress, a Monthly Magazine* 1 (June 1887): 137. The advertisement listed eleven agents in the following states: New York, Massachusetts, New Jersey, Illinois, Iowa, Connecticut, and Colorado.

22. Annie Jenness Miller, "What Others Are Doing for Improved Dress," *Dress, a Monthly Magazine* 1 (Nov. 1887): 292–93.

23. *The Battle Creek Sanitarium Dress System* (Battle Creek, Mich.: Sanitary and Electrical Supply Co., [1890]), 46–59. See also John Kellogg, *Influence of Dress on Producing the Physical Decadence of Women* (Battle Creek: Modern Medical Pub. Co., 1891).

24. *Battle Creek Sanitarium*, 7.

25. Frances Mary Steele and Elizabeth Livingston Steele Adams, *Beauty of Form and Grace of Vesture* (New York: Dodd, Mead and Co., 1892), 78–79, 83.

26. Ibid., 94–95, 224. Steele and Adams noted the companies that offered knit underwear: "Hay & Todd, Ypsilanti Manufacturing Company, Ypsilanti, Michigan; Phillis Manufacturing Company, Schlesinger & Meyer, agents, State Street, Chicago. The Jaros and Jaeger Companies also are widely advertised" (ibid., 225).

27. Helen G. Ecob, *The Well-Dressed Woman* (New York: Fowler and Wells, 1892), 132–37.

28. Frances Stuart Parker, *Dress, and How to Improve It* (Chicago: Chicago Legal News Company, 1897), 4, 30–35.

29. Ibid., 32–37.

30. Angelica Schuyler, "The New Fashions for Summer," *Needlecraft* 2 (June 1911): 1–2.

31. Oscar Wilde, *Art and Decoration* (London: Methuen, 1920), 60–61, 79. For further discussion of dress reform in England, see Stella Mary Newton, *Health, Art, and Reason: Dress Reformers of the Nineteenth Century* (London: John Murray, 1974).

32. Dora de Blaquière, "Modern Dress Reformers," *Leisure Hour* 33 (1884): 557–59; "Gazetta de Hygiene," in *Townsend's Monthly Museum of Parisian Fashion* (Nov. 1849): 331.

33. Richmond Leigh, "Corset Wearing" (letter), *Knowledge* (Nov. 10, 1882): 393.

34. E. M. King, "Principles of Dress Reform," *Knowledge* (July 27, 1883): 91–92.

35. E. M. King, "Rational Dress," *Knowledge* (Aug. 10, 1883): 92.

36. *The Exhibition of the Rational Dress Association. . . . Catalogue of Exhibits and List of Exhibitors* (1883), reprint (New York: Garland Press, 1978), 6, 9, 12, 16.

37. See *Rational Dress Society's Gazette,* Apr. 1888–July 1889.

38. Ibid., July 1889, 7; Apr. 1888, 6; Jan. 1889, 6–7.

39. Ada S. Ballin, *The Science of Dress in Theory and Practice* (London: Sampson Low, Marston, Searle & Rivington, 1885), 3–4.

40. Ibid., 6, 269.

41. Ibid., 9–10.

42. Ibid., 154.

43. Ibid., 167–68.

44. Ibid. The name "Girton" comes from the stays designed and worn by the female students in Girton College, Oxford.

45. Ibid., 141–42.

46. Ibid., 140.

47. Ibid., 172.

48. Ibid., 184–85, 187–88. See also Newton, *Health, Art, and Reason,* 98–102; and Dora de Blaquière, "How Should We Dress? New German Theories of Clothing," *Leisure Hour* 33 (1884): 735–37.

49. De Blaquière, "How Should We Dress?" 735.

50. De Blaquière, "Modern Dress Reformers," 563. See also Gustav Jaeger, *Die Normalkleidung als Gesundheitsschutz* (*Normal Clothing as a Protector of Health*) (Stuttgart, 1880).

51. De Blaquière, "How Should We Dress?" 735.

52. De Blaquière, "Modern Dress Reformers," 562.

53. Brigitte Stamm, "Das Reformkleid in Deutschland" ("Reform Dress in Germany") (Ph.D. diss., Technical University, Berlin), 1976, 14–15.

54. Stamm, "Das Reformkleid," 17–18; Heinrich Lahmann, *Die Reform der Kleidung* (*The Reform of Clothing*) (Stuttgart, 1903), 35. Other German reformers who advocated the reform of underclothing were C. H. Stratz, *Die Frauenkleidung* (*Women's Clothing*) (Stuttgart, 1900), Otto Neustatter, *Die Reform der Kleidung auf Gesundheitlicher Grundlage* (*The Reform of Clothing Based on Health Theories*) (Munich, 1903); and Anna and Heinrich Jäger, *Hygiene der Kleidung* (*Hygiene of Clothing*) (Stuttgart,

1906). See also Leonie von Wilckens, "Künstlerkleid und Reformkleid—Textilkunst in Nürnberg" ("Artistic Clothing and Reform Clothing—Textile Art in Nürnberg"), in *Peter Behrens und Nürnberg* (Nürnberg: Prestel Verlag, 1980), 198.

55. Stamm, "Das Reformkleid," 45–47.

56. Ibid.

57. Ibid., 200.

58. Ibid., 50–51. See chap. 4 for a discussion of the efforts made by Liberty's and its founder, Arthur Lasenby Liberty, in support of artistic dress reform.

59. Minna Cauer, "Dress Reform in Germany," *Independent* 63 (1907): 995–96.

60. Ibid., 996.

61. Ibid., Editor's note, 993.

62. Ibid., 996. See also Else Oppler-Legbaud, "The German Dress Reform Movement," *Independent* 59 (1905): 490–91.

63. "Dress Reform in Sweden," *Dress, a Monthly Magazine* 1 (1887): 68–69.

64. Ibid.

65. Stamm, "Das Reformkleid," 45.

4. Artistic Dress in England: Visions of Beauty and Health

1. Charles Spencer, ed., *The Aesthetic Movement, 1869–1890* (London: Academy Editions, 1973), 9.

2. William Gaunt, *The Aesthetic Movement and the Cult of Japan* (London: Fine Arts Society, 1972), 4–8.

3. John Ruskin, "'A Joy Forever,' Lecture I, The Discovery of Art," in *The Words of John Ruskin*, vol 16, ed. E. T. Cook and Alexander Wedderburn (London: George Allen, 1905), 52. Lucy Crane, *Art and the Formation of Taste* (London: Macmillan, 1882), 134–35.

4. W. Holman Hunt, *Pre-Raphaelitism and the Pre-Raphaelite Brotherhood*, 2 vols. (London, 1905–6), 1:51.

5. Leonée Ormond, "Dress in the Painting of Dante Gabriel Rossetti," *Costume* 8 (1974): 26.

6. Ibid., 27.

7. Roger Smith, "Bonnard's *Costume Historique*—Pre-Raphaelite Source Book," *Costume* 7 (1973): 22. See also Jennifer Smith, "Medieval Dress in Pre-Raphaelite Painting," in *William Morris and the Middle Ages*, ed. Joanna Banham and Jennifer Harris (Manchester, Eng.: Manchester University Press, 1984), 46–58.

8. Ormond, "Dress in the Painting of Dante Gabriel Rossetti," 26.

9. Holman Hunt, *Pre-Raphaelitism*, 2:349. See also Raymond Watkinson, *Pre-Raphaelite Art and Design* (Greenwich, Conn.: New York Graphic Society, 1970), 129–30.

10. M. H. Spielman, *Millais and His Works,* 25, 85; N. M. Merchant, *Shakespeare and the Artist* (London: 1865), 113; Smith, "Bonnard's *Costume Historique,*" 28–29.

11. William Hogarth, *An Analysis of Beauty,* ed. Joseph Burke (Oxford: Clarendon Press, 1955), title page. See also Deborah Cherry, "The Hogarth Club: 1858–1861," *Burlington Magazine* 122 (Apr. 1980): 237–44.

12. Hogarth, *Analysis,* 174.

13. Stella Mary Newton, *Health, Art, and Reason: Dress Reformers of the Nineteenth Century* (London: John Murray, 1974), 34.

14. Walter Hamilton, *The Aesthetic Movement in England* (London: 1882); Walter Crane, *Ideals in Art* (London: George Bell, 1905), 175. Part of this essay originally appeared in *Aglaia* 3 (Autumn 1894) as "Of the Progress of Taste in Dress: I. In Relation to Art Education." See also Newton, *Health, Art, and Reason,* 35.

15. See Newton, *Health, Art, and Reason,* 24–35; Susan P. Casteras, *Substance or the Shadow: Images of Victorian Womanhood* (New Haven: Yale Center for British Art, 1982), 41–42; and Stephen Jones, "Attitudes, Leighton and Aesthetic Philosophy," *History Today* 37 (June 1987): 31–37.

16. Mary Haweis, *Art of Beauty* (London: Chatto and Windus, 1878), 232; Wilkie Collins, *Woman in White* (New York: Harper, 1860), 3, 15–16; Elizabeth Aslin, *The Aesthetic Movement Prelude to Art Nouveau* (New York: Excalibur Books, 1981), 1, 157; and Isobel Spencer, *Walter Crane* (New York: Macmillan, 1975), 48, 60.

17. Annie Jenness Miller, "Our English Sisters," *Dress, a Monthly Magazine* 2 (1888): 588; *The Exhibition of the Rational Dress Association. . . . Catalogue of Exhibits and List of Exhibitors,* 1883, reprint (New York and London: Garland Press, 1978), 7. In the catalog, the firm of Grace et Cie., offered a dinner dress "to be worn without stays." The design is similar to tea gowns of the same period. "Correspondence," *Rational Dress Society's Gazette* (Oct. 1888): 8.

18. Zuzanna Shonfield, "Miss Marshall and the Cimabue Browns," *Costume* 13 (1979): 63–65.

19. Ibid., 69–70.

20. "Dress at the Private View Day at the Grosvenor Gallery," *Demorest's Monthly Magazine* 21 (July 1885): 608.

21. Newton, *Health, Art, and Reason,* 87.

22. Ibid., 53.

23. Mary Haweis [Mrs. H. R.], "Dress, Hints to Ladies," *Saint Pauls* 12 (1873): 45.

24. Mary Haweis, "The Two D's; or Decoration and Dress," *Temple Bar* 67 (1883): 124.

25. Mary Haweis, "The Aesthetics of Dress," *Art Journal* 42 [London] (Apr. 1880): 97–99, 137–39, 205–7.

26. Lucy Crane, *Art and the Formation of Taste,* 138–40.

27. Oscar Wilde, *Art and Decoration* (London: Methuen, 1920), 64.

28. Ibid., 75–76.

29. G. F. Watts, "On Taste in Dress," *Nineteenth Century* 13 (1883): 47.

30. Ibid., 55. See also, Hogarth, *Analysis,* 48.

31. W. Pajet, "Common Sense in Dress and Fashion," *Nineteenth Century* 13 (Mar. 1883): 462–64.

32. Wilde, *Art and Decoration,* 63.

33. Haweis, "Aesthetics of Dress," 99.

34. Haweis, "Dress Hints," 46–47.

35. Percy Fitzgerald, "The Art of Dressing and of Being Dressed," *Art Journal* 3, n.s. (1877): 380.

36. "Eccentricities of Costume," *All the Year Round* (May 16, 1863) 280.

37. "High Art in Women's Dress," *American Agriculturist* 38, no. 8 (Aug. 1878): 304.

38. Dr. Reveille-Parise, "The Use of the Corset" (letter), *Chamber's Edinburgh Journal* (Aug. 15, 1846): 103. See also *Godey's Lady's Book* 68 (May 1864): 527.

39. Watts, "On Taste in Dress," 52.

40. Haweis, "Dress Hints," 47.

41. William Fowler, "Fashion in Deformity," *Popular Science Monthly* 17 (1880): 741.

42. Newton, *Health, Art, and Reason,* 23. Andrew Combe, *The Principles of Physiology Applied to the Preservation of Health and to the Improvement of Physical and Mental Education* (London, 1834), 182.

43. Newton, *Health, Art, and Reason,* 97.

44. John Leighton [Luke Limner], *Madre Natura versus the Moloch of Fashion* (London, 1874).

45. Richmond Leigh, "Corset Wearing" (letter), *Knowledge* (Nov. 10, 1882): 393.

46. Lucy Crane, *Art and the Transformation of Taste,* 132–33.

47. R. A. Proctor, "Corset Wearing," *Knowledge* (Dec. 1, 1882): 430.

48. The Observer, "Corset Philosophy," *Knowledge* (Dec. 22, 1882): 478–79; and "Anti-Corset Philosophy and History," *Knowledge* (Jan. 26, 1883): 50.

49. Richard A. Proctor, "Stays and Strengths," *Knowledge* (Jan. 26, 1883).

50. F. W. Harberton, "Rational Dress Reform," *Macmillan's Magazine* (Apr. 4, 1882): 457–59; Annie Jenness Miller, "Our English Sisters," 588. See also Newton, *Health, Art, and Reason,* 97–98.

51. Newton, *Health, Art, and Reason,* 104.

52. "Editorial Note," *Rational Dress Society's Gazette,* no. 1 (Apr. 1888): 1. See also Newton, *Health, Art, and Reason,* 117.

53. On page 55 of the July 27, 1883, issue of *Knowledge*, there was a notice from Mrs. King that she had broken away from the Rational Dress Society to form the Rational Dress Association.

54. "Introduction," *Aglaia, the Journal of the Healthy and Artistic Dress Union* 1 (July 1893): 4; and *Henry Holiday 1839–1927* (London: Borough of Waltham Forest: Libraries and Arts Dept., 1989), 18.

55. "Introduction," *Aglaia* 1 (July 1893): 4; and *Henry Holiday*, 18.

56. *Henry Holiday*, 18. See also Henry Holiday, *Reminiscences of My Life* (London: Heinemann, 1914), 403–4; and Newton, *Health, Art, and Reason*, 140–45.

57. Arthur Lasenby Liberty, "On the Progress of Taste in Dress, III. In Relation to Manufacture," *Aglaia* 3 (Autumn 1894): 27–31.

58. *Liberty's 1875–1975, An Exhibition to Mark the Firm's Centenary* (London: Victoria and Albert Museum, 1975), 4–5. See also Alison Adburgham, *Liberty's: A Biography of a Shop* (London: George Allen and Unwin, 1975), 9–17, 27–34, 51–58.

59. "Costumes," *Liberty Art Fabrics, Liberty & Co. Ltd. Catalogue*, no. 9 (1886): 13, 23; and Adburgham, *Liberty's*, 27–34; BETA (author), "Costume Department," *Liberty Lamp* 7 (Oct. 1931): 97–98; "Preface," *Dress and Decoration, Liberty & Co. Ltd. Catalogue*, no. 98, 1905.

60. "Preface," *Dress and Decoration*.

61. Ibid.

62. *"Liberty" Developments in Form and Colour, Liberty & Co. Ltd. Catalogue*, no. 9 (1886).

63. *Evolution in Costume, Liberty & Co. Ltd. Catalogue* (Nov. 25, 1893), 5. The full title of this catalog is *Evolution in Costume, Illustrated by Past Fashion Plates and Present Adaptations of the Empire and Early Victorian Period*. The place of publication is given as London and Paris. This catalog included an essay, titled "How was the Empire Mode Reintroduced?" that claimed that Liberty's Paris shop introduced the mode before the fashion was reintroduced to England from Paris (ibid., 8).

64. Ibid.

65. Ibid. Illustrations for this Liberty catalog included color plates, which was unusual.

66. The classical elements of the design of the gown suggest that it would fit under the category of "Picturesque Gowns" or "Gowns Never Out of Fashion."

67. "Preface," *Dress and Decoration*. See also E. W. Godwin, *Dress and Its Relation to Health and Climate* (London: William Clawes & Sons Ltd., 1884).

68. BETA, "Costume Department," 97.

69. *"Liberty" Developments in Form and Colour*, 3–6.

70. *Evolution in Costume*, 8; Liberty Catalogue, no. 13, 1–6; B. O. Flower, "Fashion's Slaves," *Arena* 4 (1891): 429.

71. Walter Crane, "Of the Progress of Taste in Dress," 8; Walter Crane, *From William Morris to Whistler* (London: G. Bell, 1911), 212–13.

72. *Henry Holiday*, 19; Holiday, *Reminiscences*, 404–12.

73. Paris Branch Papers, 788/147a, Westminster City Archives, London.

74. Adburgham, *Liberty's*, 116–17.

75. Mary Newbery Sturrock, letter to Alison Adburgham, n.d. [1975], Westminster City Archives, London; and Margaret Swain, "Mrs. Newbery's Dress," *Costume* 12, no. 6 (1978): 69, 73 n6.

76. Swain, "Mrs. Newbery's Dress," 66, 68.

77. Ibid., 66, 71.

5. Artistic Dress in America

1. *American Agriculturist* 33 (Dec. 1874): 464, and 34 (Feb. 1875): 63–64. See also "Counter-Fashion Movements: Nineteenth-Century Examples," *New Perspectives on the History of Western Dress*, ed. Mary Ellen Roach and Kathleen Ehle Hollander (New York: NutriGuide, Inc., 1980).

2. See Judith Ann Fuller, "Artistic Reform Dress from Wisconsin Collections: 1880–1890" (master's thesis, University of Wisconsin, 1977); Sally Kinsey, "A More Reasonable Way to Dress," in Wendy Kaplan, ed., *"The Art That Is Life": The Arts and Crafts Movement in America* (Boston: Little, Brown, and Co., 1987), 358–69; and Mary Blanchard, *Oscar Wilde's America: Counter Culture in the Gilded Age* (New Haven: Yale University Press, 1998).

3. See Oscar Wilde, *Art and Decoration* (London: Methuen, 1920), 69–75, 70, 100; William Gaunt, *The Aesthetic Movement and the Cult of Japan* (London: Fine Art Society, 1972); and Mary Blanchard, "Boundaries and the Victorian Body: Aesthetic Fashion in Gilded Age America," *American Historical Review* 100, no. 1 (Feb. 1995): 21–50.

4. See Mary [Mrs. H. R.] Haweis, *The Art of Dress* (London: Chatto and Windus, 1879), and "Aesthetics of Dress," *Art Journal* 42 (Apr. 1880), 97–99, 137–39, 205–07.

5. See Alicia Finkel, "Edward William Godwin: A Tribute" *Dress* 12 (1986): 30, 38–40. On Sarah Bernhardt's aesthetic approach to dress compared with Lily Langtry's dependence on corsets, see "A Great Art," *Dress, a Monthly Magazine* 1 (1887): 33–34. See also Blanchard, *Oscar Wilde*, 141–42.

6. For a report on a Grosvenor Gallery opening, see "Dress at the Private View Day at the Grosvenor Gallery," *Demorest's Monthly Magazine* 21 (July 1885): 608.

7. Fuller, "Artistic Reform Dress," 58–59.

8. B. O. Flower, "Fashion's Slaves," *Arena* 4 (1891): 429. See also "Symposium on Women's Dress," *Arena* 6 (1892): 488–507.

9. Fuller, "Artistic Reform Dress," 58–59; and Flower, "Fashion's Slaves," 429.

10. Abba Goold Woolson, *Dress Reform* (Boston: Roberts Brothers, 1874); Fuller, "Artistic Reform Dress," 36; and Mary Abigail Dodge [Gail Hamilton], *Twelve Miles from a Lemon* (New York: Harper and Row, 1874).

11. See Patricia A. Cunningham, "Annie Jenness Miller and Mabel Jenness: Promoters of Physical Culture and Correct Dress," *Dress* 16 (1990): 48–62.

12. Woolson, *Dress Reform*, 138.

13. Amy Louise Reed, "Female Delicacy in the Sixties," *Century Magazine* 90 (Oct. 1915): 864; and Ludlow, Vermont, Probate Court Decree, Jan. 29, 1921.

14. See Richard A. Meckel, "Henrietta Russell: Delsartean Prophet to the Gilded Age," *Journal of American Culture* 12, no. 1 (Spring 1989): 65–78.

15. See Frances M. Steele and Elizabeth Livingston Steele Adams, *Beauty of Form and Grace of Vesture* (New York: Dodd, Mead and Co., 1892); Frances Stuart Parker, *Dress, and How to Improve It* (Chicago: Chicago Legal News Company, 1897), 7, 13, 25; Annie Jenness-Miller, *Physical Beauty, How to Obtain and How to Preserve It* (New York: Charles L. Webster, 1892), 11, 49–62; and Lydia Hoyt Farmer, *What America Owes to Women* (Buffalo: Charles W. Moulton, 1893).

16. See Woolson, *Dress Reform*, 142; Annie Jenness-Miller, "Liberty, Beauty and Art," *Dress, a Monthly Magazine* 2 (June 1888): 9–12; Ada Cone, "Art Principles Applied to Dress," *Dress, a Monthly Magazine* 1 (Feb. 1888): 451–54; and Steele and Adams, *Beauty of Form*, chap. 4 and 8.

17. See Cunningham, "Annie Jenness-Miller and Mabel Jenness," 48–62. Little information regarding Annie Jenness-Miller or her sister, Mabel Jenness, appears in general American biographies. However, the women lectured together throughout the United States, and at one time both were listed as editors of *Dress*.

18. Annie Jenness-Miller, "Our Purposes as a Stock Company," *Dress, a Monthly Magazine* 1 (Nov. 1887): 257; and E. L. Benedict, "A Few Comparisons," *Dress, a Monthly Magazine* 1 (July 1887): 105.

19. See Meckel, "Henrietta Russell," 68–70. See also Percy Mackaye, *Epoch: The Life of Steele Mackaye, Genius of the Theater, In Relation to His Times and Contemporaries*, 2 vols. (New York: Boni and Liverwight, 1927).

20. John M. Coffee Jr. and Richard L. Wentworth, *A Century of Eloquence* (Boston: Alternative Pub., 1982), 11–

14; *Monroe College of Oratory Catalogue, 1884–1885* (Boston: Monroe College of Oratory), 5.

21. Dr. Charles Wesley Emerson, "Aesthetic Physical Culture," *Dress, a Monthly Magazine* 1 (May 1887): 8–9.

22. Farmer, *What America Owes to Women*, 151–53.

23. Mabel Jenness, *Comprehensive Physical Culture* (New York: Jenness-Miller Co., 1891), 37. See also Annie Jenness-Miller, *Physical Beauty*, 49–62. Mabel Jenness wrote at length regarding the ancient Greeks' appreciation for the human form, observing that "the old time reverence of the Greeks for the human form must be revived before the present age can realize its possibilities" (*Physical Culture*, 11).

24. Parker, *Dress, and How to Improve It*, 13. Mrs. Parker stated her debt to Annie Jenness-Miller, whose ideas "opened up to me artistic possibilities of women's dress" (ibid., 7). See also Meckel, "Henrietta Russell."

25. Pupils of the Senior Class, "Some Thoughts on Hygienic and Aesthetic Dress," *Emerson College Magazine* 5 (Dec. 1896): 48–51, and *Emerson College Magazine* 5 (Nov. 1897): 2.

26. Annie Jenness-Miller, "How, What, When, and Where," *Dress, a Monthly Magazine* 1 (June 1887): 57.

27. "Announcement," *Jenness Miller Magazine* 5 (Nov. 1890): 244.

28. Annie Jenness-Miller, "Editorial Comment," *Jenness Miller Magazine* 5 (Sept. 1890): 142–43.

29. Fuller, "Artistic Dress Reform," 45–56. See Blanchard, "Boundaries," 38–39.

30. Steele and Adams, *Beauty of Form*, 26.

31. Ibid., 107–8.

32. S. L. S., "Dress Reform and Dress Gossip," *Dress, a Monthly Magazine* (Nov. 1887): 276.

33. Steele and Adams, *Beauty of Form*, 108; Rose E. Cleveland, *Social Mirror* (Detroit: Sun Publishing Co., 1888), 282–83. See also Gerilyn G. Tandberg, "Towards Freedom in Dress for Nineteenth-Century Women," *Dress* 11 (1985): 11–30; and Dee Brown, *The Gentle Tamers: Women of the Old Wild West* (New York: Putnam's Sons, 1958), 136.

34. Steele and Adams, *Beauty of Form*, 119.

35. Fuller, "Artistic Reform Dress," 64–67; "Mirror of Fashion," *Demorest's Monthly Magazine* (Apr. 1878): 209; "Curtains," *Delineator* (Nov. 1880): 309; Haweis, *Art of Dress*, 116; and "Artistic Dress," *Demorest's Magazine* (Nov. 1878): 609.

36. Jenness-Miller, "Artistic Dress Notes," *Dress, a Monthly Magazine* 1 (Apr. 1888): 601.

37. On the adoption of classical dress, see Aileen Ribeiro, *The Art of Dress: Fashion in England and France 1750–1820* (New Haven: Yale University Press, 1995);

and Patricia A. Cunningham, "Classical Revivals in Dress," in *Fashioning the Future: Our Future from Our Past* (Columbus, Ohio: Dept. of Consumer and Textile Sciences, 1997), 3–11.

38. Steele and Adams, *Beauty of Form*, 108–9.

39. Jenness Miller, "Artistic Dress Notes," 601.

40. Bastien Le Farge, "Artistic Clothing," *Jenness Miller Magazine* 5 (Jan. 1891): 353.

41. Ibid. See also Alicia Finkel, "Edward William Godwin: a Tribute," *Dress* 12 (1986): 28–42. Annie Jenness Miller suggested that women study Greek artistic principles ("Current Comment," *Dress, a Monthly Magazine* 1 [June 1887]: 133).

42. See especially chap. 4, "True Standards of Beauty," and chap. 8, "Grace and Design," in Steele and Adams, *Beauty of Form*.

43. Ibid., 165–66.

44. Ibid., 168, 173–74.

45. Ibid., 166–67; Parker, *Dress, and How to Improve It*, 45–46. The unabridged rules appear in the *Physical Culture and Correct Dress Society's Gazette* [Chicago, n.d.], 2–4.

46. Parker, *Dress, and How to Improve It*, 50–51.

47. Ibid.

48. Ibid., 124.

49. "Advertisement," *Dress, a Monthly Magazine* 1 (Sept. 1887): 189, and 1 (Nov. 1887): 293. See also Steele and Adams, *Beauty of Form*, 223.

50. "Fashion Notes," *Dress, a Monthly Magazine* 1 (Feb. 1888): 456.

51. Parker, *Dress, and How to Improve It*, 30–37; Steele and Adams, *Beauty of Form*, 27, 94–95, 223; and *The Delineator* (Aug. 1893): 123.

52. Fuller, "Artistic Reform Dress," 45–56.

53. For a discussion of individuals who wore aesthetic dress and pushed social boundaries, see Blanchard, "Boundaries"; and Meckel, "Henrietta Russell." While it is true that women and men no doubt felt that they were making an "individualized expression of art and beauty," they also were conforming to styles worn by like-minded people who believed that they were reforming their clothing to improve health and meet an artistic ideal.

54. Frances E. Russell, "Women's Dress," *Arena* 5 (1890–91): 360.

55. *Dress* 1 (Sept. 1887): 165.

56. Frances E. Russell, "A Brief Survey of the American Dress Reform Movement of the Past with Views of Representative Women," *Arena* 6 (1892): 339.

57. Blanchard, "Boundaries," 31; "In Memoriam," *Smith Alumnae Quarterly* (Aug. 1951): 226.

58. Blanchard, "Boundaries," 32–34.

59. Fuller, "Artistic Reform Dress," 88–97.

60. See *Woman's World and Jenness Miller Monthly* for Aug., Sept., and Oct., 1896.

61. Fuller, "Artistic Reform Dress," 45–56.

62. Ibid. See also Agnes James, "Paste and Diamonds," *Peterson's Magazine* (July 1881); Katherine Keene, "A Mount Desert Episode," *Peterson's Magazine* (June 1882); Fanny Driscoll, "Two Wise Guardians," *Peterson's Magazine* (June 1882); Emma Garrison Jones, "Dot's Farewell," *Peterson's Magazine* (Sept. 1882); and Mary Hayes, "An Esthete's Heart," *Peterson's Magazine* (Nov. 1882).

63. Fuller, "Artistic Reform Dress," 49, 52–53. See also Frances Hodgson Burnett, "Lindsay's Luck" and "Miss Crespigny," in *Earlier Stories* (New York: Scribner, 1891).

64. Cleveland, *Social Mirror*, 285–86.

65. See *Dress*, "The Ruth Tea Gown" (Apr. 1888): 653; "Fashion Notes" (Feb. 1888): 456; and S. L. S., "Dress Reform and Dress Gossip" (Nov. 1887): 276. See also Parker, *Dress, and How to Improve It*, 67; and Steele and Adams, *Beauty of Form*.

66. "On Forming Dress Clubs," *Dress, Jenness Miller Magazine* 2 (July–Aug. 1888): 42. See also Annie Jenness Miller, "The Constitution of Clubs," *Dress, a Monthly Magazine* 2 (Jan.–Feb. 1888): 141–42.

67. "On Forming Dress Clubs," 42.

68. Mrs. Frances Russell, "The Rational Dress Movement in the Columbian Year," *Arena* 9 (1893): 308–309. See also Jenness Miller, "The Constitution of Clubs," 142.

69. Steele and Adams, *Beauty of Form*, 57–58; and Parker, *Dress, and How to Improve It*, 21.

70. Russell, "Rational Dress Movement," 310–11.

71. Frances M. Steele, "Artistic Dress," *Arena* 4 (1892): 506.

72. Russell, "Rational Dress Movement," 306–309. See also "Dress Reform at the World's Fair," *Review of Reviews* 7 (Apr. 1893): 312–16.

73. Ibid.

74. Parker, *Dress, and How to Improve It*, 23.

75. Jenness Miller, "Is This a Rich or Poor Woman's Reform?" *Dress, a Monthly Magazine* 1 (Sept. 1887): 178.

76. Ted Shawn, *Every Little Movement* (New York: Dance Horizons, 1963), 81.

6. Artistic Dress and the Modern Design Movement on the Continent

1. Jane Kallir, *Viennese Design and the Wiener Werkstätte* (New York: Galerie St. Etienne/George Braziller, 1986), 22. See also Alfred Mohrbutter, *Das Kleid der Frau* (*The Dress of Women*) (Darmstadt: Alexander Koch, 1904); reprint ed. (Hannover: Th. Schafer, 1985).

2. Daniele Baroni and Antonio D'Auria, *Kolo Moser, Graphic Artist and Designer* (New York: Rizzoli, 1986), 12–13. See also Leonie von Wilckens, "Künstlerkleid und Reformkleid—Textilkunst in Nürnberg" ("Artistic Clothing and Reform Dress—Textile Art in Nürnberg"), in *Peter Behrens in Nürnberg* (Nürnberg: Prestel Verlag, 1980), 198–99.

3. Kallir, *Viennese Design*, 20–21.

4. See Kathryn Bloom Heisinger, *Art Nouveau in Munich* (Philadelphia and Munich: Philadelphia Museum of Art and Prestel Verlag, 1988).

5. The most comprehensive study regarding the development of women's dress reform in Germany is a Ph.D. dissertation by Brigitte Stamm, "Das Reformkleid in Deutschland" ("Reform Dress in Germany") (Technical University, Berlin, 1976). For discussion in English, see Else Oppler-Legbaud, "The German Dress Reform Movement," *Independent* 59 (1905): 487–93; and Minna Cauer, "Dress Reform in Germany," *Independent* 63 (1907): 993–97. See also Penny Johns, "Regeneration Reform and the Cultural Imperative: The Theory and Practice of Dress Reform in Germany, 1890–1919" (master's thesis, Winchester School of Art, England, 1997).

6. Cauer, "Dress Reform," 994–96; Heisinger, *Art Nouveau*, 95.

7. See *Encyclopedia of World Art*, 3d ed., "Henry van de Velde," 730.

8. See Henry van de Velde, "Das Neue Kunst-Prinzip in der Moderner Frauen-Kleidung" ("New Art Principles in Modern Women's Clothing") *Deutsche Kunst und Dekoration* 10 (1902): 362–86.

9. Ibid., 369. Henry van de Velde became artistic adviser to the Grand Duke of Saxe-Weimer and lived in Weimer until the outbreak of the First World War. In Weimer van de Velde directed the Kunstgewerbeschule (School for Arts and Crafts) and revolutionized the teaching of arts and crafts. The school merged with the Kunstschule to become the Bauhaus School. See "Henry van de Velde," *Encyclopedia*, 730.

10. Van de Velde, "Neue Kunst-Prinzip"; and Maria van de Velde, "Sonderausstellung Moderner Damenkostume" ("Special Exhibition of Modern Women's Costumes), *Dekorative Kunst* 7 (1901): 44. See also von Wilckens, "Künstlerkleid und Reformkleid." Deneken had the idea for an exhibition in 1899, but instead of having the exhibition at that time, he experimented with the performance of living pictures. For these he asked a friend, the painter Alfred Mohrbutter, to design pictures that deviated completely from the usual historical style.

11. Maria van de Velde, "Sonderausstellung," 46–47; Henry van de Velde, "Neue Kunst-Prinzip," 364.

12. Maria van de Velde, "Sonderausstellung," 46–47.

13. Ibid. See also Henry van de Velde, "Neue Kunst-Prinzip," 364.

14. Ibid.

15. R. Martin Strand, "Henry van de Velde, Extractions from His Memoirs, 1881–1901," *Architectural Review* (Sept. 1952): 153.

16. von Wilckens, "Künstlerkleid und Reformkleid," 198–99.

17. Ibid., 199–200; Brigitte Stamm, "Richard Riemerschmid: Unveröffentlichte Entwürfe zur Reformierung der Frauenbekleidung um 1900," *Waffen und Köstumkunde* 20 (1978): 51–56.

18. "Die Austellung 'Die Neue Frauentracht' in Berlin" ("The Exhibition of 'the New Women's Costume' in Berlin"), *Dekorative Kunst* 6 (1903): 76. See also Paul Schultze-Naumburg, "Die Bewegung zur Bildung einer Neuen Frauentracht" ("The Movement toward the Formation of a New Women's Costume"), *Dekorative Kunst* 11 (1903).

19. Schultze-Naumburg, "Die Bewegung," 66 "Die Austellong 'Die Neue Frauentradit,'" 76–79.

20. See Oppler-Legbaud, "German Dress Reform."

21. von Wilckens, "Künstlerkleid und Reformkleid," 202; Oscar Ollendorf, "Austellung Deutscher Künstlerischer Frauenkleidung" ("Exhibition of German Artistic Women's Dress"), *Dekorative Kunst* 11 (1903): 108–11.

22. von Wilckens, "Künstlerkleid und Reformkleid," 201.

23. Ibid., 198–99, 201. See also Anna Muthesius, "Die Ausstellung Künstlerischer Frauenkleider im Waren-Haus Wertheim-Berlin" ("The Exhibition of Artistic Women's Costume at Wertheim's Store in Berlin"), *Deutsche Kunst und Dekoration* 14 (1904): 441–43; and Anna Muthesius, *Das Eigenkleid der Frau* (*The Proper Dress of Women*) (Krefeld: Kramer & Baum, 1903).

24. See Alfred Mohrbutter, *Das Kleid der Frau*; and Heinrich Pudor, *Die Frauen Reformkleidung. Ein Beitrag zur Philosophie, Hygiene und Aesthetic das Kleides* (*Women's Reform Clothing. A Contribution toward a Philosophy of Hygiene and Aesthetics of Dress*) (Leipzig, 1903) and Adolf Thiele, *Zur Philosophie des neuen Frauentracht* (*Toward a Philosophy of New Women's Dress*) (Leipzig, 1903).

25. See Mohrbutter, *Das Kleid der Frau*.

26. Pudor, *Die Frauen Reformkleidung*; Oppler-Legbaud, "German Dress Reform," 490; and Adolf Thiele, *Zur Philosophie des Neuen Frauentracht*.

27. C. H. Stratz, *Die Frauenkleidung* (*Women's Clothing*) (Stuttgart: Ferdinand Enke, 1900), 167–86.

28. See Elsa Bruckmann, "Die Austellung moderner Damenkleider noch Künstlerentwürfen in Krefeld" ("The Exhibition of Modern Women's Clothing by Artist-Designers in Krefeld"), *Illustrierte Frauen-Zeitung* 27 (1900): 118–19.

29. von Wilckens, "Künstlerkleid und Reformkleid," 200–201; Stamm, "Das Reformkleid," 50–51. See also Richard Flachs, "Geschichte der Vereine für Verbesserung der Frauenkleidung" ("History of the Associations to Improve Women's Dress"), *Die Neue Frauentracht* 4 (1907): 68.

30. Oppler-Legbaud, "German Dress Reform," 487–91.

31. Ibid., 490–91.

32. Ibid., 493.

33. Ibid.

34. See Kallir, *Viennese Design*, 15–19; and Werner J. Schweiger, *Wiener Werkstätte* (New York: Abbeville Press, 1984).

35. See Schweiger, *Wiener Werkstätte;* Baroni and D'Auria, *Kolo Moser;* and Trude Hansen, *Wiener Werkstätte Mode* (Vienna, Munich: Christian Brandstätter, 1984).

36. *Hohe Warte*, 1905/1906, 78; Udo Kultermann, "Gustav Klimt, Emilie Flöge und die Modereform in Wien um 1900" ("Gustav Klimt, Emilie Flöge and Dress Reform in Vienna around 1900"), *Alte und Moderne Kunst* 23 (1978): 35–36.

37. Ibid.

38. See *Emilie Flöge and Gustav Klimt* (Wien: Stadt Museum, 1988); Kultermann, "Gustav Klimt," 34–36; and Kallir, *Viennese Design*, 32–33.

39. Kultermann, "Gustav Klimt," 35–36.

40. Baroni and D'Auria, *Kolo Moser*, 7–19.

41. Ibid. See also *200 Jahre Mode in Wien* (*200 Years of Vienna Fashion*) (Vienna: Müseen der Stadt Wien, 1976).

42. Baroni and D'Auria, *Kolo Moser*, 44.

43. Ibid., 11. See also Kallir, *Viennese Design*, 8–9, 22–23.

44. Baroni and D'Auria, *Kolo Moser*, 11, 17–21.

45. Josef Hoffmann, "Das individuelle Kleid" ("The Individual Dress"), *Die Wage* 1 (Apr. 9, 1898): 25–52.

46. Alfred Roller, "Gedanken über Frauenkleidung, ein Brief" ("Thoughts on Women's Clothing, a Letter"), *Dokumente der Frauen* 1 (Mar. 1902): 649–54.

47. Ibid.

48. Hermann Bahr, "Zur Reform der Tracht" ("Toward Reform of Clothing"), *Dokumente der Frauen* 1 (Mar. 1902): 664–66.

49. Adolf Loos, "Damenmode" ("Women's Fashion"), *Dokumente der Frauen* 1 (Mar. 1902): 660–64.

50. Kallir, *Viennese Design*, 25–26.

51. Ibid., 29.

52. Ibid., 25–33.

53. Kirk Varnedoe, *Vienna 1900, Art, Architecture and Design* (New York: Museum of Modern Art, 1986), 101.

54. Kallir, *Viennese Design*, 25–33; Schweiger, *Wiener Werkstätte*, 223–26, 241–43.

55. Kallir, *Viennese Design*, 90–91.

56. Ibid., 92–93.

57. Ibid.

58. Ibid., 94.

59. Carin Schnitger, "Reformkleding in Nederland" ("Women's Dress Reform in the Netherlands"), *Textile History* 24 (1993): 75–77.

60. Ibid., 83. See also *Maandblad* (Nov. 1899): 4; (Apr. 1901): 43; (May 1901): 51; (Nov. 1901): 7; (July 1902): 68; and (June 1903): 74, 89. The "models" by Madame de Vroye illustrated in 1901 are all cut in a variation of the princess-style reform dress with a high waist. For further discussion of dress reform in the Netherlands, see Carin Schnitger and Inge Goldhoorn, *Reformkleding in Nederland* (*Reform Clothing in the Netherlands*) (Utrecht: Centraal Museum Utrecht, 1984).

61. Schnitger, "Women's Dress Reform," 84–85.

62. Ibid. See also "Die Ausstellung 'Die Neue Frauentracht' in Berlin," 77–78.

63. Schnitger, "Women's Dress Reform," 87.

64. Ibid.; Marianne Carlano, "Wild and Waxy, Dutch Art Nouveau Artistic Dress," *Art Journal* (spring 1995): 30–33. See also Margaret Swain, "Mrs. Newbury's Dress," *Costume* 12, no. 6 (1978): 68.

65. Schnitger, "Women's Dress Reform," 83–84.

66. Stamm, "Das Reformkleid," 45; "Verbesserte Frauenkleidung, 1900," *Illustriertes Konversations-Lexicon der Frau* (Berlin 1900): 625.

67. Schweiger, *Wiener Werkstätte*, 234–36.

68. See Swain, "Mrs. Newbery's Dress"; and June Bedford and Ivor Davies, "Remembering Charles Rennie Macintosh, a Recorded Interview with Mary Sturrock," *Connoisseur* 183 (Aug. 1973): 280–88.

7. FASHION, DRESS REFORM, AND THE NEW WOMAN

1. On the adoption of trousers and other changes in women's dress during the First World War, see Susan V. Lab, "'War'drobe and World War I," in *Dress in American Culture*, ed. Patricia A. Cunningham and Susan V. Lab (Bowling Green, Ohio: Bowling Green State University Popular Press, 1993), 200–219.

2. Helen G. Ecob, "A New Philosophy of Fashion," *Chautauquan* 31 (Sept. 1900): 604–608.

3. Ibid., 606–608.

4. Ibid., 608.

5. See issues of *Dress, a Monthly Magazine*, 1887–88; *Jenness Miller Magazine [Dress]*, 1889–93; and *Jenness Miller Monthly* 1893–96.

6. Diana DeMarly, *The History of Haute Couture, 1850–1950* (New York: Holmes & Meier, 1980), 77–79.

7. Ibid., 77; Jean Philippe Worth, *A Century of Fashion* (Boston: Little, Brown, 1928), 53.

8. *Exhibition of the Rational Dress Association. . . . Catalogue of Exhibits and List of Exhibitors* (1883), reprint (New York and London: Garland Press, 1978), 16, 29, 33.

9. See "Fashion as a Dress Reformer," *Independent* 76 (Oct. 23, 1913): 151–52.

10. For biographical information, see Paul Poiret, *King of Fashion: the Autobiography of Paul Poiret,* trans. Stephen Haden Guest (Philadelphia and London: J. P. Lippincott, 1931).

11. Valerie Steele, *Paris Fashion: A Cultural History* (New York and Oxford: Oxford University Press, 1988), 226; and Poiret, *King of Fashion,* 76–77.

12. Yvonne Deslandres, *Poiret* (New York: Rizzoli, 1987), 259.

13. Werner J. Schweiger, *Wiener Werkstätte: Design in Vienna 1903–1932* (New York: Abbeville, 1984), 224; and Deslandres, *Poiret,* 259.

14. Schweiger, *Wiener Werkstätte,* 100.

15. Ibid., 224.

16. Leonie von Wilckens, "Künstlerkleid und Reformkleid—Textilkunst in Nürnberg" ("Artistic Clothing and Reform Dress: Textile Art in Nürnberg"), in *Peter Behrens in Nürnberg* (Nürnberg: Prestal Verlag, 1980), 201. See also Jane Kallir, *Viennese Design and the Wiener Werkstätte* (New York: Galerie St. Etienne/George Braziller, 1986), 91.

17. Kallir, *Wiener Werkstätte,* 91–92.

18. Guillermo De Osma, *Mariano Fortuny: His Life and Work* (New York: Rizzoli, 1980), 86–88, 95.

19. Ibid.

20. Ibid., 94–95.

21. Ibid.

22. Worth, *Century of Fashion;* De Osma, *Fortuny,* 126.

23. De Osma, *Fortuny,* 94– 95, 132.

24. Belle Armstrong Whitney, *What to Wear, a Book for Women* (Battle Creek, Mich.: Good Health Pub. Co., 1916), 137; and De Osma, *Fortuny,* 137–38.

25. De Osma, *Fortuny,* 140–41.

26. Dorothy Behling, "The Russian Influence on Fashion, 1909–1925," *Dress* 5 (1979): 2.

27. Poiret, *King of Fashion,* 157–59; and Schweiger, *Wiener Werkstätte,* 224–28.

28. De Osma, *Fortuny,* 85–86, 93–94, 122–43; Alice Mackrell, *Paul Poiret* (New York: Holmes and Meier, 1990), 16–17, 28–30.

29. Elizabeth Dryden, "How Athletics May Develop Style in Women," *Outing* (July 1903): 413.

30. Anna G. Noyes, "A Practical Protest against Fashion," *Independent* 63 (Aug. 29, 1907): 503.

31. Dudley A. Sargent, "Hygiene, Dress and Dress Reform," *Journal of Home Economics* 2 (June 1910): 302–4, 305.

32. Marguerite Wilkinson, "Relation of Clothes to the Body," *Craftsman* 26 (Apr. 14, 1914): 122.

33. "Fashion as a Dress Reformer," 151–52.

34. Edith M. Burtis, "Has *your* Figure Suffered *By* Corset Fads, *or the* No-Corset Habit? *We* Fear *It* Has!" *Ladies Home Journal* (Sept. 1915): 72.

35. Jane Barr, "Women's Clothes," *Health* (Oct. 1922): 89–91.

36. See Jacques Damase, *Sonia DeLaunay, Fashion and Fabrics,* trans. Shaun Whiteside (New York: Harry N. Abrams, 1991), 57–58.

37. Patricia C. Warner, "The Gym Suit: Freedom at Last," in *Dress in American Culture,* ed. Patricia A. Cunningham and Susan V. Lab (Bowling Green, Ohio: Popular Press, 1993), 141–42.

Bibliography

"A Healthful Corset." *Demorest's Monthly Magazine* (March 1874): 109.

Adburgham, Alison. *Liberty's: A Biography of a Shop.* London: George Allen and Unwin, 1975.

Advertisement. *Dress, a Monthly Magazine* 1 (June 1887): 137.

Advertisement. *Dress, a Monthly Magazine* 1 (September 1887): 189, and 1 (November 1887): 293.

Advertisement for the Ferris "Good Sense" Corset. *Dress, a Monthly Magazine* 1, no. 4 (Sept. 1887): 185.

Alcott, William A., "*Health Journal and Independent Magazine* 1 (1843): 29.

———. *The Laws of Health.* Boston: Jewett, 1843.

———. *The Young Mother.* Boston: Light & Stearns, 1836.

American Agriculturist 33 (Dec. 1874): 464.

American Agriculturist 34 (Feb. 1875): 63–64.

"American Free Dress League." *Geauga Republican,* Sept. 16, 1874.

Announcement. *Jenness Miller Magazine* 5 (November 1890): 224.

"Anti-Corset Philosophy and History." *Knowledge* (Jan. 26, 1883): 50.

Architectural Review (Sept. 1952): 148–53.

Armytage, G. "Modern Dress." *Littell's Living Age* 153 (1883): 165–67.

"Artistic Dress." *Demorest's Monthly Magazine* (November 1878): 609.

Aslin, Elizabeth. *The Aesthetic Movement Prelude to Art Nouveau.* New York: Excalibur Books, 1981.

"Die Austellung 'Die Neue Frauentracht" in Berlin" ("The Exhibition of 'the New Women's Dress' in Berlin") *Dekorative Kunst* 11 (1903): 76–79.

Bahr, Hermann. "Zur Reform der Tracht." ("Toward Reform of Dress.") *Dokumente der Frauen* 1 (Mar. 1902): 664–66.

Ballin, Ada S. *The Science of Dress in Theory and Practice.* London: Sampson Low, Marston, Searle & Rivington, 1885.

Banner, Lois. *American Beauty.* New York: Alfred Knopf, 1983.

Baroni, Daniele, and Antonio D'Auria. *Kolo Moser, Graphic Artist and Designer.* New York: Rizzoli, 1986.

Barr, Jane. "Women's Clothes." *Health* (Oct. 1922): 89–91.

The Battle Creek Sanitarium Dress System. Battle Creek, Mich.: Sanitary and Electrical Supply Co., [1890].

Bedford, June, and Ivor Davies. "Remembering Charles Rennie Macintosh, a Recorded Interview with Mary Sturrock," *Connoisseur* 183 (August 1973): 280–88.

Beecher, Catharine. *Physiology and Calisthenics for Schools and Families.* New York: Harper Bros., 1856.

Behling, Dorothy. "The Russian Influence on Fashion, 1909–1925." *Dress* 5 (1979): 2.

Benedict, E. L. "A Few Comparisons." *Dress, a Monthly Magazine* 1 (July 1887): 105.

Benson, Susan. *Counter Cultures: Saleswomen, Managers, and Customers in American Department Stores, 1890–1940.* Urbana: University of Illinois Press, 1986.

Benton, Mona Hodges. "History of South Newbury, Geauga County, Ohio." Typescript, 1947.

BETA, "Costume Department." *Liberty Lamp* 7 (Oct. 1931): 97–98.

Bissonette, Anne. "At Home at Tea Time: The Distinctive Tea Gown of the Victorian Era." *Lady's Gallery* 4, no. 5 (1997): 8–14, 58.

Blackwell, Elizabeth. *The Laws of Life, with Special Reference to the Physical Education of Girls.* New York: G. P. Putnam, 1852.

Blanchard, Mary. "Boundaries and the Victorian Body: Aesthetic Fashion in Gilded Age America." *American Historical Review* 100, no. 1 (Feb. 1995): 21–50.

———. *Oscar Wilde's America: Counter Culture in the Gilded Age.* New Haven: Yale University Press, 1998.

Bloomer, D. C. *Life and Works of Amelia Bloomer.* New York: Schocken Books, 1975.

"The Bloomer Costume." *Chamber's Edinburgh Journal* (Oct. 15, 1851): 280–81.

"Bloomerism." *Lily* 4, no. 10 (October 1852): 85.

"Bloomerism." *Sibyl* 1 (Aug. 1856): 23.

"Bloomerism, or the Female Invasion." *Bartley's Miscellany* 30 (1851): 644.

Brown, Dee. *The Gentle Tamers: Women of the Old Wild West.* New York: G. P. Putnam's Sons, 1958.

Bruckmann, Elsa. "Die Ausstellung moderner Damenkleider noch Künstlerentwürfen in Krefeld." ("The Exhibition of Modern Women's Clothes by Artist-Designers in Krefeld.") *Illustrierte Frauen-Zeitung* 27 (1900): 118–19.

Buchan, Dr. William. *Advice to Mothers.* Boston, 1809.

Burnett, Frances Hodgson. "Lindsay's Luck." In *Earlier Stories.* New York: Scribner, 1891.

———. "Miss Crespigny." In *Earlier Stories.* New York: Scribner, 1891.

Burtis, Edith M. "Has *your* Figure Suffered *By* Corset Fads, *or the* No-Corset Habit? *We* Fear *It* Has!" *Ladies Home Journal* (Sept. 1915): 72.

Carlano, Marianne. "Wild and Waxy, Dutch Art Nouveau Artistic Dress." *Art Journal* 54 (spring 1995): 30–33.

Casteras, Susan P. *Substance on the Shadow: Images of Victorian Womanhood.* New Haven: Yale Center for British Art, 1982.

Cauer, Minna. "Dress Reform in Germany." *Independent* 63 (1907): 993–97.

Cayleff, Susan E. *Wash and Be Healed. The Water-Cure Movement and Women's Health.* Philadelphia: Temple University Press, 1987.

Cherry, Deborah. "The Hogarth Club: 1858–1861." *Burlington Magazine* 122 (April 1980): 237–44.

Cleveland, Rose E. *Social Mirror.* Detroit: Sun Publishing Co., 1888.

Coffee, John M., Jr., and Richard L. Wentworth. *A Century of Eloquence.* Boston: Alternative Pub., 1982.

Coleman, Elizabeth Ann. "Acquiring a French Wardrobe." *With Grace & Favour.* Ed. Otto Charles Thieme. Cincinnati: Cincinnati Art Museum, 1993: 1–3.

Collins, Wilkie. *The Woman in White.* New York: Harper, 1860.

Cone, Ada. "Art Principles Applied to Dress." *Dress, a Monthly Magazine* 1 (Feb. 1888): 451–54.

Connelly, Dolly. "Bloomers and Blouses Plus Waving Alpenstocks." *Smithsonian Magazine* 7, no. 7 (1976): 126–31.

Combe, Andrew. *The Principles of Physiology Applied to the Preservation of Health and to the Improvement of Physical and Mental Education.* London, 1834.

"Corset Philosophy." *Knowledge* (Dec. 22, 1882): 478–79.

"Costumes." *Liberty Art Fabrics, Liberty & Co. Ltd. Catalogue,* no. 9 (1886): 13, 23.

Crane, Lucy. *Art and the Formation of Taste.* London: Macmillan, 1882.

Crane, Walter. *From William Morris to Whistler.* London: George Bell, 1911.

———. *Ideals in Art.* London: George Bell, 1905.

———. "Of the Progress of Taste in Dress, I. In Relation to Art Education." *Aglaia* 3 (Autumn 1894): 8.

Cunnington, C. Willet, and Phillis. *The History of Underclothes.* London: M. Joseph, 1951.

Cunningham, Patricia A. "To Be Healthy, Artistic, and Correct: Alternatives to the Fashionable Ideal." *With Grace & Favour,* 14–25.

———. "Annie Jenness Miller and Mabel Jenness: Promoters of Physical Culture and Correct Dress." *Dress* 16 (1990): 48–62.

———. "Classical Revivals in Dress." *Fashioning the Future, Our Future from Our Past.* Columbus, Ohio: Dept. of Consumer and Textile Sciences, 1997. 3–11.

———. "Simplicity of Dress: A Symbol of American Ideals." *Dress in American Culture.* Ed. Patricia A. Cunningham and Susan V. Lab. Bowling Green, Ohio: Popular Press, 1993. 180–99.

Damase, Jacques. *Sonia DeLaunay, Fashion and Fabrics.* Trans. Shaun Whiteside. New York: Harry N. Abrams, 1991.

de Blaquière, Dora. "How Should We Dress? New German Theories on Clothing." *Leisure Hour* 33 (1884): 735–37.

———. "Modern Dress Reformers." *Leisure Hour* 33 (1884): 557–63.

DeMarly, Diana. *The History of Haute Couture, 1850–1950.* New York: Holmes & Meier, 1980.

De Osma, Guillermo. *Mariano Fortuny: His Life and Work.* New York: Rizzoli, 1980.

Deslandres, Yvonne. *Poiret.* New York: Rizzoli, 1987.

Dodge, Mary Abigail [Gail Hamilton], *Twelve Miles from a Lemon.* New York: Harper and Row, 1874.

Donegan, Jane B. *"Hydropathic Highway to Health": Women*

and Water-Cure in Antebellum America. New York: Greenwood Press, 1986.

"Dress and Decoration." *Liberty Catalogue*, no. 98 (1905): Preface.

"Dress at the Private View Day at the Grosvenor Gallery." *Demorest's Monthly Magazine* 21 (July 1885): 608.

"Dress Reform at the World's Fair." *Review of Reviews* 7 (Apr. 1893): 312–16.

"Dress Reformers in Congress." *Northern Ohio Journal* 5 (September 1874): 3.

"Dress Reformers in Sweden." *Dress, a Monthly Magazine* 1 (1887): 68–69.

Dryden, Elizabeth. "How Athletics Develop Style in Women." *Outing* (July 1903): 413–18.

Dufay, Pierre. *Le Pantalon Feminin.* Paris: Charles Carrington, 1906.

Dulles, Foster R. *America Learns to Play.* New York: Appleton-Century Co., 1940.

"Eccentricities of Costume." *All the Year Round* (May 16, 1863): 280.

Ecob, Helen Gilbert. "A New Philosophy of Fashion." *Chautauquan* 31 (Sept. 1900): 604–608.

———. *The Well-Dressed Woman: A Study in the Practical Application to Dress of the Laws of Health, Art, and Morals.* New York: Fowler and Wells, 1892.

"Editorial Note." *Rational Dress Society's Gazette*, no. 1 (Apr. 1888): 1.

Emerson, Charles Wesley. "Aesthetic Physical Culture." *Dress, a Monthly Magazine* 1 (May 1887): 8–13.

Emilie Flöge and Gustav Klimt. Wien: Müseen der Stadt Wien, 1988.

Evolution in Costume, Illustrated by Past Fashion Plates and Present Adaptations of the Empire and Early Victorian Period. Liberty & Co. Ltd. Catalogue, no. 25 (1893).

Ewing, Elizabeth. *History of Children's Costume.* New York: Charles Scribner's and Sons, 1977.

The Exhibition of the Rational Dress Association. . . . Catalogue of Exhibits and List of Exhibitors. 1883. Reprint. New York and London: Garland Press, 1978.

Farmer, Lydia Hoyt. *What America Owes to Women.* Buffalo: Charles W. Moulton, 1893.

"Fashion as a Dress Reformer." *Independent* 76 (Oct. 23, 1913): 151–52.

"Fashionable Vagaries." *Chamber's Edinburgh Journal* (July 15, 1871): 418.

"Female Attire." *Lily* 3 (Feb. 1851): 2.

Finkel, Alicia. "Edward William Godwin: A Tribute." *Dress* 12 (1986): 28–42.

"The First Union Suit." *Textile World* (July 29, 1905): 139.

Fischer, Gayle V. "'Pantalets' and 'Turkish Trousers': Designing Freedom in the Mid-Nineteenth-Century

United States." *Feminist Studies* 23, no. 1 (spring 1997).

———. *Pantaloons and Power. A Nineteenth-Century Dress Reform in the United States.* Kent, Ohio, and London: The Kent State University Press, 2001.

Fitzgerald, Percy. "The Art of Dressing and of Being Dressed." *Art Journal* 3, n.s. (1877): 316–18, 345–46, 378–80.

Flachs, Richard. "Geschichte der Vereine für Verbesserung der Frauenkleidung" ("History of the Associations to Improve Women's Dress"). *Die Neue Frauentracht* 4 (1907): 65–79.

Fletcher, Shiela. *Woman First: The Female Tradition in English Physical Education, 1880–1980.* London; Dover, N. H.: Athlone Press, 1984.

Fletcher, Robert. *History of Oberlin College.* Oberlin, Ohio: Oberlin College, 1943.

Flower, B. O. "Fashion's Slaves." *Arena* 4 (1891): 401–30.

Foote, Shelly. "Bloomers." *Dress* 6 (1980): 1–10.

Fowler, William. "Fashion in Deformity." *Popular Science Monthly* 17 (1880): 721–42.

Fuller, Judith Ann. "Artistic Reform Dress from Wisconsin Collections: 1880–1890." Master's thesis, University of Wisconsin, 1977.

Gaunt, William. *The Aesthetic Movement and the Cult of Japan.* London: Fine Art Society, 1972.

"Gazetta de Hygiene." *Townsend's Monthly Museum of Parisian Fashion* (Nov. 1849): 331.

"Geauga County Had a 'Bloomer Girl' Too, in the 1870s." *Cleveland Plain Dealer Pictorial Magazine* (June 20, 1948).

Godwin, E. W. *Dress and Its Relation to Health and Climate.* London: William Clawes and Sons Ltd., 1884.

Graham, Sylvester. *Lectures on the Science of Human Life.* Boston: Marsh, Capen, Lyon and Webb, 1839.

Green, Harvey. *Fit for America.* New York: Pantheon Books, 1986.

Halttunen, Karen. *Confidence Men and Painted Women: A Study of Middle-Class Culture in America, 1830–1870.* New Haven and London: Yale University Press, 1982.

Hamilton, Walter. *The Aesthetic Movement in England.* London: 1882.

Hansen, Trude. *Wiener Werkstätte Mode.* Vienna, Munich: Christian Brandstätter, 1984.

Harberton, F. W. "Rational Dress Reform." *Macmillan's Magazine* (Apr. 4, 1882): 456–61.

Haweis, Mary [Mrs. H. R.] "The Aesthetics of Dress." *Art Journal* 42 (Apr. 1880): 97–99, 137–39, 205–7.

———. *The Art of Beauty.* London: Chatto and Windus, 1878.

———. *The Art of Dress.* London: Chatto and Windus, 1879.

———. "Dress, Hints to Ladies." *Saint Pauls* 12 (1873): 45–47.

———. "The Two D's; or Decoration and Dress," *Temple Bar* 67 (1883): 124.

Hayes, Mary. "An Esthete's Heart." *Peterson's Magazine* (Nov. 1882).

Heisinger, Kathryn Bloom. *Art Nouveau in Munich.* Philadelphia and Munich: Philadelphia Museum of Art and Prestel Verlag, 1988.

Helvenston, Sally. "Fashion on the Frontier." *Dress* 16 (1990): 41–45.

Henry Holiday 1839–1927. London: Borough of Waltham Forest: Libraries and Arts Dept., 1989.

"High Art in Women's Dress." *American Agriculturist* 38, no. 8 (Aug. 1878): 304.

Hoffmann, Josef. "Das Individuale Kleid" ("Individual Dress"). *Die Wage* 1 (Apr. 9, 1898): 25–52.

Hogarth, William. *An Analysis of Beauty.* London: T. Reeves, 1753. Reprint, ed. Joseph Burke. Oxford: Clarendon Press, 1955.

Holiday, Henry. *Henry Holiday, Reminiscences of My Life.* London: Heinemann, 1914.

"How to Begin," *Godey's Lady's Book* (July 1841).

Hunt, W. Holman. *Pre-Raphaelitism and the Pre-Raphaelite Brotherhood.* 2 vols. London, 1905–1906.

"In Memoriam." *Smith Alumnae Quarterly,* Aug. 1951, 226.

"Introduction." *Aglaia, the Journal of the Healthy and Artistic Dress Union* 1 (July 1893):4.

Jaeger, Gustav. *Die Normalkleidung als Gesundheitsschutz.* (*Normal Clothing as a Protector of Health*). Stuttgart, 1880.

Jäger, Anna, and Heinrich Jäger. *Hygiene der Kleidung* (*Hygiene and Clothing*). Stuttgart, 1906.

James, Agnes. "Paste and Diamonds." *Peterson's Magazine* (July 1881).

Jenness, Mabel. *Comprehensive Physical Culture.* New York: Jenness Miller Co., 1891.

Jenness-Miller, Annie. "Artistic Dress Notes." *Dress, a Monthly Magazine* 1 (Apr. 1888): 601.

———. "The Constitution of Clubs." *Dress, a Monthly Magazine* 2 (Jan.–Feb. 1888): 1–42.

———. "Current Comment." *Dress, a Monthly Magazine* 1 (June 1887): 133.

———. "Editorial Comment." *Jenness Miller Magazine* 5 (Sept. 1890): 142–43.

———. "How, What, When, and Where." *Dress, a Monthly Magazine* 1 (June 1887): 56–58.

———. "Is This a Rich or Poor Woman's Reform?" *Dress, a Monthly Magazine* 1 (Sept. 1887): 178.

———. "The Jenness-Miller System of Dress." *Jenness Miller Monthly* 7 (Mar. 1894): 22.

———. "Liberty, Beauty and Art." *Dress, a Monthly Magazine* (June 1888): 9–12.

———. "On Forming Dress Clubs." *Dress, Jenness Miller Magazine* 2 (July–Aug. 1888): 42.

———. "Our English Sisters." *Dress, a Monthly Magazine* 2 (1888): 588–89.

———. "Our Purposes of a Stock Company," *Dress, a Monthly Magazine* 1 (Nov. 1887): 257–58.

———. *Physical Beauty, How to Obtain and How to Preserve It.* New York: Charles L. Webster, 1892.

———. "The Reason Why." *Dress, a Monthly Magazine* 1 (May 1887): 7–8.

———. "What Others Are Doing for Improved Dress." *Dress, a Monthly Magazine* 1 (Nov. 1887): 292–93.

Johns, Penny. "Regeneration Reform and the Cultural Imperative: The Theory and Practice of Dress Reform in Germany, 1890–1919." Master's thesis, Winchester School of Art, England, 1997.

Jones, Emma Garrison. "Dot's Farewell." *Peterson's Magazine* (Sept. 1882).

Jones, Mrs. M. M. *Woman's Dress: Its Moral and Physical Relations.* New York: Miller Wood Pub., 1865.

Jones, Stephen. "Attic Attitudes, Leighton and Aesthetic Philosophy." *History Today* 37 (June 1987): 31–37.

Kaiser, Susan. *The Social Psychology of Clothing.* New York: Macmillan, 1992.

Kallir, Jane. *Viennese Design and the Wiener Werkstätte.* New York: Galerie St. Etienne/George Braziller, 1986.

Keene, Katherine. "A Mount Desert Episode." *Peterson's Magazine* (June 1882).

Kellogg, John. *Influence of Dress on Producing the Physical Decadence of Women.* Battle Creek, Mich.: Modern Medical Pub. Co., 1891.

Kesselman, Amy. "The Freedom Suit: Feminism and Dress Reform in the United States, 1848–1875." *Gender and Society* 5, no.4 (Dec. 1991): 495–510.

Kidwell, Claudia. *Women's Bathing and Swimming Costume in the United States.* Washington, D.C.: Smithsonian Institution Press, 1968.

———. "Paper Patterns." *1876, A Centennial Exhibition.* Ed. Robert C. Post. Washington D.C.: Smithsonian Institution, 1976. 126–29.

Kidwell, Claudia, and Margaret C. Christman. *Suiting Everyone: The Democratization of Clothing in America.* Washington, D.C.: Smithsonian Institution Press, 1974.

King, E. M. "Principles of Dress Reform." *Knowledge* (July 27, 1883): 91–92.

———. "Rational Dress." *Knowledge* (Aug. 10, 1883): 92.

Kinsey, Sally. "A More Reasonable Way to Dress." *"The Art That Is Life": The Arts and Crafts Movement in America.*

Ed. Wendy Kaplan. Boston: Little, Brown and Co., 1987. 358–69.

Kultermann, Udo. "Gustav Klimt, Emilie Flöge und die Modereform in Wien um 1900" ("Gustav Klimt, Emilie Flöge and Dress Reform in Vienna around 1900"). *Alte und Moderne Kunst* 23 (1978): 34–36.

Kunzle, David. "Dress Reform as Antifeminism: A Response to Helene E. Roberts, 'The Exquisite Slave: The Role of Clothes in the Making of the Victorian Woman." *Signs* 2, no. 3. (1977): 570–79.

Lab, Susan V. "'War'Drobe and World War I." *Dress in American Culture.* Ed. Patricia A. Cunningham and Susan V. Lab. Bowling Green, Ohio: Bowling Green State University Popular Press, 1993. 200–19.

Lahmann, Heinrich. *Die Reform der Kleidung* (*The Reform of Clothing*). Stuttgart, 1903.

Lauer, Jeanette C., and Robert H. Lauer. "The Battle of the Sexes, Fashion in 19th Century America." *Journal of Popular Culture* 13, no. 4 (Spring 1980): 248–58.

Leach, William. *Land of Desire: Merchants, Power and the Rise of a New American Culture.* New York: Pantheon Books, 1983.

———. *True Love and Perfect Union: The Feminist Reform of Sex and Society.* New York: Basic Books, 1980.

Le Farge, Bastien. "Artistic Clothing." *Jenness Miller Magazine* 5 (Jan. 1891): 345–53.

Leigh, Richmond. "Corset Wearing" (letter). *Knowledge* (Nov. 10, 1882): 393.

Leighton, John [Luke Limner]. *Madre Natura versus the Moloch of Fashion.* London, 1874.

Letters. *Sibyl* 1 (Aug. 1856): 23.

Levitt, Sarah. "From Mrs. Bloomer to the Bloomer: The Social Significance of the Nineteenth-Century English Dress Reform Movement." *Textile History* 24, no. 1 (1993): 27–37.

Lewis, Dio. *Five Minute Chats with Young Women and Certain Other Parties.* New York: Harper & Brothers, 1874.

———. *New Gymnastics for Men, Women, and Children.* Philadelphia: Ticknor and Fields, 1862.

Liberty, Arthur Lasenby. "On the Progress of Taste in Dress, III. In Relation to Manufacture." *Aglaia* 3 (Autumn 1894): 27–31.

"Liberty" Developments in Form and Colour, Liberty & Co. Ltd. Catalogue (1890).

Liberty of London. Paris Branch Papers, 788/147a, Westminster City Archives, London.

Liberty's 1875–1975, An Exhibition to Mark the Firm's Centenary. London: Victoria and Albert Museum, 1975.

"List of Dress Reformers." *Sibyl* (Sept. 1, 1858) and (July 15, 1859).

Lockwood, Allison. "Pantsuited Pioneer of Women's Lib., Dr. Mary Walker." *Smithsonian Magazine* 7, no. 12 (Mar. 1977): 113–19.

Loos, Adolf. "Damenmode" ("Lady's Fashion"). *Dokumente der Frauen* 1 (Mar. 1902): 660–64.

Luck, Kate. "Trouble in Eden with Eve: Women, Trousers, and Utopian Socialism in Nineteenth Century America." *Chic Thrills: A Fashion Reader.* Ed. Juliet Ash and Elizabeth Wilson. Berkeley: University of California Press, 1993. 200–12.

Macdonald, Anne L. *Feminine Ingenuity, Women and Invention in America.* New York: Ballantine Books, 1992.

Mackaye, Percy. *Epoch: The Life of Steele Mackaye, Genius of the Theater, in Relation to His Times and Contemporaries,* 2 vols. New York: Boni and Liverwight, 1927.

Mackrell, Alice. *Paul Poiret.* New York: Holmes and Meier, 1990.

Mactaggart, P., and R. A. Mactaggart. "Some Aspects of the Use of Non-Fashionable Stays." In *Strata of Society,* 20–28. London: Costume Society, 1974.

Meckel, Richard A. "Henrietta Russell: Delsartean Prophet to the Gilded Age." *Journal of American Culture* 12, no. 1 (Spring 1989): 65–78.

Mechant, N. M. *Shakespeare and the Artist.* London, 1865.

Merritt, Angeline. *Dress Reform, Practically and Physiologically Considered.* Buffalo, N.Y.: Jewett, Thomas and Co., 1852.

Milbank, Caroline R. *Couture, The Great Designers.* New York: Stewart, Tabori, & Chang, 1985.

Miller, Elizabeth Smith. "Reflections on Woman's Dress, and the Record of a Personal Experience" in "Symposium on Women's Dress, Part 1." *Arena* 6 (1892): 491–95.

Miller, Michael B. *The Bon Marché: Bourgeois Culture and the Department Store, 1869–1920.* Princeton: Princeton University Press, 1981.

Mohrbutter, Alfred. *Das Kleid der Frau* (*The Dress of Women*). Darmstadt: Alexander Koch, 1904; Reprint, Hannover: Th. Schafer, 1985.

Monroe College of Oratory Catalogue, 1884–1885. Boston: Monroe College of Oratory.

Mott, Frank L. *A History of American Magazines.* Cambridge: Harvard University Press, 1938–68.

Murray, Anne Wood. "The Bloomer Costume and Exercise Suits." *Waffen und Köstumekunde* 24 (1982): 103–18.

Muthesius, Anna. *Das Eigenkleid der Frau* (*The Proper Dress of Women*). Krefeld: Kramer & Baum, 1903.

———. "Die Ausstellung Künstlerischer Frauenkleider in Waren-Haus Wertheim, Berlin" ("The Exhibition of Artistic Women's Costume at Wertheim's Store in Berlin"). *Deutsche Kunst und Dekoration* 14 (1904): 441–56.

Myers, Annie E. *Home Dressmaking: A Complete Guide to Household Sewing.* Chicago: Chas. H. Sergel & Co., 1892.

Neustatter, Otto. *Die Reform der Kleidung auf Gesundheitlicher Grundlage* (*The Reform of Clothing Based on Health Theories*). Munich, 1903.

Neuwirth, Waltraud. *Wiener Werkstätte, Avantgarde, Art Deco, Industrial Design.* Vienna: W. Neuwirth, 1984.

Newton, Stella Mary. *Health, Art, and Reason: Dress Reformers of the Nineteenth Century.* London: John Murray, 1974.

Nisbet, Hugh. "Fin de Siècle Dress and Its Effects." *Englishwoman* 3 (1896): 265–68.

Novak, Barbara. *Nature and Culture.* New York: Oxford University Press, 1980.

Noyes, Anna G. "A Practical Protest against Fashion." *Independent* 63 (Aug. 29, 1907): 503–9. In *Prophetess of Health: Ellen G. White and the Origins of Seventh-Day Adventist Health Reform.* Ed. Ronald L. Numbers. Knoxville, Tenn.: University of Tennessee Press, 1992.

Observer, The. "Corset Philosophy." *Knowledge* (Dec. 22, 1882): 478–79.

Ollendorf, Oscar. "Ausstellung Deutscher, Künstlerischer Frauenkleidung" ("Exhibition of German Artistic Women' Dress"). *Dekorative Kunst* 11 (1903): 108–11.

Oppler-Legbaud, Else. "The German Dress Reform Movement." *Independent* 59 (1905): 487–93.

Ormond, Leonée. "Dress in the Painting of Dante Gabriel Rossetti." *Costume* 8 (1974): 26–29.

———. "Female Costume in the Aesthetic Movement of the 1870s and 1880s." *Costume* 4 (1970): 47–52.

Pajet, W. "Common Sense in Dress and Fashion." *Nineteenth Century* 13 (Mar. 1883): 462–64.

Parker, Frances Stuart. *Dress, and How to Improve It.* Chicago: Chicago Legal News Company, 1897.

Pennell, Mrs. E. R. "Cycling." In *Ladies in the Field.* Ed. Lady Greville. London: Ward & Downey, 1894.

Perrot, Philippe. *Fashioning the Bourgeoisie.* Trans. Richard Bienvenu. Princeton: Princeton University Press, 1994.

Phelps, Elizabeth Stuart. *What to Wear.* Boston: J. R. Osgood, 1873.

Physical Culture and Correct Dress Society's Gazette [Chicago n.d.], 2–4.

Pioneer and General History of Geauga County. Geauga County Historical and Memorial Society, 1953.

Poiret, Paul. *King of Fashion: The Autobiography of Paul Poiret.* Trans. Stephen Haden Guest. Philadelphia and London: J. P. Lippincott, 1931.

"Preface," *Dress and Decoration, Liberty & Co. Ltd. Catalogue,* no. 98, 1905.

Proctor, R. A. "Corset Wearing." *Knowledge* (Dec. 1, 1882): 429–30.

Proctor, Richard A. "Stays and Strength." *Knowledge* (Jan. 26, 1883): 50–51.

Pudor, Heinrich. *Die Frauen Reformkleidung. Ein Beitrag zur Philosophie, Hygiene und Aesthetic des Kleides* (*Women's Reform Clothing. A Contribution toward a Philosophy of Hygiene and Aesthetics of Clothing*). Leipzig, 1903.

Pupils of the Senior Class. "Some Thoughts on Hygienic and Aesthetic Dress." *Emerson College Magazine* 5 (Dec. 1896): 48–51, and 5 (November 1897): 2.

"Rational Dress," *Knowledge* (Oct. 16, 1885): 333–34.

Reed, Amy Louise. "Female Delicacy in the Sixties." *Century Magazine* 90 (Oct. 1915): 855–64, 904.

Reichley, Lilah. "Lucy Webb Hayes: An Advocate of Republican Simplicity in Dress." Master's thesis, Bowling Green State University, 1994.

Reveille-Parise, Dr. "The Use of the Corset" (letter). *Chamber's Edinburgh Journal* (Aug. 15, 1846): 103.

Reynolds, Sir Joshua. *Discourses on Art.* Ed. Robert R. Work. New Haven: Yale University Press, 1975.

Ribeiro, Aileen. *The Art of Dress: Fashion in England and France 1750–1820.* New Haven: Yale University Press, 1995.

Riegel, Robert E. "Women's Clothes and Women's Rights." *American Quarterly* (1963): 390–401.

Roach, Mary Ellen, and Kathleen Ehle Hollander, eds. *New Perspectives on the History of Western Dress.* New York: NutriGuide, Inc., 1980.

Roberts, Helene E. "The Exquisite Slave: The Role of Clothes in the Making of the Victorian Woman." *Signs: Journal of Women in Culture and Society* 2, no. 3 (1977): 554–69.

Roller, Alfred. "Gedanken über Frauenkleidung, ein Brief" ("Thoughts on Women's Clothing, a Letter"). *Dokumente der Frauen* (Mar. 1902): 649–54.

Rousseau. Jean-Jacques. *Émile; or, Treatise on Education.* Trans. William H. Payne. New York: Appleton, 1904.

Ruskin, John. *Lectures on Art: Delivered before the University of Oxford in Hilary Term, 1870.* London: G. Allen, 1910.

———. *Modern Painters.* New York: John Wiley, 1847–62.

———. *The Works of John Ruskin.* Vol. 16. Ed. E. T. Cook and Alexander Wedderburn. London: George Allen, 1905.

Russell, Frances E. "A Brief Survey of the American Dress Reform Movements of the Past, with Views of Representative Women." *Arena* 6 (1892): 325–39.

———. "Freedom of Dress for Women." *Arena* 8 (1893): 70–77.

———. "The Rational Dress Movement in the Columbian Year." *Arena* 9 (1893): 305–16.

———. "Women's Dress." *Arena* 5 (1890–91): 352–60.

Sargent, Dudley A. "Hygiene, Dress and Dress Reform." *Journal of Home Economics* 2 (June 1910): 298–305.

Sargent, Shirley. *Pioneers in Petticoats: Yosemite's Early Women, 1856–1900.* Los Angeles: Trans-Anglo Books, 1966.

Scarce, Jennifer. *Women's Costume of the Near and Middle East.* London: Unwin Hyman, 1987.

Schlesinger, Arthur. *Learning How to Behave: An Historical Study of American Etiquette Books.* New York: Macmillan, 1946.

Schnitger, Carin. "Reformkleding in Nederland" ("Women's Dress Reform in the Netherlands"). *Textile History* 24 (1993): 75–89.

Schnitger, Carin, and Inge Goldhoorn. *Reformkleding in Nederland (Reform Clothing in the Netherlands).* Utrecht: Centraal Museum Utrecht, 1984.

Schultze-Naumburg, Paul. "Die Bewegung zur Bildung einer Neuen Frauentracht" ("The Movement toward the Formation of a New Women's Costume"). *Dekorative Kunst* 11 (1903): 63–69.

———. *Die Kultur des Weiblichen Körpers als Grundlage der Frauenkleidung (The Development of Women's Bodies in Relation to Theories about Women's Clothing).* Leipzig, 1902.

Schuyler, Angelica. "The New Fashions for Summer." *Needlecraft* 2 (June 1911): 1–2.

Schweiger, Werner J. *Wiener Werkstätte: Design in Vienna 1903–1932.* New York: Abbeville, 1984.

Severa, Joan. *Dressed for the Photographer: Ordinary Americans and Fashion, 1840–1900.* Kent, Ohio: Kent State University Press, 1995.

Shawn, Ted. *Every Little Movement.* New York: Dance Horizons, 1963.

Shonfield, Zuzanna. "Miss Marshall and the Cimabue Browns." *Costume* 13 (1979): 63–70.

Simmel, George. "Fashion." *International Quarterly* 10 (1904): 130–55.

Sims, Sally. "The Bicycle, the Bloomer and Dress Reform." *Dress and Popular Culture.* Ed. Patricia A. Cunningham and Susan V. Lab. Bowling Green, Ohio: Popular Press, 1991. 125–45.

S. L. S., "Dress Reform and Dress Gossip." *Dress, a Monthly Magazine* 1 (Nov. 1887): 275–77.

Smith, Jennifer. "Medieval Dress in Pre-Raphaelite Painting." In *William Morris and the Middle Ages,* 46–58. Ed. Joanna Banham and Jennifer Harris. Manchester, Eng.: Manchester University Press, 1984.

Smith, Roger. "Bonnard's *Costume Historique*—Pre-Raphaelite Source Book." *Costume* 7 (1973): 22–29.

Snyder, Charles M. *Dr. Mary Walker, the Little Lady in Pants.* New York: Arno Press, 1974.

Sokolow, Jayme A. *Eros and Modernization. Sylvester Graham, Health Reform, and the Origins of Victorian Sexuality in America.* London and Toronto: Associated University Presses, 1983.

Sombart, Werner. *Wirtschaft und Mode (Economics and Fashion).* Berlin, 1902.

Spencer, Charles, ed. *The Aesthetic Movement, 1869–1890.* London: Academy Editions, 1973.

Spencer, Isobel. *Walter Crane.* New York: Macmillan, 1975.

Spielman, M. H. *Millais and His Works.* London, 1898.

Stamm, Brigitte. "Das Reformkleid in Deutschland" ("Reform Dress in Germany"). Ph.D. diss., Technical University, Berlin, 1976.

———. "Richard Riemerschmid: Unveröffentlichte Entwürfe zur Reformierung der Frauenbekleidung um 1900." *Waffen und Köstumkunde* 20 (1978): 51–56.

Stearns, Bertha Monica. "Reform Periodicals and Female Reformers: 1830–1860." *American Historical Review* 37 (July 1932): 697–99.

Steele, Frances M. "Artistic Dress." *Arena* 4 (1892): 503–7.

Steele, Frances Mary, and Elizabeth Livingston Steele Adams. *Beauty of Form and Grace of Vesture.* New York: Dodd, Mead and Co., 1892.

Steele, Valerie. *Fashion and Eroticism.* New York and Oxford: Oxford University Press, 1985.

———. *Paris Fashion: A Cultural History.* New York and Oxford: Oxford University Press, 1988.

Stern, Radu. *A Contre-Courant: Vêtements d'artistes/ Gegen den Strich: Kleider von Küntstlern, 1900–1940.* Bern: Benteli, 1992.

Strand, R. Martin. "Henry van de Velde, Extractions from His Memoirs, 1881–1901." *Architectural Review* 111 (Sept. 1952): 148–53.

Stratz, C. H. *Die Frauenkleidung (Women's Clothing).* Stuttgart: Ferdinand Enke, 1900.

Sturrock, Mary Newbury. Letter to Alison Adburgham, ca. 1975. Westminster City Archives, London.

"Suitable Corsets." *Demorest's Monthly Magazine* (May 1874): 188.

Swain, Margaret. "Mrs. Newbery's Dress." *Costume* 12, no. 6 (1978): 66–73.

Tandberg, Gerilyn G. "Towards Freedom in Dress for Nineteenth-Century Women." *Dress* 11 (1985): 11–30.

Thiele, Adolf. *Zur Philosophie des Neuen Frauentracht (Philosophy about New Women's Costume).* Leipzig, 1903.

Thieme, Otto Charles. "With Grace & Favour, Victorian and Edwardian Fashion in America." *With Grace & Favour: Victorian and Edwardian Fashion in America.* Ed. Otto Thieme. Cincinnati: Cincinnati Art Museum, 1993. 26–86.

Thomson, Samuel. *New Guide to Health Prefixed by a Narrative of the Life and Medical Discoveries of the Author,* 2d ed. Boston: E. G. House, 1825.

Tillotson, Mary E. *History ov[sic] the First Thirty-Five Years ov[sic] the Science Costume Movement in the United States.* Vineland, N.J.: Weekly Independent and Job Office, 1885.

Tinling, Marian. "Bloomerism Comes to California." *California History* 61 (spring 1982): 18–25.

200 Jahre Mode in Wien. Vienna: Museem der Stadt Wien, 1976.

Reveille, Parise, Dr. "The Use of the Corset" [letter]. *Chamber's Edinburgh Journal* (August 15, 1846): 103.

van de Velde, Henry. "Das Neue Kunst-Prinzip in der Modernen Frauen-Kleidung" ("New Art Principles in Modern Women's Clothing). *Deutsche Kunst und Dekoration* 10 (1902): 362–86.

van de Velde, Maria. "Sonderausstellung Moderner Damenkostume" ("Special Exhibition of Modern Women's Costume"). *Dekorative Kunst* 7 (1901): 41–47.

Varnedoe, Kirk. *Vienna 1900, Art, Architecture and Design.* New York: Museum of Modern Art, 1986.

Veblen, Thorstein. "The Economic Theory of Women's Dress." *Popular Science Monthly* 46 (1894): 198–205.

———. *Theory of Leisure Class.* New York: Macmillan, 1899.

"Verbesserte Frauenkleidung 1900," *Illustriertes Konversations-Lexicon der Frau* (Berlin 1900), 625.

Verbrugge, Martha H. *Able-Bodied Womanhood: Personal Health and Social Change in Nineteenth-Century Boston.* New York: Oxford University Press, 1987.

Vertinsky, Patricia. "Rhythmics—A Sort of Physical Jubilee: A New Look at the Contributions of Dio Lewis." *Canadian Journal of History of Sport and Physical Education* 96 (1978): 31–41.

von Wilckens, Leonie. "Künstlerkleid und Reformkleid—Textilkunst in Nürnberg" ("Artistic Clothing and Reform Dress—Textile Art in Nürnberg"). *Peter Behrens in Nürnberg.* Nürnberg: Prestel Verlag, 1980. 198–203.

Walsh, Margaret. "The Democratization of Fashion: The Emergence of the Women's Dress Pattern Industry." *Journal of American History* 66, no. 2 (Sept. 1979): 299–313.

Warner, Deborah J. "Fashion, Emancipation, Reform and Rational Undergarments." *Dress* 4 (1978): 24–29.

———. "The Women's Pavilion." In *1876: A Centennial Exhibition,* 165–73. Ed. Robert C. Post. Washington, D.C.: National Museum of History and Technology, Smithsonian Institution, 1976.

Warner, Patricia C. "The Gym Suit: Freedom at Last." In *Dress in American Culture,* 140–79. Ed. Patricia A. Cunningham and Susan V. Lab. Bowling Green, Ohio: Popular Press, 1993.

Watkinson, Raymond. *Pre-Raphaelite Art and Design.* Greenwich, Conn.: New York Graphic Society, 1970.

Watts, G. F. "On Taste in Dress." *Nineteenth Century* 13 (1883): 45–61.

Weimann, Jeanne M. *The Fair Women.* Chicago: Academy Chicago, 1981.

Weiss, Harry B., and Howard R. Kemble, *The Great American Water Cure Craze.* Trenton, N.J.: Past Times Press, 1967.

White, Ellen G. *Health, or How to Live.* Battle Creek, Mich.: Steam Press, 1865.

Whitman, Allen. "Caroline Maria Seymour Severance." In *American Reformers, an H. W. Wilson Biographical Dictionary,* 733–34. New York: H. W. Wilson, 1985.

Whitney, Belle Armstrong. *What to Wear, a Book for Women.* Battle Creek, Mich.: Good Health Pub. Co., 1916.

Whorton, James C. *Crusaders for Fitness. The History of American Health Reformers.* Princeton: Princeton University Press, 1982.

Wilde, Oscar. *Art and Decoration.* London: Methuen, 1920.

Wilkinson, Marguerite. "Relation of Clothes to the Body." *Craftsman* 26 (Apr. 14, 1914): 120–22.

Wilson, Dr. George. *Healthy Life and Healthy Dwellings.* Edinburgh, Scotland, 1880.

"Women in Trousers." *American Agriculturist* 36, no.9 (Sept. 1877): 344.

Woolson, Abba Goold. *Dress Reform: A Series of Lectures Delivered in Boston, On Dress as It Affects the Health of Women.* Boston: Roberts Brothers, 1874.

Worth, Jean Philippe. *A Century of Fashion.* Boston: Little, Brown and Co., 1928.

Bodice, 22; model, 84, 84–85. *See also* Equipoise Waist; Freedom waist
Bohemians, 155–56, 167
Bon Marché, 13
Bonnard, Camille, 108
Bosom support, 23, 84, 84–85, 89, 91, 205
Boston Rational Dress, 64
Boston Society of National History, 158
Boston University, 143, 144, 158
Boston, 28, 29, 64, 80, 143, 162
Braces. *See* Suspenders
Brassiere, 91, 211, 221
British Aesthetic. *See* Aesthetic Movement.
Brown, Ford Madox, 105, 108, 114–15
Bryant, Sophie, 132
Burne-Jones, Edward, 105, 126
Burnett, Frances Hodgson, 145, 163
Burtis, Edith M., 219
Bust supporter, 23, 89, 91, 205
Bustle style, 16, 17, 18, 20–21, 23
Butterick Pattern Company, 9, 138
Butterick, Ebenezer, 12

Cage crinoline, 10, 11, 15, 16
Calisthenics, 28–30, 32, 37, *38*, 58, 61, 70–71, 72
Carte, D'Oyly, 136
Cauer, Minna, 99–100, 171
Cayleff, Susan A., 26–27
Centennial Exhibition in Philadelphia (1876), 81
Chamber's Edinburgh Journal, 67, 120
Chanel, 133
Checkley, Edwin, 88
Chemilette, 84, 84–85, 89
Chemiloon, 80, 89
Chemise, 20, 22, 96
Chicago Society for the Promotion of Physical Culture and Correct Dress, 89
Chicago World's Fair (1893), 61, 62, 64, 74, 81, 138, 165, 166
Chinese influence on dress, 108
Chiton. *See* Greek revival dress
Christianity, 29
Cincinnati Art Museum, 159
Civil War, 12, 28
Cleveland, Rose, 147, 163
Clothing reform, 4–5, 5–6, 24–25, 82, 214, 220; American review of, 217–19; health-reform movement and, 24–25, 26, 51, 55, 57, 88–89; house gowns in, 10, 155–56; police arrests for, 55; street wear and, 10, 183; undergarments in, 6, 10, 75–76, 91, 205, 221; undergarments in American, 5, 76–91, 101; undergarments in English, 92–97; water-cure movement and, 50, 51–52, 53, 57. *See*

also Aesthetic dress; Artistic reform dress; Skirt(s); Trousers; Undergarments
Clothing: health and, 3–4, 20, 22, 24, 25, 51, 82, 88–89; modernity and, 1, 3, 5, 23–24, 130, 204, 207–208; nineteenth-century farm labor, 9–10; nineteenth-century women's, 43, 44, 220; public arena and, 3; social status and, 5, 11, 12, 22, 23–24; social values and, 1, 3; suppressed by decree, 10. *See also* Fashion; Women
Club for People's Hygiene, 183
Club for the Improvement of Clothing, 183
Club for the Improvement of Women's Clothing, 99
Color, for reform dress, 117, 148, 152
Columbian Exposition. *See* Chicago World's Fair.
Combe George, 27
Combe, Andrew, 25, 121, 122
Combination garment. *See* Union suit
Communal societies, 33, 35, 35, 37
Converse, Susan Taylor, 79–80, 80, 84, 86
Cornforth, Fanny, 107, 111
Corset, 20, 22–23, 75–76, 96, 219, 221; Ada Ballin on, 95–96; beauty and, 4, 120–21; Demorest, 81; as Emancipation Suit component, 79–80, 80; eroticism and, 22–23; "good sense," 81–82; ill health from, 51, 95, 121, 122; Philadelphia Centennial Exhibition and, 81; rational, 92; as stays for health, 22; "tight-lacing" of, 20, 24, 25, 28, 95, 95, 121, 122–23, 193. *See also* Anti-corset societies
Crane, Lucy, 116, 117–18, 122
Crane, Walter, 104, 112, 113, 113–14, 116, 126, 132, 190. 214
Croly, Jane C., 81
Cruikshank, George, 67
"Cult of Beauty," 109, 111–12, 124, 135
Cunningham, Lula, *13*
Cunnington, Phillis, 22

D'Annunzio, Gabriele, 215
D'Auria, Antonio, 188, 189–90
D'ora, 185
Dagnan-Boureret, M., 208
Dahl, Christine, 100, 201–202
Davis, Paulina Wright, 26
de Blaquière, Dora, 71, 92, 97
De Osma, Guillermo, 213–14
de Vroye, Madame, 198–99
Delacroix, 37
DeLaunay, Sonia, 219
Delphos Robe, 213, 213, 215
Delsarte physical exercise principles, 88, 89, 141, 142, 143, 144, 166, 167

Delsarte, François, 84, 141
Demorest, Ellen, 12, 78, 81
Demorest, William, 12
Demorest's Monthly Magazine, 12, 78, 81, 137–38, 148
Denmark, 99, 100, 101
Department stores, 12–13
Der Bazar, 12
Der Jugend (periodical), 170–71, 189, 201, 202
Dexter, C. H., 66
Die Modenwelt, 12
Die Wage, 191
Directoire. *See* Empire style
Divided skirt, 67, 68, 84, 84–87
Dodge, Mary Abigail, 138
Dokumente der Frauen, 184, 193
Donegan, Jane B., 50, 51, 52, 53
Dresden Crafts Workshop, 194
Dress (periodical), 82, 84, 100, 139, 142, 143, 144, 146, 149, 154, 156, 157, 163–64; international influence of, 100, 101
Dress reform undersuit, 79, 79
Dress Reform, 78
Dress: blouse, 174, 179, 180, 183; Delphos, 213, 213, 215; human shape and, 1; reform in: (see Clothing reform); "tied-back," 21–22. *See also* Skirt(s)
Dressmakers, in dissemination of fashion, 12, 152. *See also* Liberty and Company; Worth et Cie.
Dryden, Elizabeth, 217–18
Dual skirt. *See* Divided skirt
DuMaurier, George, 112, 113
Duncan, Isadora, 167, 208, 214–15
Dunn, Treffry, 107
Duse, Eleanora, 208, 214–15
Dutch Society for the Improvement of Women's Dress, 198

Eames-Story, Emma, 162
Eckmann, Otto, 171
Ecob, Helen Gilbert, 64, 65, 88, 89, 139, 164, 203, 206–207
Economic arena, and clothing, 3, 5
Economic development, and fashion, 15
Economic oppression, and fashion, 1
Economic position, and fashion, 11, 12, 22
Emancipation Suit, 79–80, *80*
Emerson College, 143, 144
Emerson, Charles Wesley, 142–43, 144
Emery, Mary E., 62
Émile, 7
Empire style, 9, 15, 121, 128–29, 146, 148–49, *149*, 158, 175, 178, 198, 206, 221
English bifurcated garments, 65–70, 71, 72–73
Equipoise Waist, 81, 89, 155